Love in the Lav

In the series *Sexuality Studies*,
edited by Janice M. Irvine and Regina Kunzel

ALSO IN THIS SERIES:

AVERILL EARLS

Love in the Lav

A Social Biography of Same-Sex
Desire in Ireland, 1922–1972

TEMPLE UNIVERSITY PRESS
Philadelphia • Rome • Tokyo

TEMPLE UNIVERSITY PRESS
Philadelphia, Pennsylvania 19122
tupress.temple.edu

Library of Congress Cataloging-in-Publication Data

Names: Earls, Averill, 1986– author.
Title: Love in the lav : a social biography of same-sex desire in Ireland,
1922–1972 / Averill Earls.
Description: Philadelphia : Temple University Press, 2025. | Series:
Sexuality studies | Includes bibliographical references and index. |
Summary: "Drawing upon a wide variety of sources, including police
records, fictional narratives, religious sermons, and beyond, historian
Averill Earls offers a social biography of male same-sex desires and the
state forces that policed them in Ireland from the 1920s through the
1970s"— Provided by publisher.
Identifiers: LCCN 2024054234 (print) | LCCN 2024054235 (ebook) | ISBN
9781439924150 (cloth) | ISBN 9781439924167 (paperback) | ISBN
9781439924174 (pdf)
Subjects: LCSH: Gay men—Ireland—Dublin—History—20th century. | Gay
men—Sexual behavior—Ireland—Dublin. | Gay
men—Ireland—Dublin—Social conditions.
Classification: LCC HQ76.3.I73 E27 2025 (print) | LCC HQ76.3.I73 (ebook)
| DDC 306.76/6209418350904—dc23/eng/20250219
LC record available at https://lccn.loc.gov/2024054234
LC ebook record available at https://lccn.loc.gov/2024054235

The manufacturer's authorized representative in the EU for product safety is
Temple University Rome, Via di San Sebastianello, 16, 00187 Rome RM, Italy
(https://rome.temple.edu/).
tempress@temple.edu

Printed in the United States of America

9 8 7 6 5 4 3 2 1

To all the men I love.

Contents

Acknowledgments

There are really too many people to thank for the help, guidance, feedback, support, and cheerleading that made the completion of this book possible.

My initial research for this book was funded by my doctoral program at the University at Buffalo as well as a Mark Diamond Research Fellowship and a University at Buffalo Gender Institute Fellowship. More recently, my work has been supported by a Summer Stipend from the National Endowment for the Humanities, a course development grant from the St. Olaf Smith Center for Global Engagement, and the NACBS-GALE Digital Scholar Lab Fellowship.

The research and writing has taken a decade, and everything I did was made possible by the assistance, feedback, and support of others. I'm thankful for every archivist and archive staff member who answered my emails, gave me suggestions, and brought me files from the depths. Elizabeth, Ciara, Simon, Brian, Michael, Jennifer, and every one of the National Archives staff members—thank you for making this work possible. My advisers, Susan Cahn, Paul Deslandes, and Patrick McDevitt, read countless drafts of my writing and encouraged me to keep on with this academic life. Somewhere along the way, they all became dear friends, for which I am unendingly thankful. Every summer for the past six years, the Beatties have given me, Dan, and Curie a peaceful place to relax, take in the sunsets, read, swim, and write. I am thankful for every hour spent in North Hero. This book would not have been finished without the students of my 2024 January Term study abroad course,

Love and Sex in Modern Irish History. I was working furiously in every down moment of our trip to get this manuscript finished for my deadline and being able to talk about the broader history of love and sex in the twentieth century with my nineteen students, spend time in the archives with them, and read their research into these topics was essential to the final preparation of these chapters. Stef, Erin, Katie B., Julia, Kali, Lucy, Soph, Theo, Raena, Corrin, Elias, Phoebe, Piper, Gracia, Celeste, Asia, Leo, Katie W., and Alex—thank you for your time, for choosing this course and adventure, and for investing in the work. And Jillian, thanks for helping me keep them all safe and for making the nonwork time an absolute blast.

The history of sex between men in Ireland led Tom Hulme to me in 2019, a relationship that has delightfully evolved into a friendship and our joint book tour, coming to a gay bookstore near you. He's one of my most important sounding boards and encouraged me to finish this book at every turn. Our writing group with Martha Robinson Rhodes and Gil Englestein was essential in working out the ideas in the last chapter of this book as I wrote it.

Each of these chapters were forged in conversations with colleagues. My award-winning article that became Chapter 4, "The Solicitor," is only as good as it is because of the feedback and support of Rachel Hope Cleves and Nick Syrett. I have to thank the conference organizers who accepted my papers and gave me space to talk through my arguments and evidence: the North American Conference on British Studies, the Queer History Conference, the Ireland and Sexualities in History Conference, and the Big Berkshire Conference of Women Historians. At each of these conferences, I received invaluable feedback on my work, and so, for every audience member whose name I didn't catch, thank you. I'm also grateful to Chuck Upchurch for recommending that I submit my proposal to Temple University Press and for giving me feedback on my proposal.

In Ireland, a number of academics and activists have been immeasurably supportive of my work. Kieran Rose has honored me on countless occasions with his praise and thanks, arranging for me to give public talks virtually and when I happened to be in Ireland, and always pushing for the recognition of LGBTQ struggles (and love) in Ireland. I'm also grateful to Mary McAuliffe and Ciara Breathnach for being incredible role models as Irish academics and scholars and for the way they've welcomed me into the Irish women historians circle. Karl Hayden, Charles Duggan, and Abby O'Reilly are champions of bringing LGBTQ Irish history to the public, and I am thankful for their enthusiasm and support.

And there are so many people in my life who've helped me balance my ambitions with my hobbies, relaxation, and fun. My book clubs: the original DBC—Kathryn, Claire, Nathan, Rachel, Hilary, and Sarah—and the St. Olaf librarians; the Dreamer's Vault board gamer group in MN, and the WNY/

FL/Canadian gamers—Jenna, Scott S., Shelia, Scott N., Don, and Mark; my Yayas—Else, Janet, Lya, Heather, Katie; my RAs—Gwen, Aaren, Kayleigh, Ashley, Andy; my Oles—Eric, Jake, Steph, Jaden, Mariana, Jill, Emily, Anna, Patrick; Co-Caboteers—Berta, Wendy, Jen, Joey, Rachael; my Lakers—EmmaLeigh, Katie, Adam, Verna; and my family—Dad, Brennan, Tonya, Jenny, Evelyn, Buddy, Kyle, Kate, Johnny, Paige, Kennedy (born a few days before I finished this manuscript), Archie, Bear, Mer, and Bri. My mom, Jenny, who passed in 2017, made me into a teacher. My grandmothers, Connie and Virginia, who passed in 2011 and 2019, gave me a love for reading and history. You've all been instrumental in keeping me sane, driving me crazy, and giving me life. Thank you, thank you, thank you. I love you all.

My friends and forever writing group Sarah Handley-Cousins, Elizabeth Garner Masarik, and Marissa Rhodes read too many drafts of these chapters to count, and our work together on *Dig: A History Podcast* teased out ideas and directions of historiographical inquiry that were essential to this book. These women are my foundation, my coven, and my heroes.

And none of this would have been possible without Dan, my partner, research assistant, doggy co-parent, laundry doer, carpenter, and best friend. Thank you for loving me these past twenty years.

Love in the Lav

Introduction

The Historian

In the opening of John Broderick's *The Waking of Willie Ryan*, the titular character walks down the road toward his hometown. He's just escaped the mental institution where he's been held for twenty-five years, and, with death knocking at his door, he plans to face down his family members and see his midlands Irish home one last time. As noted by the Irish politician and gay rights activist David Norris, who introduces the reprint of the novel, Willie Ryan suffered "his brother Michael's precocious sexual advances" as a boy. Then, as a teen, Willie fell in love with the boy next door, Roger Dillon. Roger ran with a group of wild "homosexual" boys, and Willie was reluctantly pulled into their orbit. When the local priest got wind of the little gang's activities, he used his considerable presence to break them up. But Willie and Roger continued their affair in secret. In the picturesque village where they grew up, it was inevitable that someone would find out about their illicit—and illegal—affair. When Willie, unsure of how to repair his reputation and relationship with his family, clumsily tried to kiss his sister-in-law, she cried rape, and his family committed Willie to a lifetime in an asylum.

In all the years he was institutionalized, Willie never confessed the "sin" for which he'd been sent away. The priest of his hometown wanted him to admit and repent for what he'd done to his sister-in-law, but Willie refused. He wouldn't admit to a crime he didn't commit, and he spent his life keeping his youthful love of Roger to himself. His entire town believed that Roger had given up his sinful ways when the priest broke up the ring of troublemakers. But Willie Ryan harbored the truth, whether out of spite, or defiance, or fear, or shame. It wasn't until his deathbed that he whispered the truth about Roger and him, shattering the priest's self-congratulating belief that he could persuade the sinners to a "right" path. Willie's declaration serves to highlight just how false the outward practice of Catholicism was in his town. Everyone performed piety and religiosity, but, in their hearts, they were liars and sinners, filled with spite, envy, lust, and rage. The tragedy of Willie's life, loss, and love is the heart of John Broderick's best novel.[1]

Willie Ryan's sad and brave tale is a fascinating mirror for the experiences of same-sex-desiring men in independent Ireland. Willie spent his life locked up. For hundreds of same-sex-desiring men, the legal and social condemnation of sex between men was a literal and figurative prison. Between 1922 and 1972, at least four hundred men were arrested for crimes of "gross indecency" or "sodomy" in Dublin alone.[2] Significantly, however, neither formal nor informal policing was complete. While the Free State and community members might be able to police their bodies, for many, like Willie Ryan, their hearts and minds were their own. Willie held on to his secret, the joy and pain of his love for Roger, until the day he died. And though the historical records demonstrate that there were hundreds of lives interrupted, inconvenienced, and, yes, ruined, when we look closer, it's clear that there were many more who slipped through the cracked facade of the Irish postcolonial moral regime. After Willie was institutionalized, Roger went on with his life, seemingly conforming to the social expectations of his community, secretly taking lovers, and never again getting caught. Yes, they're fictional characters. But the author, John Broderick, a man who lived, worked, and maybe even loved men in the nascent Irish state, wrote these characters from the well of his own observations, experiences, and fantasies. The world he crafted from ink and paper was, I think, not so far removed from the one in which he lived.

For better or worse, few of Ireland's same-sex-desiring men left records of their lives or loves before 1972. A lucky researcher (not me) might stumble on a diary in their local library or archive or come into possession of family papers that include love letters between soldiers, or some equally fortuitous and once in a lifetime find. Because sex between men was illegal in Ireland until 1993, and socially unacceptable even after that, those kinds of records weren't

---

1. Broderick, *The Waking of Willie Ryan*.
2. These statistics are calculated from the state files and books of the Dublin Criminal Circuit Courts as well as newspapers from 1922 to 1972. It is important to note that one-fourth of those returns involved children under fourteen; most cases involving boys were demarcated with an additional "indecent assault" charge to indicate an unwanted sexual overture involved in the "gross indecency." I expand on these issues, and the issue of age more broadly in the court records, later and in Chapter 5. Also, notably, though I say "Dublin alone" here, the majority of all of Ireland's arrests for same-sex sex took place in Dublin; that is why this book is focused on Dublin.

being donated proudly to archives and libraries. There is living memory, of course, but there are, to my knowledge, no oral histories for the pre-1970 period that are publicly accessible.[3] As an American, a junior academic at a small Midwest private college, and a woman, I haven't been the ideal person to launch such a project up to this point. The limitation of the sources is painfully evident in the historiography, and even more so for social histories of same-sex desire in Ireland.[4] My approach with this book is to write a history of people. To recover the histories, before 1972, of same-sex-desiring men in Ireland, I had to be creative. I was fortunate to locate at the National Library of Ireland (NLI) some of the letters and ephemera of Micheál Mac Liammóir and Hilton Edwards, a couple who lived in Dublin for most of their lives.[5] They are the subject of Chapter 7. But, for the rest of this book, most chapters are built first and foremost from court records.

Scholars have been using court records to write subaltern histories for decades.[6] Most people, especially marginalized people, left little to no record of their lives. So, to understand how people who expressed marginalized sexualities lived, loved, and butted up against the mainstream, historians have often gone first to the arrests, prisons, and courts. If we're lucky, the men who loved men left bits of themselves in the records of the state. But they are records of the *state* and so colored and shaped by legal and cultural conditions and authorities. Statements given under the duress of interrogation, "witness" depositions extracted under the judging gaze of jury and audience, and the "observations" of gardaí are as much records of violence inflicted on these men as they are a record of same-sex desire.[7] We must grapple with the

---

3. Director Edmund Lynch collected oral histories from 168 LGBT people for his documentary, *A Different Country* (2017), but has not yet released his private collection to a public archive. It is my understanding that he willed the collection to the historian Patrick McDonagh, and, since Lynch's death in November 2023, the status of that collection is up in the air. The documentary can be screened on RTE's video player: available at https://www.rte.ie/culture/2017/0629/883884-a-different-country-the-story-of-irelands-lgbt/.

4. In addition to Lacey and Ferriter, discussed later, there is actually a pretty robust tradition of queer Irish scholarship in literary studies. Éibhear Walshe, in particular, has led the way in mapping the work of Ireland's queer literary, artistic, and theatrical figures. While I am indebted to Walshe's work, this book aims to be a social history, even when I utilize and discuss literature.

5. NLI, Micheál Mac Liammóir Papers.

6. Notable among the scholars who used legal records to write histories of same-sex desire: Boag, *Same-Sex Affairs*; Boyd, *Wide-Open Town*; Houlbrook, *Queer London*; Chauncey, *Gay New York*; Smith, *Masculinity, Class and Same-Sex Desire in Industrial England*; and Peniston, *Pederasts and Others*. In Irish history, Denton and Luddy both utilized court records for developing histories of the women who sold sex in Ireland in the nineteenth and twentieth centuries. See Luddy, *Prostitution and Irish Society*; and Denton, "Open Secrets."

7. The Civic Guard was founded in 1921 following Irish independence from Britain. They were renamed An Garda Síochána in 1923, and the DMP was merged with Garda Síochána

long-term damage inflicted by the laws themselves, but so too must we acknowledge the centrality of these records in allowing us to reconstruct the
queer past.

The representatives of the "justice" system in this book—the Garda Síochána, the attorney general, and the circuit court judges—brought to each
of these cases their own perceptions about sex between men and the state's
purpose regarding sex between men. Their perspective is, really, *the* perspective communicated in the recorded history.[8] Less clear is the self-perception
of the men put on trial. While I can read against the grain, as have countless
historians before me, I don't want to replicate the ideological anxieties of the
state that generated these court documents in the first place, so, for the most
part, I discuss "same-sex desire" and "sex between men," rather than homosexuality or gay identities, because I simply don't know how these men self-
identified.[9] I use "queer" throughout this book, in its umbrella form, to refer
to the subaltern, subcultural, or nonnormative expressions of desire, community, and self-definition, because it is useful for communicating that the cases
I discuss here reveal more about Ireland's history than just a record of sex.

Following independence, the new Irish Free State took on the task of deciding which and how much of the British institutions and laws they'd carry over.
Much of the "change" in the nascent state was rebranding rather than revision. And some things—like the laws used to police sex between men—were
simply carried over with no revision. Significantly, the Irish state started to
utilize some of those laws with greater force and emphasis than the British
ever had in Ireland. I've combed through newspapers, prison records from
before and after independence, Crown and Peace files containing the circuit
court files for the period under British rule, and the state files and books for
the circuit courts containing court files under Irish rule. An explosion and
fire at the Four Courts building in 1922, during the Irish Civil War, destroyed
many records held on-site, including the census records going back to 1821,
and some of the Crown and Peace files may have been lost in this tragedy as
well. But enough corroborating evidence has been preserved that I didn't
have much trouble finding what I was looking for across archives.[10]

---

in 1925. A singular member of the force is called a "garda." A group of Irish police are "gardaí."
Informally, gardaí are called "guards," but, in this text, I'll use the formal garda and gardaí.

8. For discussions of the limitations of court records, see, e.g., Brickell, "Court Records
and the History of Male Homosexuality"; and Robertson, "What's Law Got to Do with It?"

9. E.g., in the United States, as Margot Canaday has demonstrated, the state asserted that
sexual identity was a legal category rather than a medical condition. While this was intended
to allow the state to repress the same-sex desiring, it also served to build a basis for same-sex-
desiring people to agitate for citizenship rights. Canaday, "Who Is a Homosexual?"

10. A warning to future researchers: most of the court records from all centuries are held
off-site and can take up to three days to arrive at the reading room for you to look at. Researching this topic, then, is not something one can easily do over a couple of days in Dublin. It will

The cases I was interested in were the ones that would produce the most extensive investigations and evidence packets: cases involving "sodomy," as prosecuted under the 1861 Offenses against the Person Act, and cases involving "gross indecency," as prosecuted under the 1885 Criminal Law Amendment Act.[11] The police used a range of other lesser offenses to harass, arrest, and imprison men who had sex with men, including loitering, covered by the Offenses against the Person Act, the Vagrancy Law Amendment Act 1898, and the Town Police Clauses Act 1847. Men were imprisoned quite regularly under both British and Irish rule for "loitering" and "loitering with intent to commit a felony," but the surviving accounts aren't particularly detail rich. They could just as well have been loitering with intent to commit a felony like larceny or causing grievous bodily harm. Constables could arrest individuals or small groups of men who were hanging out where they weren't supposed to be, too late at night, or in a way that seemed menacing. Or, after 1898, they could have been arrested on suspicion of being in the company of a prostitute.[12] A lot of these laws were created in response to Irish rural agitation under British rule, as angry tenant farmers, starving laborers, and militant nationalists were inclined to cause trouble at any given moment. It's harder to parse out which loitering arrests and imprisonments were motivated by a man's search for violence, thieving, or sex. Suffice it to say that under British rule, the Irish were policed extensively; but, when it came to the use of the sodomy and gross indecency laws, not very much at all.[13] For this book, I've focused on the cases under both the "sodomy" and the "gross indecency" laws. A quantitative study of these cases demonstrates the public-facing initiatives of the postcolonial state to strike fear into the hearts of and eradicate same-sex-desiring men. I also use these court records qualitatively in this book, in an effort to better understand the lives and experiences of men who had sex with men in twentieth-century Ireland.

My intent is to reconstruct a history specifically on Dublin's men who had sex with men, the gardaí who policed them, and the teen boys who sold sex to them. To resist replicating the gaze of the homophobic state, I adopted the

take weeks or even months to sift through all the records, even if you follow the reference information contained in the footnotes of this book.

11. To streamline the case file information in citations, especially the file/docket numbers, they are styled this way: e.g., National Archives of Ireland (NAI), Dublin Circuit Court, State Files, File #1C-94-81 / Docket #30, 23-Sep-29, the State v. Francis McPartland. In a citation with multiple cases, additional cases will be shorthanded like this: 1C-94-89/61, 20-Jan-31, the State v. James Hand.

12. "The Law Reform Commission 1985: Report on Vagrancy and Related Offences," The Law Reform Commission, Ardilaun Centre, 111 St. Stephen's Green, Dublin 2, available at https://www.lawreform.ie/_fileupload/reports/rvagrancy.htm.

13. Allen, *Garda Síochána*; Conway, *Policing Twentieth Century Ireland*; and McNiffe, *History of the Garda Síochána*.

methodology of social biography to write about the lives of the men of my case studies beyond their arrest.[14] As a methodology, social biography permits historians to infer a narrative of individual experiences through the larger contexts in which they are embedded. I draw my models for social biography from examples like Camilla Townsend, Saidaya Hartman, and Jonathan Ned Katz.[15] All demonstrate that comprehensive use of the public record combined with "educated speculation" can be a useful way of reconstructing the lives of people who left few or no records of their thoughts and experiences.

In *Malintzin's Choices*, for example, Townsend introduces Malintzin as a woman who never wrote down her own thoughts and about whose life we know little, except for the conflicting reports from the literate men—indigenous and conquistador—around her. Townsend takes what we know about Malintzin's origins and supplements those scraps of a life with scholarship on indigenous gender roles, naming conventions, daily life, customs, traditions, and politics to weave together a plausible tapestry of what Malintzin's life was like. Every firsthand account about Malintzin was written by someone who knew her or of her, but we have no surviving documents written by Malintzin herself. Even the names we know her by—La Malinche, Malintzin, Maria—are names given to her by others. I am fortunate, in some ways, because my subjects are not quite so silent. Though I have, perhaps, fewer firsthand accounts of their lives, because they were not the primary translator for Spanish conquistadors, in most court records there is something written by the subjects themselves. Court records might include a teen sex worker's written statement, a Garda's court deposition, or sometimes even letters or telegraphs between lovers or friends. But, like the firsthand accounts of Malintzin, the conditions of those records are heavily biased by the institution that created them and further still in how and what have been preserved.[16]

---

14. Nick Salvatore, "Biography and Social History: An Intimate Relationship," *Labour History* no. 87 (November 2004): 187–192; and Edmund Burke III, "Social Biographies as World History," Center for World History, UC Santa Cruz, available at https://cpb-us-e1.wp mucdn.com/sites.ucsc.edu/dist/f/704/files/2019/05/Writing-Social.Biographies.pdf; other scholars refer to this methodology as "speculative biography."

15. Townsend, *Malintzin's Choices*; Hartman, *Wayward Lives, Beautiful Experiments*; Katz, *Love Stories*.

16. For more on archival silences and violences, see Trouillot, *Silencing the Past*; Jacques Derrida, *Archive Fever: A Freudian Impression* (Chicago: University of Chicago Press, 1995); Anne Strachan Cross, "'The Time Has Now Gone by When Things of This Nature Are to Be Hidden from the Public': Mediating Bodily and Archival Violence," *Panorama* 1 (2022); and Katharine Gebner, "Archival Violence, Archival Capital: Ethics, Inheritance, and Reparations in the Thistlewood Diaries," *William and Mary Quarterly* 79, no. 4 (October 2022): 595–624. For a discussion of the Irish Queer Archive, including what has been preserved and what has not, see Madden, "Queering Ireland, in the Archives." Notably, the Irish Queer Archive is currently limited in scope, with materials focused almost exclusively on 1970 to the present, with particular emphasis on community building in that period as well as the rights move-

Social biography allows us to push beyond the confines of archival records, to breathe life into these people who would otherwise be swallowed
by time. For the men whose stories I am bringing to the fore in the following
chapters, the social biographical methodology supplements the gaps left by
genealogical and public records. Close readings of courtroom testimonies, police records, and family history archives allow me to locate these men in their
historical moment. But social biographical methods invite the historian to
reach beyond what is known in recorded fact and blend contextual expertise
and contemporary (but not specific) sources to fill in the gaps where a biographical subject's words, thoughts, and motivations are absent. I use contemporary memoir, fiction, and public discourses in Irish newspapers, as well
as the broad strokes and niche scholarship of Ireland's historians and social
scientists, to offer "educated speculation" in the biographies of these men.
My goal is to tell the stories of these men not as mere "gross indecency offenders" but as more whole and complete people who lived before and after
their day in court.

Sometimes ordinary people left little more than imprints in the historical records. From archival records, I can tell you the details of James Hand's
gross indecency trial: the night he was apprehended in Phoenix Park while
locked in an intimate embrace with a lover, or the teen rent boys he connected
with his out-of-town friends. But James Hand was more than some criminal.[17] Though he didn't speak about his work, his friendships, or his neighborhood in the court records, by seeking him out through genealogical research,
I have been able to tease out the details of where he came from and what his
life might've been like in the nascent Irish state. In this book, I present a fuller
picture of James Hand than the court records could ever provide.[18] And, as
someone who served as a networker for men like him, James Hand becomes
for us—those trying to understand the ordinary men who loved other men
in the Free State—a window onto the queer subculture of 1930s Dublin.

In my focus on developing a more complete picture of these men, for the
most part I have elected to use real names in this book. All the court records
I'm using are unsealed and publicly available at the National Archives of Ireland (NAI), so there is no legal reason that I shouldn't. But like many historians of sexuality before me, I have grappled with the ethics of using the
names of subjects whose lives were preserved in the historical record because

---

ments in the Republic for LGBTQ+ people. The pre-1970 period is particularly silent in that
collection.

17. NAI, Dublin Circuit Court, State Files, 1C-94-89, 21-Jan-31, The State v. James Hand,
Frank North, Michael Corr; James Hand is the primary biographical focus of Chapter 3.

18. See Chapter 3.

they committed a crime.[19] There is a validity to wanting to anonymize the victims of state violence in these histories. They've already been violated by the justice system, the press, and the sociolegal culture. What right does a historian have to capitalize on these snapshots of pain? None, of course. I have no explicit or inherent right to these stories. But, like many scholars before me, I feel a responsibility to tell these stories. To hide behind or fictionalize with pseudonyms feels like agreeing that what these men did was wrong and that they should be ashamed. As Tom Hulme points out, "If we prioritise the anticipated negative feelings of descendants when writing small queer histories, we might 'skew' our narratives or, much worse, reinforce homophobic or transphobic discourses of shame that aim to keep sexual and gender diversity hidden."[20] Just because the Free State upheld the British laws and kept same-sex sex illegal until 1993 does not mean that policing consensual sex between men was *right*. Morality is socially constructed and changes over time. And, even though the state-sponsored position was against same-sex sex, that doesn't mean everyone felt or believed the same thing at the time. Laws that punish people for whom they love, what they look like, how they talk, where they live, and how they present themselves to the world *should* be challenged and resisted. Was cruising Dublin's quays for a lavatory hook-up a revolutionary act of resistance? Maybe. I won't say it *wasn't* resistance. Overtly or covertly, consciously or subconsciously, same-sex-desiring people beat quietly at the cage of Ireland's postcolonial moral project in the small everyday ways they lived their lives. Simply existing, in many cases, was resistance. So I won't use pseudonyms to shore up systems that shame sex work, sex between men, or poverty. The history of all the men in this book is the history of resistance, even if it didn't feel like it at the time, and deserves to be told as fully as possible.

Historians have learned to approach these problematic sources with care, and I have worked to build on those strategies with this book, because court records are not exactly capturing people in their finest moment. Being harassed by the police, arrested, and put on trial is harrowing, a violence that *might* not leave physical scars (though, as we know in both the United States and Ireland right now, it certainly can), but which does leave emotional, psychological, financial, and social wounds. Some men arrested for gross indecency in Ireland lost their jobs, fled the country, or were disowned by their families.[21]

19. See, e.g., Adrian Bingham, Lucy Delap, Louise Jackson, and Louise Settle, "Historical Child Sexual Abuse in England and Wales: The Role of Historians," *History of Education* 45, no. 4 (2016).

20. Hulme, "Queering Family History and the Lives of Irish Men before Gay Liberation," 5.

21. Queen's University Belfast Ph.D. student Michael Lawrence is currently tracing the queer men who emigrated after encounters with the judicial system for his doctoral thesis; I expect that his work will be available shortly after this book is published.

Judicial records are not just repositories of life stories; they are repositories of trauma. I am transparent in this book about the sources I use, and their limitations and possibilities, and so there are places where I write explicitly about the courtroom, the "crime scene," the interrogation room, and the experience of policing and being policed. I want future scholars of Irish sex between men to know what is out there, how to find it, and at least one way to use it. At the same time, I do not want to replicate the harm done. If one of the subjects of the case studies in this book is alive, and if they read this book (I realize this is a lot of really unlikely "ifs"), my writing could reopen the wounds of their trauma. To the best of my knowledge, all the individuals highlighted in this book have passed. I hope that the lengths I've gone to locate these people in death records, probate, and cemeteries will reduce the possibility of retraumatizing the living.

Fortunately, the parameters of this project are already doing a lot of mitigating work for me. I selected 1922 as the start of this study because it marks the start of the Free State, and this book is a history of how the postcolonial state attempted to eliminate visible sexual immorality. I picked 1972 for three reasons. First, the most complete policing records that are publicly available end in the early 1970s. Second, to push beyond that scope I'd be pushing into an era when the subjects might still be alive. Finally, 1972 is about the time the Irish gay rights movement (IGRM) got off the ground; from there the landscape of queer community, organizing, and advocacy changed dramatically in Ireland. There were meetups in pubs, personal ads, gay newspapers, the mention of homosexuality on television, the founding of formal gay and lesbian social and political groups, a small but mighty group of people advocating for the decriminalization and, more importantly, the normalization of queer sexualities. These people completely transformed Ireland, bit by bit. And there are others who are already doing or have done that history: among the academics, Páraic Kerrigan and Patrick McDonagh have published extensively on the era; and among the activists themselves, Kieran Rose, Tonie Walshe, Clodagh Boyd, Declan Doyle, Bill Foley, Brenda Harvey, Annette Hoctor, Maura Molloy, and Mick Quinlan were publishing on the history of the IGRM and LGBTQ Irish communities as the liberation movement was happening.[22] There is too much work to do on the pre-1972 period. I am happy to leave the post-1972 period to these other fabulous historians.

My focus on Dublin in this book is also practical. Even at the height of emigration, Dublin always had the biggest population, the greatest population density, the most Garda, and the most public conveniences. Unsurpris-

---

22. A lot of the early books were a blend of history and personal reflection. See, e.g., Boyd et al., *Out for Ourselves*; Ide O'Carrol and Eoin Collins, eds. *Lesbian and Gay Visions of Ireland: Towards the Twenty-First Century* (UNKNO, 1995); and Rose, *Diverse Communities*.

ingly, then, Dublin had the most arrests for gross indecency and sodomy crimes at any given period in the twentieth century. I looked at Cork and Galway, and the material was not robust enough to have done a stand-alone project on either, or even really to serve as a point of comparison. In Galway, for example, I found just four gross indecency/sodomy case files between 1917 and 1942, and all involved children under fourteen. Further, most of the crimes that went through the Galway Criminal Circuit Court were crimes that would not have required much active policing (as in surveillance, baiting, etc.) of the Garda Síochána. There were many larcenies, woundings, attempted murders, suicide attempts, and fraud, plus the occasional cases of concealment of birth and men sexually assaulting girls under thirteen, between thirteen and sixteen, or over sixteen. In perusing the archives, I was interested to find one case of a man on trial for trying to help a woman miscarry (a.k.a. providing abortion services), but that's a story for another day.[23] Finally, beyond the limitations of sources, Dublin is simply an interesting focus for study in and of itself.

In the period leading up to Irish independence, Irish nationalism coalesced around Catholicism. This meant that, while not every citizen was Catholic, the will and whims of the Catholic hierarchy and ideals impacted all Irish men and women. Two chapters of *Love in the Lav* examine the ways that the Catholic nationalist ethos shaped the development of the new Irish police force, An Garda Síochána. Because sex between men was illegal, it fell to the gardaí to enforce the anti-sex laws. This put officers in close contact with same-sex-desiring men, sometimes in compromising situations. Most studies of Irish masculinity are focused on the colonial period. Aidan Beatty, Joanna Bourke, Michael Patrick LaPointe, Patrick McDevitt, and Joseph Nugent examine the period when the debates about Home Rule and Irish nationalisms were palpable influences on the ideals of Irish manliness.[24] In two chapters spanning two key periods in the development of the modern Irish police force, I consider the role of masculine ideals and early state building in the Gardaí policing of Dublin's same-sex-desiring world: as the "bait" in the state's trap for queer men, and the "predators" of Dublin's streets. I demonstrate the ways that regulating sexuality impacted both the men who did the policing and the men who were policed.

---

23. NAI, Galway Circuit Courts, State Books and Files, 1917–1924, inclusive of reference numbers 1D-15-63 (1927–30); 1D-16-66 (1935); 1D-36-36 (1941–42).

24. Bourke, "The Ideal Man"; McDevitt, "Muscular Catholicism"; LaPointe, *Between Irishmen*; Nugent, "The Sword and the Prayerbook"; and Valente, *The Myth of Manliness in Irish National Culture*. For works that transcend the colonial/postcolonial period, see Beatty, "The Life That God Desires"; J. Foster, "Masculinities in Life and Literature"; and Montgomery, "They Were the Men."

Like most cities, there were two kinds of boys in queer Dublin: the "rent boys," who sold sex to get by, and the boys seeking to affirm their own sexual desire by networking among men who had sex with other men. Rent boys moved in and out of urban sexual economies, as demonstrated by both Katie Hindmarch-Watson in her work on the London General Post Office and telegraph messenger boys, and Steven Maynard in his work on working-class male youths in urban Ontario.[25] Significantly, Irish rent boys were able to slip under the onus of responsibility in independent Ireland.[26] In the economic and social stagnation of the twentieth century, Dublin was teeming with under- and unemployed teen (thirteen to nineteen) boys. Some found odd jobs running messages or selling newspapers, making enough money for a few nights lodging or a meal. Many knew of the network of same-sex-desiring men who'd pay for a boy's nightly "company." In Chapter 5, I argue that the Irish state was willing to go to great lengths to forgive teen boy's their trespasses and that the consequences were dire when those boys didn't grow out of their transgressions. This chapter also demonstrates how Dublin's vagrant teen boys were both essential to and a product of Ireland's same-sex-desiring urban subculture.

Problematically, the laws that criminalized sex between men did not differentiate between consensual sex and rape. Technically speaking, too, any party could be charged with gross indecency or sodomy, regardless of age or enthusiasm for the crime. There were even, occasionally, fifteen- and sixteen-year-olds charged with gross indecency in Dublin.[27] These cases were rare and exceptional but evidence just how fluid and in development the judicial system was between 1922 and 1972 when it came to same-sex sex. To further complicate things, "boy" was a nebulous category in the court records that could refer to any male under the age of twenty-one. Emotionally, physically, and intellectually, a boy of twelve would have been quite different from a "boy" of twenty-one. In practice, the agents of the justice system implemented their own age-based hierarchy for dealing with juveniles (fourteen to sixteen) and juvenile-adults (seventeen to twenty-one). Judges, for example, exercised their

25. Hindmarch-Watson, "Male Prostitution and the London GPO," 594–617; and Maynard, "Horrible Temptations," 191–235.

26. See Walkowitz, *Prostitution in Victorian Society*.

27. Matthew Nyhan, charged at aged fifteen (NAI, Dublin Circuit Court State Files, 1C-94-88, docket 43, 31-Jan-31, the State v. Matthew Nyhan and Robert Byrne); Lawrence Donnelly, charged at age fifteen (NAI, Dublin Circuit Court State Files, 1C-94-82, docket 19, 4-Dec-29, the State v. John Patrick Redmond, John Kelly, and Lawrence Donnelly); Patrick McCarton, charged at age sixteen (NAI, Dublin Circuit Court State Files, 1C-94-88, docket 36, 14-Apr-31, the State v. Patrick McCarton and John Healy); Michael Russell, charged at age sixteen (NAI, Dublin Circuit Court State Files, 1D-44-28, docket 71, 10-Apr-34, the State v. Michael Russell and Patrick Houlihan); and John Kenne, charged at age sixteen (NAI, Dublin Circuit Court, State Files, 1D-55-70/71, docket unknown, 6-Oct-36, the State v. John Kenne).

discretion in meting out punishments. The state never charged boys under fifteen with gross indecency, even though they were regular participants in the sexual economy of Dublin.

For historians of sexuality, intergenerational sex, whether consensual or coerced, is a difficult subject. As Rachel Hope Cleves has argued, we live in a moment when any discussion of child sexuality is taboo, and that makes historian's jobs hard, dangerous, and essential. Few have tried.[28] Cleves's careful examination of Norman Douglas's sexual relationships with children is an exemplary model for how one can tackle this taboo. It requires equal parts excellent historianing, the job security of tenure, and clarity of purpose. I made a deliberate (perhaps cowardly) choice not to include qualitative case studies involving boys under fifteen in this book.[29] I picked fifteen because that was the age of the youngest person himself charged with gross indecency in Ireland between 1922 and 1972.[30] My choice to include even fifteen-year-olds in this book will be controversial.[31] Fifteen isn't the current age of consent in most English-speaking countries.[32] I personally find it challenging to discuss sex between fifteen-year-olds and men twice their age; I am, after all, a

---

28. On children's sexuality, see Angelides, *The Fear of Child Sexuality*; and Cleves, *Unspeakable*. For case studies in intergenerational sex, see the collection of essays in *Historical Reflections* 46, no. 1 (2020), coedited by me, Rachel Hope Cleves, and Nick Syrett, with contributors from two panels at the 2019 Queer History Conference in San Francisco.

29. I considered including the case of repeat offender Michael Moore in this book, in part because there are so few repeat offenders—none, actually, that I've found besides Moore, who was first arrested at the age of eighteen—that survive in the court records, which makes him a particularly rich case study. Moore was arrested at least seven times. But, as an adult, he sought sex partners by placing false wanted ads in the newspaper seeking boys aged twelve to fourteen. Sometimes he advertised for a page boy, sometimes a shepherd, and always he lured those boys into some remote part of the county, proposed that he pay them for sex, and proceeded depending on if they agreed or not. On all the occasions he was arrested, it was because the boys had objected and immediately gone to an adult to intervene. But, as Moore noted, his victims agreed more often than not. Rather than wade into the weeds on this troubling case study, I've left Moore out for the time being. Grappling with the complexity of his case, and how it does and doesn't fit with the other cases in this book, would have derailed my goals for this project. I hope I can come back to his case in another project, but I'm also happy to offer up the reference numbers from the NAI for a braver soul who is interested in pursuing this inquiry: NAI, Dublin Circuit Courts, State Files, 1C-90-39/45, 17-Apr-28; 1D-20-112/31, 19-Jan-34; 1D-20-112, 21-Apr-36; 1D-20-112/12, 9-Apr-40; 1D-20-112/31, 19-Oct-42; 1D-27-12/68, 17-Apr-45; V14-30-22/41, 15-Jan-51.

30. NAI, Dublin Circuit Court, State Files, 1C-124-40, docket 43, 6-Jun-31, the State v. Matthew Nyhan and Robert Byrne.

31. My goal here is to report my findings from the recorded history of Ireland and offer some contextualization to help understand this world that we're peering into. I am not championing pederasty.

32. It is currently sixteen for boys in the United Kingdom, sixteen or seventeen in various Australian territories, sixteen to eighteen for boys in the United States, seventeen for boys in Ireland, sixteen for boys in South Africa, etc.

product of a culture that marks those relationships as taboo. Though we live in a moment when postpubescent teen sexuality is becoming less controversial as a subject, most people have pretty strict parameters of what makes an "acceptable" partner for teens to explore their sexuality. I, too, have my own personal beliefs about when someone can make informed and healthy decisions about sex. But what I think and feel about "age" as an adequate boundary for sex and sexual relationships is, ultimately, irrelevant. There are thirty-eight cases in the NAI in which a party to the gross indecency was aged fifteen to twenty-one. Nearly all of those youths had sex with someone substantially older.[33] In this book, I need and want to facilitate an interrogation of the past, specifically of Ireland's social, legal, and cultural constructions of "boyhood," masculinity, and same-sex desire, all through the experiences of the boys and men who are snapshotted in the court records, and whose life stories I've worked to expand beyond the criminal.

Conversely, at least sixty-eight of the court records I collected from the NAI involved a boy under fifteen, none younger than nine.[34] Many of the boys aged nine to fourteen took money from men who wanted sex. An indecent assault charge was a way that the state discerned coercive sex from (ostensibly) consensual sex between males. When two men were charged with *just* gross indecency or sodomy, and not "indecent assault," the details of the case seem to indicate that both parties were willing participants. But when children under fifteen were involved, the adult was almost always charged with indecent assault. Even in cases where the children testified that they willingly engaged in some kind of exchange, the attorney general's office stacked the "indecent assault" as well as "gross indecency" charges against the adult. Though the laws weren't necessarily designed to protect children, in practice, the agents of the justice system developed their own criteria that harshly punished men who sexually assaulted prepubescent boys.

In total, of the gross indecency and sodomy court records I found in the NAI and in newspapers, just under one-quarter involved boys under fifteen. This means that 75 percent of cases involve boys and men fifteen and over, and those case studies—rather than the ones involving boys under fifteen— are the focus of this book. In places where I discuss the broader statistics of the total number of "gross indecency" and "sodomy" court records, I do so

---

33. I discuss these nuances again in Chapter 5.

34. The police and courts used different criminal statutes to deal with men who assaulted boys under the age of nine. Charges like "carnal knowledge of a child" were used to frame a crime as one enacted by one party (the defendant) on another. "Gross indecency" and, indeed, "sodomy" seem to have been framed in the courts as requiring two to tango. If there wasn't an indecent assault attached—which was usually bolstered by one man/boy turning witness against the other in the case—it is very likely that a gross indecency or sodomy crime was consensual. That could, depending on the judge, be better or worse for those involved.

not because *I* equate the adult sexual assault of children with "homosexuality" but because many in Ireland (and Britain, the United States, Germany, etc.) in the early twentieth century, like Judge Cahir Davitt, *did* equate all male same-sex desire with pederasty and pedophilia.[35] Those numbers help us understand how policing all expressions of same-sex sex exploded under the Free State. And, in comparison with the court records that survive from 1890 to 1920, which show the inverse ratio when it comes to policing sex between adult men versus sexual assaults of boy children, those statistics are particularly staggering.[36]

In Dublin, over a ten-year period of British rule, 1899–1909, only ten men were arrested for sodomy or gross indecency crimes. There were a handful more between 1910 and 1913, but the police in Dublin were understandably busy dealing with other issues between 1914 and 1922. Seven, or 70 percent, of the cases from 1899 to 1909 were cases of men who'd sexually assaulted male children under the age of fourteen. Only 30 percent were cases of sex between two adult men. Jump to the Irish Free State: between 1924 and 1934 in Dublin, 135 men were charged under the gross indecency and sodomy laws. Of those, twenty-nine cases were of men charged with sexual assault on a child under fourteen, and fifteen cases involved youths aged fifteen to twenty-one. The remaining ninety-one cases in that single decade were men arrested for seeking or having sex with other adult men. As far as I can tell from the testimonies and statements, only one of those ninety-one cases was launched because a man made a pass at an unwilling adult stranger.[37] This means that under the Free State, in addition to an astounding increase in overall policing, the motivation for policing same-sex sex flipped from mostly protecting children, under British rule (70 percent of the time), to mostly targeting men who desired consensual sex with other men, in about 67 percent of the cases, under Irish rule. This baseline would continue for the rest of the period I am focusing on in this book, through the early 1970s.[38]

Before 1970, men who loved other men were rendered invisible. Two chapters of *Love in the Lav* are dedicated to men whose sexual partners were

---

35. "Vice Prevalent in Dublin," *Irish Times*, 13 February 1931, 13; see also Jenkins, *Moral Panic*; and Evans, "Bahnhof Boys," 605–636.

36. For a more detailed discussion of the total number of arrests and convictions in Dublin between 1922 and 1972, see Chapter 1.

37. NAI, Dublin Circuit Court, State Files, 1C-94-84, 6-May-30. There are a number of cases where the gardaí baited men into crimes, but because of the tactics used I would not count those among the "unwilling strangers" category. I discuss these cases at length in Chapter 2.

38. For statistics on policing sex between men in Ireland after 1970, see McDonagh, *Gay and Lesbian Activism*. Some statistics are also included in the newly deposited files at the NAI associated with David Norris's suit against Ireland in the European Human Rights Court. See NAI, Dudgeon v. Northern Ireland / Norris v. Ireland in the European Human Rights Court, 2023/16/1, 2023/16/2, and 2023/16/3.

over the age of consent and whose partners described the sexual contact as consensual. But sex was not something Irish men and women were able to give away freely without consequence; sex was formally and informally policed. The Irish struggle for independence was built on a rhetoric that asserted same-sex desire was English, an unnatural affliction imported by those colonial oppressors, and thus not Irish.[39] This specter of Otherness haunted the same-sex-desiring men and women who forced themselves into uncomfortable marriages, drank themselves into early graves, estranged themselves from family and kin, or fled the island for the promise of anonymity or opportunity in faraway lands. Of course, we know that same-sex-desiring people lived in Ireland prior to 1973, but we don't know anything *about* those people. By examining twentieth-century Ireland through the lived experiences of ordinary same-sex-desiring Irish men who've been relegated to obscurity by history, this book reveals the contradictions, possibilities, and magnitude of postcolonial Irish Catholic nationalism.

Chapter 7 and the Conclusion of this book are focused on men whose lives were *not* interrupted by the formal policing system of Ireland's postcolonial moral project. A few public figures—Micheál Mac Liammóir, Hilton Edwards, and John Broderick—provide a glimpse into the unregulated queer Irish world. But, by the very nature of who they were, and what their privilege afforded them, their biographies are as representative as and no more than those of the men who clashed with the authorities. Their experiences were both unique and mundane. When offered alongside the others highlighted in this book, Mac Liammóir, Edwards, and Broderick help paint a more complete picture of life as a same-sex-desiring man in postcolonial Ireland. Mac Liammóir, Edwards, and Broderick were men who had sex with men, who lived most of their lives in Ireland, and who never once ran afoul of the Garda. Mac Liammóir and Edwards lived together for fifty years in Dublin. John Broderick (though he was evasive about it most of the time) admitted on television to being bisexual. Their stories, which overlap and intersect, are so profoundly different from those of the other men in this book that it doesn't seem fair. But theirs are important foils for understanding the limitations, allowances, and hypocrisies of Ireland's sexual purity campaigns. And, in that way, their stories actually are like the majority of queer Ireland's stories.[40]

---

39. Earls, "Unnatural Offenses of English Import," 396–424.

40. Despite the morality and even postcolonial campaigns opposing and criminalizing same-sex desire, no states have ever been fully successful in eradicating LGBTQ people. That's not to say that state-based violence and terror isn't effective in creating shame, fear, and internalized homophobia and destroying families, tanking careers, and filling prisons. It certainly is. But I think it's important to remember that people will resist, persist, and survive in even the bleakest conditions of oppression.

In many ways, the study of sex and sexuality in Ireland—as elsewhere—has been stagnated by the conservative "habitus and ethos" that shaped the policing of Ireland in the twentieth century.[41] There are very few histories of Irish same-sex desire, and those that have been written tend to focus on the IGRM from the 1960s through the 1990s. The earliest works on Irish same-sex sex were published in the 1990s by founding members of the IGRM. Literary scholars have examined the writings of queer Irish authors like Oscar Wilde, Brendan Behan, and Kate O'Brien, but historians have only come to these studies very recently.[42] Sonja Tiernan's *Marriage Equality in Ireland* and Patrick McDonagh's *Gay and Lesbian Activism in the Republic of Ireland, 1973–93* emphasize the "liberalization" period of Irish LGBTQ history. McDonagh, Tiernan, and others draw on the robust Irish Queer Archive at the NLI, the collections of which are focused almost entirely on the post-1960s period. Brian Lacey's *Terrible Queer Creatures* was the first monograph dedicated to locating same-sex-desiring people across the centuries of Irish history, focusing on case studies of famous or forgotten men and women rather than on the impact of policing on ordinary same-sex-desiring people.[43] Conversely, the historian Diarmaid Ferriter's sweeping *Occasions of Sin* (2009) raises as many questions as it answers. Though Ferriter also utilizes court records for the pre-1960 period, he glosses over the detailed testimonies of defendants, police, and witnesses, missing out on the crucial social history of sexuality layered in those records. He neglects much of the nuance of same-sex-desiring experiences, particularly as they might be shaped by age, class, or postcolonial ideology. More to the point, his book, which is invaluable as a jumping-off point for those interested in the history of sexuality in Ireland, is more a sketch of the "habitus and ethos" surrounding sex and less a history of the people. The "hidden" histories of these ordinary Irish men and boys haven't been written yet. We don't know who they were, how they lived, or who they loved. *Love in the Lav* is the first social history of same-sex-desiring men prior to 1973.

Because little has been written about same-sex desire in Ireland before 1970, there's a sort of Whiggish slant in the historiography that suggests things were really bad for LGBTQ people before the "thaw" of the 1960s, and then things slowly got better thanks to the due diligence of activists who worked tirelessly to build community and networks and advocate for decriminalization and rights. This isn't untrue, but it's also not that simple. By the 1970s, when the IGRM and the feminist movement got off the ground,

---

41. Inglis, *Lessons in Irish Sexuality.*
42. Sinfield, *Wilde Century*; Walshe, "First Gay Irishman?" 38–57; Walshe, *Kate O'Brien: A Writing Life* (Irish Academic Press, 2006); and Walshe, *Oscar's Shadow.*
43. Lacey, *Terrible Queer Creatures.*

there was a collective sense among the people who shared their experiences that things had been bad in Ireland for a long time.[44] And it had been. Men were made examples of in the courts, imprisoned for kisses and caresses with lovers. Women were forced into Magdalene laundries and Mother and Baby Homes for unwed pregnancies, perceived sexual "immorality," and without reason. It's hard to say whether men and women in the 1930s, 1940s, or 1950s felt the weight of the postcolonial moral project, which was a clear effort through state and church apparatuses to erase the visible signs of sex and construct a pure "Irish" Ireland. There are snippets in the court records of men who felt they were always being watched. The women who survived the systems of oppression have, since the 1990s, shared their harrowing experiences. The way people reflected on the prior decades, Ireland's homophobia and misogyny were all encompassing, total, and unyielding.

The collective memory of Ireland's LGBTQ people and, more broadly, women is important and real. But I hope in this book to chronicle both the postcolonial moral project *and* the ways people resisted, carved out space for themselves, and lived. In the face of the socioreligious pressure to conform to Catholic anti-sex ideologies, expanded under Archbishop John Charles McQuaid's campaign to Catholicize Dublin in the 1940s, Irish people still sought and had sex. Despite the threat of arrest and social censure, queer people lived and loved in Ireland. Same-sex-desiring men took advantage of irregular policing, juries unwilling to convict "gross indecency" offenders, public space, and, for the fortunate middle-class Dubliners, private residences for their affairs and relationships. The existence of queer Irish people persistently, subversively, and daily challenged the nationalist mythology that same-sex desire was not Irish.

While the statistics that I present in this book are shocking—with arrests and trials increasing 1,000 percent in the shift from British rule to the Irish Free State—I want to be sure to communicate the nuance of this history. The heaviest policing of same-sex sex happened in waves, between 1930 and 1932, during World War II, and in 1950. Most other years the gardaí might arrest five or fewer men in Dublin for the entire year.[45] Inconsistent policing proved

44. NAI, Norris v. Ireland, 2023/16/1-11; see also McDonagh, *Gay and Lesbian Activism*; and Kerrigan, *LGBT Visibility, Media, and Sexuality*.

45. These numbers are based on the court records that have survived in the NAI. It is possible, even likely, that some files are lost or were destroyed, but these numbers are still fairly representative based on the rare instances of sex crime statistics produced by the Garda Commissioners. E.g., Eoin O'Duffy put together a sex crimes dataset for the Carrigan Commission in 1931, which shows anywhere from 40 percent to 150 percent more same-sex sex crimes in Dublin than I found files for in the NAI. NAI, Carrigan Report, Reference JUS-2004-32-105. E.g., O'Duffy reported six sodomy, indecent assault, or gross indecency crimes in 1924, and I found just three of those case files in the newspapers and/or Dublin Circuit Court records:

opportunistic for same-sex-desiring men. The waves were devastating, for sure, and publicized enough that they conditioned a lot of people into hiding and avoiding those landmarks of queer sociality. But the threat of arrest was never enough to eradicate sex between men, not in public, and not in private.

Love in the Lav as a title represents equal parts author and subject. When I started research for this project in 2013, I went to the NAI knowing I'd find something if I looked hard enough, even without a road map to get there. Ferriter's *Occasions of Sin* offered a shorthand I wasn't then equipped to decipher, so I started in the Circuit Court State Books, and followed those to the full Circuit Court State Files. It was in a public lavatory—described in Garda testimony and "crime scene" photographs—that I found the first men whose experiences would drive my doctoral dissertation and now this book. The labor of love that is working on a project for over a decade is indescribable. For all that I mourned the disruption to their intimate moments, without these court records describing men having sex in lavatories, I wouldn't have been able to get this far. I hope that the care and consideration I've put into writing about Dublin's same-sex-desiring men, the Gardaí who policed them, and the teens who sold sex to them goes some way toward rectifying the wrongs of the past. More than simply revealing the extent of state-based violence against same-sex-desiring men, I endeavor here to fold these men into Ireland's history.

For my subjects, *Love in the Lav* nods not to the police officer's gaze but to the reality of life for same-sex-desiring men in Ireland and elsewhere in this period. Of course, Ireland (like most Christian-leaning countries in the twentieth century) had both formal and informal modes of policing its citizens' sexuality. Gardaí enforced the law and moral regime by surveilling the spaces that men were known to cruise. The Catholic Church exerted its own influence both at the grassroots level, by preaching brimstone and hellfire from the pulpit and in the confessional, and at the state level, with its "special place" in the Irish 1937 Constitution.[46] Between church and state, the two-pronged approach created an oppressive culture and ensured that ordinary queer Irish people—people without social status or wealth to protect—suffered. For some, perhaps even many, the only place they could find the physical touch they craved was in Dublin's public and urban spaces: in parks, alleyways, and, yes, public lavatories.

---

in 1927, he reported twenty, of which I found fourteen, and, in 1929, he reported thirty-one cases, while I found records of only fifteen.

46. Constitution Act (1937), Oireachtas, available at https://www.oireachtas.ie/en/bills/bill/1937/41/; for a discussion of Catholicism's place in the constitution and constructions of citizenship, see Ronit Lentin, "'Irishness,' the 1937 Constitution, and Citizenship: Gender and Ethnicity View," *Irish Journal of Sociology* 8 (1998): 5–24.

Recently, when I was sitting in the NAI lobby waiting for the reading room to open, I encountered a group of self-described "nosy" Irish women who were getting trained to volunteer at the archives. They asked if I was there for the training, and I said, "No, I'm an academic historian here doing research." They said, "Oh, how lovely, what are you researching?" I said, "Men who had sex with men in the Free State." One immediately (and jokingly) said, "Well there were none here, of course!" I said (with a friendly wink to assure her I'm in on the joke), "I've found a few!" And another said (with enthusiasm), "Sure, but what does the National Archive have about that?" And I told them about the court records for men who were arrested for having sex with men. Surprised, but interested, they peppered me with questions for the next ten minutes until their guide came down to collect them for the training and tour.

I've had many similar conversations. The joke that there were no gay people in Ireland (before when? before marriage equality? before decriminalization in 1993? before the IGRM in 1973? before the British came?) is a tongue-in-cheek nod to (or, in some nastier cases, a serious assertion about) Ireland's recent history, shaped as it was by Catholic nationalism and a particularly virulent brand of hypocritical sexual morality policing. The Irish take their history seriously, and every student can recite the names of the martyred heroes of the 1916 Easter Rising. But Ireland's history of queer people—the wide spectrum who didn't conform to the gender or sexuality norms of the state and country—is woefully understudied by academics.[47] So queer history is not integrated or really even included in the history of Irish nationalism, *An gorta mor*, the Land Wars, the Home Rule movement, the War of Independence and Civil War, Fianna Fáil's political domination, and the other key events, people, and themes of Ireland's history. There have, in recent years, been notable exceptions of same-sex-desiring individuals being celebrated on a national scale. Roger Casement, made infamous when the British government released excerpts of his diaries chronicling his participation in cruising culture everywhere he went, was highlighted among the 1916 heroes during the Decade of Centenaries events.[48] Oscar Wilde is on the literature curriculum in most secondary schools, and most people (including my archive vol-

47. Exceptions being, as previously mentioned, Ferriter's *Occasions of Sin*, Hug's *The Politics of Sexual Morality in Ireland*, McAuliffe's recent biography *Margaret Skinnider*, Kerrigan's *LGBTQ Visibility, Media, and Sexuality*, the sociologist Paul Ryan's work on homosexuality and sex work in Ireland, McDonagh's *Gay and Lesbian Activism*; and, of course, my two articles (Earls, "Solicitor Brown and His Boy" and "Unnatural Offenses of English Import").

48. There's been a "Roger Casement Summer School" every year since 2017; 2023's took place Friday 5–6 May 2023; schedule of events accessed on 9 September 2023, available at https://www.decadeofcentenaries.com/2023-roger-casement-summer-schoolfri-5-sat-6-may/. A list of 2017 Roger Casement events during the Decade of Centenaries is available at https://www.decadeofcentenaries.com/tag/roger-casement/.

unteer friends) are aware that he was charged and imprisoned under the gross indecency law.[49] But, in highlighting high-profile outliers, the ordinary and everyday people are further marginalized.

I hope to rectify that with this book. Moreover, as Ireland continues to embrace its queer past, I hope that relatives will deposit the personal papers and beautiful love stories of their same-sex-desiring ancestors with publicly accessible archives. I hope that funding bodies will enable scholars to do more substantial work in finding queer women and trans lives in the archives and through oral history. But most of all, I hope that this book will just be the first of many to uncover Ireland's queer lives.

---

49. See Sinfield, *Wilde Century*; Walshe, "First Gay Irishman?"; and Walshe, *Oscar's Shadow*.

1

The City

In John Broderick's fiction, Dublin is a world apart from the suffocating self-righteous and performative Catholicism of the midlands and the rest of rural Ireland. In Broderick's Dublin, the gardaí are aware of and willing to overlook the consenting relationships of same-sex-desiring men. In *The Pilgrimage*, Tommy Baggot moves to Dublin from the country—like so many other young Irish men—and finds the independence and freedom he needed both to connect with other same-sex-desiring men and to engage with a social-sexual community. "It appears," Broderick writes in his characteristically succinct way, "young [Tommy] Baggot was known to the police, and had been warned [but never arrested] a few times before."[1] Similarly, in *The Trial of Father Dillingham*, Eddie lives in a renovated Georgian on Fitzwilliam Square, divided into four apartments and occupied by his dearest friends—a defrocked priest, an ancient kleptomaniac opera star, and Eddie's lover Maurice. Eddie and Maurice occupy separate apartments, but in a way that communicates their cohabitation.[2] In many ways, Broderick's Dublin represents a haven for men like Eddie, Maurice, Tommy, and the author himself.

In this book, I recount stories of men's lives upended and erotic dalliances destroyed by the tightfisted enforcers of the postcolonial Irish state. Yet we know prison, pain, and suffering weren't the *only* possible outcomes for men who loved men in Dublin. Not just because John Broderick imag-

1. Broderick, *Pilgrimage*, 119–120.
2. Broderick, *Trial of Father Dillingham*, 22–25.

ined same-sex relationships and desire as being made almost unremarkable by the "big city"; there are also archival shards evidencing abiding love, sexual pleasure, and contentment for men who desired other men in Ireland, though rare, in the NAI and the NLI. While most of the historical examples in this book highlight the worst case scenarios, they are also revealing of something resembling Broderick's Dublin. In Chapters 3 and 4, for example, I demonstrate just how rare it was for men to be policed for the sexual relationships they maintained in private homes and, further, how rare it was for neighbors, acquaintances, or even authority figures to turn in men who had sex with men. In Chapters 2 and 6, my discussion of the Garda reveals how gross indecency policing campaigns were infrequent, and that infrequency created space and opportunity for same-sex-desiring men to make connections, however fleeting, in the public spaces of the city. It's possible that the thrillingly mundane world Broderick reconstructed in his fiction had some kernels of truth to it. In *The Pilgrimage*, Tommy Baggot and his lover/roommate were allowed to move around the city and find sexual partners without real risk of consequences. The city provides a shelter for same-sex love and creates opportunities for casual sexual encounters. In *The Trial of Father Dillingham*, the garda Greg says that he has been instructed to root out gross indecency offenders, and yet he overlooks Eddie's dalliances so long as children are not involved.[3] The infrastructure of danger is present in Broderick's fiction, but it is toothless. Broderick's world is fantasy, and the state's postcolonial moral project had real and palpable consequences for thousands of Irish women and men. But there is nuance in this history as well, and that starts with Dublin.

In 1922, Dublin became the capital city of the Irish Free State, but before that it was the center of English power in Ireland for some eight hundred years. For the nationalists intent on forging the Free State into their ideal Ireland, Dublin was tainted. Since the Act of Union in 1801, the formal British administration in Ireland operated out of Dublin Castle. Between 1801 and 1922, the city's barracks and forts housed thousands of British (and British-employed Irish) soldiers. Even after the administrators and soldiers were expelled, the memory of Dublin's colonial past lingered. For those concerned with Ireland's moral health, men like Eámon de Valera (taoiseach 1937–1948, 1951–1954, and 1957–1959) and John Charles McQuaid (archbishop of Dublin 1940–1972), Dublin was as far from an "authentically" Irish place as London. It was where young people went and rarely found work, where Ireland's Catholic values threatened to be overwhelmed by urban decay, and where the sinful sought and found their vices.

---

3. Broderick, *Trial of Father Dillingham*, 207–208. Perhaps, significantly, Broderick dedicated *The Trial of Father Dillingham*, which includes some of the most loving and positive relationships of any of his novels, to his friend, Julien Green.

Of particular concern was the apparent prevalence of sex crimes in the city. In 1923, Ernst Blythe, minister for local government, felt that "the character of the capital will have a very important influence upon the progress and development of the state. . . . If Dublin is not as good a capital as we ought to have, the State will suffer."[4] Blythe's comment referred specifically to the alleged "vice scare" that gripped the city in the 1920s. High crime rates plagued Dublin between 1916 and 1924, largely attributable to the upheaval that accompanied the War of Independence and Civil War. The Dublin Metropolitan Police (DMP) dismissed claims that there was an increase in "abominable offences," with one spokesperson asserting, "the present outcry is what I would call a seasonal scare."[5] A year later, Justice Jonathan Pim said that "the city of Dublin was not yet what it ought to be, but it was getting, from day to day, more like what it ought to be."[6] It appeared, in reports shared with the public, that violent crimes were on the decline. The *Freeman's Journal* noted that the overall crime increase from 1923 to 1924 was only due to a rise in drunkenness.[7] Yet, Commissioner of the Garda Eoin O'Duffy's 1931 report to the Carrigan Committee showed that sex crimes, particularly rape and sexual assault of girls under fifteen, actually increased every year from 1924 to 1929.[8] While this may simply evidence the efficacy of the newly manned police force, the increase in incidents was troubling enough to the Carrigan Committee members to convince them that the information should not be shared with the public.[9] Despite the exorcism of the British, immoral and illegal sexual behavior persisted in Ireland, and Dublin appeared to be the worst of all.

Both the perception and reality of moral and physical urban decay compounded the unease created by the legacy of Dublin's place in the British subjugation of Ireland. There were slums "unfit for human habitation" throughout the city, abject poverty and disease plaguing the working class, and sexual scandals and crime that seemed to radiate from the city.[10] In the twentieth century, anxiety over these conditions translated into policies seeking to reform the physical city and police the morality of Dublin. The city was troubling. Its sexual criminals were a danger to the pure and chaste Irish Catholic-nationalist state. But it was also rife with opportunity. With the right guiding

---

4. Campbell, "Interpreting the City," 43.

5. "Dublin Vice Scare: Worse Than for 50 Years," *Irish Independent*, 20 September 1923, 6.

6. "Grand Jury Again," *Freeman's Journal* (1763–1924), 6 February 1924, 8.

7. "Grand Jury Again," 8.

8. NAI, Department of Justice, H247/41A, Eoin O'Duffy, Evidence to Carrigan Committee, 30 October 1930.

9. O'Malley, *Sexual Offences*, 6.

10. "Grand Jury Again," 8; "Dublin Shooting," *Irish Examiner* (1841–1989), 5 April 1924, 7; and "Dublin Proselytizing Vice," *Irish Independent* (1905–current), 24 December 1923, 2.

Figure 1.1 Aerial photograph of the River Liffey west of the Four Courts by Cyril Murrell, Joe Williams Collection. *(Reproduced with permission of the South Dublin Libraries.)*

force, Dublin could be reforged. Between the Catholic Church and the newly created Garda Síochána, the state could implement and exercise moral order.

The Garda was an essential component of building a new state and building up Dublin as its capital. With the Peace Preservation Act of 1814 and the Irish Constabulary Act of 1822, there were two police forces in Ireland: the Royal Irish Constabulary (RIC), which dealt with all of Ireland except Dublin, and the DMP. There were a little over one thousand DMP members in 1857, and around the same number of officers in the RIC for the rest of Ireland. In the nineteenth century, there were proportionately more crimes in Dublin than elsewhere in Ireland. Both forces were made up mostly of Catholics (DMP 88 percent, RIC 75 percent), but Protestants occupied the officer positions in both forces. The DMP was generally respected by upper- and middle-class Dubliners, while the more impoverished and working-class areas of the city clashed with the DMP more frequently, as in the Dublin Lockout of 1913. When the Irish Catholic lawyer and political hopeful Daniel O'Connell created the Catholic Association in 1823, a mass movement with thousands of Irish members, to pressure the British government to repeal the Penal Laws that disenfranchised Catholics, the British expanded the presence of the RIC throughout Ireland to deal with agrarian unrest and O'Connell's famous Monster Meetings. Thousands of Catholic Association members showed up in fields to hear O'Connell speak.[11]

11. See O'Farrell, *Catholic Emancipation*.

In times of political strife—the 1830s Tithe War, the 1848 Young Irelanders uprising, the 1867 Fenian rebellion, the Land Wars, and the 1916 Easter Rising—both the RIC and the DMP were at odds with the general population.[12] Both forces were made up of Irish natives, until the second phase of the War of Independence (March 1920 to July 1921) when the British prime minister David Lloyd George reinforced the RIC with ex-military English (66 percent) and Scottish (14 percent) recruits, also known as the Black and Tans.[13] The Black and Tans were followed by another group of special recruits, mostly English ex-officers, who became known as the Auxiliaries (the Auxiliary Division of the RIC). The DMP was an unarmed force, except for the "G men" or detective division, which dealt mostly with political crime and took up the fight against the Irish Republican Army (IRA) during the War of Independence.[14] During the War of Independence, the Provisional Government created the Irish Republican Police (IRP) who dealt to some extent with catching criminals but did little else in the way of typical police work. Sometimes the RIC or DMP worked with the IRP, but often they clashed. With the passage by the Irish parliament, or Dáil, of the Treaty with Great Britain on January 7, 1922, the British almost immediately began the process of withdrawal. The RIC was disbanded in the independent twenty-six counties and reorganized and renamed the Royal Ulster Constabulary in Ulster in 1922; the DMP was maintained as a distinct unit until 1925 when it was merged with the Garda Síochána. Though nationalized, the Dublin Metropolitan Division (DMD) of the Garda Síochána was always the largest concentration of officers, and those officers were tasked with policing the vice and foreignness of Dublin. The uneasy place that Dublin occupied in the Irish state and society was evident in the fits and starts of attempted urban renewal and haphazard attempts to impose a moral sexual regime onto Dubliners.[15]

At the same time, Dublin was Ireland's major urban center. Young people moved to Dublin seeking independence from their families. A man with a few pence could have a pint or catch a movie. Those interested in indulging a sinful urge, from gambling to drink to illicit sex, were sure to find that which they sought. The changes to the physical city—the slum clearance, construction of new public housing, and restoration of the cityscape—created new parks, lavatories, and doorways that facilitated all sorts of sexual opportunities.

---

12. See R. F. Forster, *Modern Ireland 1600–1972* (New York: Penguin Books, 1988); Alvin Jackson, *Ireland 1778–1998* (Oxford: Oxford University Press, 2007).

13. See W. J. Lowe, "Who Were the Black-and-Tans?" *History Ireland* 3, no. 12 (Autumn 2004), accessed on 3 November 2015, available at http://www.historyireland.com/20th-century-contemporary-history/who-were-the-black-and-tans/.

14. McNiffe, *History of the Garda Síochána*, 5–8.

15. Hanna, *Modern Dublin*; and Kincaid, *Postcolonial Dublin*.

Even as the state and Catholic Church sought to control Dubliners and "reclaim" the city through moral order and physical changes, same-sex-desiring men carved out their own spaces in the cityscape. Scholars like Sam Mc-Grath are tracing the modest but vital gay pub scene from the pre-1970 period, including the living memory of those establishments. Pubs were an important part of working-class queer life in midcentury Ireland. Bartley Dunne's and Rice's (both in the 1950s–1960s), and the Hotel Beresford (1930s–1940s) were known as gay-friendly spaces where men could get a pint or pick up a man.[16] Surprisingly, the gardaí didn't bother surveilling pubs for cruising men before the 1970s; presumably, the centrality of pub culture to all Irish men made it a waste of their time to police. Same-sex-desiring men also sought out parks, darkened alleyways, and public lavatories for potential lovers. We know that these were sites frequented by same-sex-desiring men because that is where gardaí arrested them. But certainly the recorded instances of "gross indecency" are merely the tip of the iceberg. Though judges promised that the Gardaí were "always watching," in reality they weren't. They had finite resources for policing vice, and surveilling public toilets for same-sex-desiring men was just one of their various responsibilities. Same-sex-desiring men were able to transform public and private spaces to meet their needs, laden with the thrilling possibilities of both pleasure and peril.

In independent Ireland, like all countries employing Section 11 of the British Criminal Law Amendment Act of 1885, same-sex sex was illegal whether it was conducted in private or in public. Historians Matt Houlbrook and Steven Maynard, in their works on London and Toronto, respectively, expound on the differentiation of public and private spaces, and in Houlbrook's case, the "public-private" spaces that fell into the gray zone of the two.[17] Broadly conceived, in a state where same-sex sex was illegal no matter the setting, the bushes and ditches of public parks, the exterior walls of buildings that create lanes and alleyways, social spaces like public houses and cinemas, a rented room in a hotel or hostel, or even a privately owned cottage, all presented their own element of danger, and their own opportunity for sexual pleasure.

In 1931, when sentencing men found guilty of keeping a "male brothel," the circuit court judge Cahir Davitt said "the offence . . . was a disgusting one, and one which, unfortunately, seemed to be spreading in the city."[18] While it's true that same-sex sex crime prosecutions rose dramatically from 1922 (when there were none) to 1926 (when there were some), they steadied from

---

16. McGrath, "Bartley Dunnes"; McGrath, "Hotel Beresford and the Seafarer's Club."

17. Houlbrook, *Queer London*; Maynard, "Through a Hole in the Lavatory Wall," 207–242; Maynard, "Horrible Temptations," 191; and Maynard, "Without Working?" 378–398.

18. "Vice Prevalent in Dublin," *Irish Times*, 13 February 1931, 13.

1926 to 1929.[19] In January 1931, when Davitt heard the male brothel case, the number of gross indecency cases he saw was fairly consistent. Davitt's hyperbole may have been intended to move the public to action or, at the very least, frighten queer men away from acting on their desires. Significantly, Davitt also pointed to the issue as a localized and urban issue; vice was "prevalent in Dublin," not in Ireland, according to the headline of that particular story.[20] For some, Dublin's foreignness and susceptibility to vice and squalor made it a site ripe for policing and reconquest, even as others—those who envisioned that Ireland was a rural state of chaste, Catholic, happily impoverished Celts—hoped to ignore it, abandon it, or destroy it.

As the historian David George Boyce notes, Ireland was a rural state with rural values and ways of life. The veneration of the rural was a sentiment that was shared by the arbiters of Irish independence.[21] Some public figures—particularly those representing the rural counties—wanted to abandon the city entirely. In 1924, one member of the Dáil, from Mayo, said, "The seat of the national Assembly should really be far removed from Dublin, as Dublin [is] a foreign town."[22] Though the *Irish Examiner* reported that laughter from the Dáil members followed the comment, the underlying sentiment was widespread. That "foreignness" was the persistence of the "taint" of the British, embodied in this physical remnant of British rule—the city itself—and the presence of those immoral sexual vices attributed to British rule.[23]

Politicians spoke of the ideal Ireland, one divorced entirely from its British colonial legacy. De Valera was the product of late nineteenth- and early twentieth-century romantic and militant nationalisms, a hero of the War of Independence, leader of the anti-Treatyites during the Civil War, and founder of Fianna Fáil, the dominant political party for most of the twentieth century.[24] In a radio broadcast in March 1943, de Valera asked listeners to turn to "that ideal Ireland that we would have." He emphasized the centrality of the Catholic Church, and "a land whose countryside would be bright with cosy homesteads" rather than cluttered with the filth and modernisms of urban centers, with a happily impoverished population of chaste men and women. "It would, in a word," he said, "be the home of a people living the life that God desires that man should live."[25] When fanciful speeches and rhetoric were

19. NAI, Department of Justice, H247.41A, Evidence from Eoin O'Duffy to the Carrigan Committee.
20. "Vice Prevalent in Dublin," 13.
21. Boyce, *Nineteenth-Century Ireland*, 5.
22. "In the Dail Today," *Irish Examiner*, 5 April 1924, 7.
23. On the "taint" of British rule, see Earls, "Unnatural Offenses of English Import," 396–424.
24. The different forms of Irish nationalism—romantic, militant, and socialist—are discussed in LaPointe, *Between Irishmen*.
25. De Valera, "The Ireland We Dreamed Of," 466–469.

translated into policy, this idealism had tangible impacts on the lives of Irish men and women. During the years of de Valera's leadership (1932–1948, 1951–1954, 1957–1959), Fianna Fáil implemented policies that emphasized his rural dream, through a focus on agriculture and small-scale native industry. The historian Tom Garvin suggests that these efforts were intended to achieve a "collective dream of a moral community which was authentic, pious, static and intellectually homogeneous."[26] Until the 1950s, a range of economic policies, including tariffs on imports and restrictions on the foreign ownership of domestic firms meant to protect the big cattle farmers and landowners of rural Ireland delayed the growth of the Irish economy.[27]

While the emphasis of Fianna Fáil policies was on the rural, conditions in Dublin could not be ignored. The decay of the capital city was, after all, a legacy of colonialism. Under British rule the majority of the once stately Georgian-style houses were allowed to become dilapidated and crowded slum tenements by the start of the twentieth century.[28] The *Irish Times* wrote that the slums were "responsible not only for disease and crime but for much of our industrial unrest" in the 1910s.[29] One of the key political issues in independent Ireland was addressing this lingering problem. Like the men having sex with other men and the "fallen" women (sex workers), the slums represented a persistent reminder of Irish subjugation and British corruption. "Slum clearance" in Dublin has over 1,500 search results in the Irish Newspaper Archive database from 1925 to 1972 for the *Irish Examiner, Irish Independent*, and the *Irish Press*. The height of concern was between 1930 and 1939, when de Valera and Fianna Fáil made slum clearance a central issue in their campaigning.[30] In 1933 alone, when Fianna Fáil came to power, there were over one hundred reports on slum clearance and the Dublin Corporation's efforts to tackle the issue.[31] According to the Irish newspapers, most of Dublin's problems, from low marriage rates to child neglect and abuse to crime, could be traced to the slums.[32]

---

26. Garvin, *Preventing the Future*, 27; Hanna, *Modern Dublin*, 7.

27. Hanna, 8.

28. Hanna, 44.

29. "Editorial," *Irish Times*, 4 September 1913, 8. References the Dublin Lockout of 1913.

30. Richard Dunphy, *The Making of Fianna Fáil Power in Ireland, 1923–1948* (Oxford: Clarenden, 1995), chaps. 4, 5.

31. The Dublin Corporation was the name of the city government and its administrative organization, which was responsible for overseeing city planning and infrastructure management in Dublin. It was renamed the Dublin City Council in 2002. Until the 1920s, the Dublin Corporation was limited in its scope to the city center and a handful of developing suburbs. The wealthiest suburbs, like Rathmines, didn't merge with the corporation's jurisdiction until the 1930s. McManus, *Dublin, 1910–1940*, 89–90.

32. "The Slum Problem," *Irish Examiner*, 4 March 1937, 14; "Untoward Events in the Saorstat," *Irish Independent*, 22 August 1931, 6; "Trim Civ Affairs," *Meath Chronicle*, 11 July 1931,

Some even saw the Georgian structures as remnants of British imperialism. As the historians Andrew Kincaid and Erika Hanna show, the way that Dublin was built and rebuilt exemplifies the struggle that persisted as the Irish government and policymakers debated what it meant to be Irish, what counted and did not count as Irish heritage in the built environment, and how the memory of British rule could or should be erased from the Dublin cityscapes.[33] According to Hanna, the Georgian buildings were said to be "unsuited to Dublin's new status as capital of an independent state and centre of Ireland's economy" because "they were not an 'authentic' part of Ireland's cultural heritage, and as such were not worth preservation."[34] Thus, clearance of the Georgian tenements was as important to the imposition of a moral order in Dublin as policing same-sex sex and female prostitution. William Cosgrave's government began the slum-clearing program but was not quick enough. Fianna Fáil turned elections in their favor by promising to clear the slums of Dublin more effectively than Cosgrove's Cumann na nGaedheal.[35] With funds from the state, the Dublin Corporation commissioned the building of sixteen hundred inner-city apartments, over five thousand houses in the northern suburbs, and thirty-two hundred two-story houses in the southwestern district of Crumlin between 1932 and 1939.[36] Housing projects developed by the Dublin Corporation enabled working-class people to achieve homeownership, through very long repayment schedules; the move to private property ownership was welcomed by church and state.[37] Still the pace and funds were never enough to match the demand, and the last uninhabitable buildings were not cleared until the late 1960s.

The crowded tenements, located deep within the immoral city center, blurred the line between public and private. Family life was thus in danger because of the lack of clearly defined boundaries between the two spheres. A. J. Humphreys, a sociologist and author of the 1966 study *New Dubliners and the Irish Family*, was commissioned in the 1950s by the Catholic Church to conduct a sociological study of the impact of urbanization and how to combat the perceived demoralization of urbanization on society.[38] In 1955, he wrote in *Christus Rex* that "urbanisation has upset the internal balance of the urban nuclear family, lessened the scope of its traditional functions, weak-

---

8; "Housing and the Poor," *Irish Press*, 27 May 1932, 6. See also Jacinta Prunty, *Dublin Slums, 1800–1925* (Dublin: Irish Academic Press, 1998).

33. See Hanna, *Modern Dublin*, and Kincaid, *Postcolonial Dublin*.

34. Hanna, 16.

35. McManus, *Dublin 1910–1940*, 41.

36. Dickson, *Dublin*, 481.

37. Dickson, 480.

38. Hanna, *Modern Dublin*, 35.

ened inter-familial solidarity and increased dependence on outside agencies."[39] Humphreys recommended that extensive social programming, led by the church, be implemented in Dublin to counteract the negative effects of urbanization. The family—the very core of the Irish Catholic state—was under threat.

Under the leadership of Archbishop McQuaid, the Catholic Church began to Catholicize Dublin in 1940, tempering its "foreignness" with the moral order of the "authentic" Irish faith. McQuaid's directives had palpable results. The diocesan clergy grew from 370 to 600, and 80 new churches and 250 Catholic primary schools were built. The expanded religious infrastructure accommodated the growing Dublin county population, which increased from 636,000 in 1946 to 859,000 in 1971. Dublin city itself only grew from 506,000 to 567,000 in that same period.[40] The church was successful in making Catholicism part of everyday life in Dublin. Almost all works of Irish fiction or memoir accounts of growing up in twentieth-century Ireland discuss attending church, skipping church, traumatizing run-ins with a priest in the confessional, or some discussion of the superiority of the Irish Catholic faith to Protestantism and the like.[41]

By no means, however, were the efforts of either the government or the church wholly successful or even consistent in their attempts to establish a moral order by shaping the physical and spiritual environments of Dublin. Urban renewal and slum clearance were projects that were picked up and put down at random in those fifty years, resulting in inefficient road systems, failed housing projects like the Ballymun Flats in the north of Dublin, and the movement of working-class families deep into the suburbs without means to transport them back to the city to their jobs.[42] Catholicism, and its capacity for inuring shame and guilt in its followers for the smallest of sins, permeated everyday life in Dublin, yet the significance of the faith and faithful in the city did not expunge sin, sinners, or Protestants from the city.

Humphreys' recommendations were taken seriously by the Irish state, and major political and economic changes in the late 1950s and throughout the 1960s radically changed the lives of Dubliners. Whereas in the two decades after independence urban planning was largely ad hoc and resistant to modernization, by the 1950s and 1960s, planners proposed ways to improve life and industrial production in Dublin's city center, as well as ad-

---

39. A. J. Humphreys, "Migration to Dublin," 199.

40. Cooney, *John Charles McQuaid*, 428; Punch and Finneran, "Changing Population Structure," 15.

41. See A. Madden, *Fear and Loathing in Dublin*; O'Callaghan, *Down by the Glenside*; A. Clarke, *Twice Round the Black Church*; McGahern, *All Will Be Well*; and O'Connor, *An Only Child*.

42. Dickson, *Dublin*, 527.

TABLE 1.1 SEX CRIME STATISTICS FOR IRELAND AND DUBLIN, 1924–1929			
Prosecutions for same-sex sex (sodomy and indecent assault on males) crimes	All of the Free State	Just Dublin	Dublin's percentage of the total
1924	13	6	46%
1925	18	8	44%
1926	24	16	67%
1927	29	20	69%
1928	41	23	56%
1929	40	31	78%
Data drawn from original report by Eoin O'Duffy to the Carrigan Committee, 1931.			

dressing the moral concerns of urbanization.[43] Hanna argues that the creation of the large suburban housing estates designed by architects like Myles Wright can be read as "the physical manifestation of an attempt to create the Christian, family-centred society as inscribed in the [1937] constitution."[44] By separating suburban residential life from productive life in the city, the family was removed from the decaying influence of the urban gray zones.

Same-sex desire was more heavily policed in Dublin than other parts of the twenty-six counties. Table 1.1 shows the number of arrests per year in all of Ireland and those just in Dublin. In 1924, for example, there were thirteen arrests for same-sex sex crimes in all of Ireland. Of those thirteen, six were in Dublin—or about 46 percent of all arrests. Only one-sixth, or 15 percent, of the total population of Ireland inhabited the Dublin County Borough in 1930.[45] Yet, between 1924 and 1929, of all of the same-sex sex crime arrests, two-thirds, or 60 percent, were in Dublin. The much higher rate of police intervention in Dublin is significant. The uneven representation of Dublin in these numbers may simply point to a higher instance of those crimes in Dublin. Perhaps same-sex-desiring men flocked to the city in search of sexual opportunities and were thus caught more frequently in Dublin. Conversely, however, these data suggest that the Free State and the Garda presumed that there would be more same-sex sex crime in Dublin, and so Gardaí were more frequently instructed to root out those criminals. Both interpretations point to a state-held perception that vice or sexual immorality were more prevalent in the city than elsewhere in Ireland.

Dublin was the target of more policing than any other county in the independent state. And yet, policing was sporadic at best between 1924 and 1964. Most years, between five and twenty arrests went to court for the entire year,

43. Hanna, *Modern Dublin*, 35.
44. Hanna, 41–42.
45. "Ceisteanna—Questions. Oral Answers.—Dublin Population, Tenants and Wage Statistics," *Dáil Éireann Debate* 194, no. 5 (28 March 1962).

and only in 1931 and 1950 were there significant spikes. The years of the Emergency (World War II) had relatively few gross indecency charges, except for 1944, when a "sex ring" was uncovered operating out of the railway station in Howth. By 1936, there were 468,103 people in Dublin city; so ten or even fifty arrests in a year seems modest. Yet the unbalanced focus on sex crime in Dublin compared to the other areas of Ireland suggests that the Irish state believed it warranted increased police presence and intervention.

Dublin was both anathema to the rural vision of an independent Ireland and inextricable from the ability to operate an independent state. The idealizations of a rural Ireland never actually meant that there was an intent to level the cities and return the land to pasture and cozy cottages, any more than the Irish politicians and newspaper editors of the nineteenth century actually believed that "unnatural crimes" were not committed by Irishmen.[46] There was always tangible evidence to the contrary: real, if slow, public spending on the rehabilitation of Dublin, and court schedules with Irish sodomy crimes published in the same newspapers as statements of Ireland's moral fortitude and chastity. The rhetoric of rural idealization and Ireland's sexual purity were tools used to influence public opinion and policy. The repeated assertion that Dublin was a place where vice—same-sex sex, particularly, but also prostitution, gambling, and drunkenness—permeated the streets, settled in the parks, and lingered outside of the pubs was easy to accept because Dublin was a city and a foreign city at that. But Irish moral authorities and politicians could believe that Dublin was a foreign city, somehow not "authentically" Irish, and still order the reconstruction of the city to effect "authentic" Irishness and the policing of vices. Meanwhile, in the spaces between the newly constructed and the decaying remnants of the city, same-sex-desiring men found each other in spaces shared with other Dubliners.

While politicians and police worried about Dublin's morality, the city took on a character of its own in the independent state. It was one of the top three ports taking emigrants out of Ireland and had temporary lodging to support any number of itinerant visitors. Dublin was where people from the rural areas and townscapes of Ireland went for culture, adventure, and economic opportunities, and it was also the locus for international travelers. Men like Micheál Mac Liammóir and Hilton Edwards, who founded the Gate Theatre Company in Dublin in 1928, saw Dublin as a welcoming city for both their artistic pursuits and, unexpectedly, their lifelong same-sex partnership.[47] Author John Broderick spent a year in Dublin as a bakery apprentice, as a teen, and visited often with his mother to take in the cultural opportunities only

---

46. See Earls, "Unnatural Offenses of English Import," 396–424.
47. Mac Liammóir and Edwards are the subject of Chapter 7.

a city could offer the well-to-do like them.[48] International travelers, like Greek citizen Constantine Kyriacco and Englishman John Bodkin, availed themselves of Dublin's poor-relief infrastructure and cruising culture.[49] The visitors, the residents, and those simply passing through tapped into the sexual economy of urban Ireland. Only half of the city's inhabitants were born there, and the shifting population created anonymity and opportunity for those seeking the pleasures of urban life.

Sex was pervasive throughout Dublin before and after Irish independence. As demonstrated by Morgan Denton, the sex worker's neighborhood known as the "Monto" district, between Gardiner, McDermott, Talbot, and Amiens, collapsed due to the harassment of the DMP in the 1920s.[50] Instead of disappearing, women sex workers were "no longer confined to a specific geographic space but spread . . . out more diffusely over the urban environment of Dublin."[51] Similarly, there were not necessarily specific neighborhoods where one might expect to find same-sex-desiring men, although, as evidenced by the arrest records, Gardaí expected to find same-sex-desiring men in and around public lavatories, in parks, and tucked into the alleyways of Dublin's many side streets.

Same-sex-desiring men appropriated spaces old and new, the remnants of an earlier city and the evidence of a slowly modernizing city. There was not a London "West End" in Dublin. Rather, the sites of sexual possibility were everywhere. Same-sex-desiring men found each other all over the city. A cursory glance at Figures 1.2 and 1.3, mapping the locations of gross indecency crimes between 1922 and 1972, shows that even while generally concentrated in the city center, same-sex sex was not limited to a single neighborhood or venue. And these maps only show where the men were caught; it is safe to assume that many more men went undetected or were simply ignored by the Garda Síochána. Though, of course, same-sex-desiring men were not entirely invisible—as suggested by the records of the arrest and charging of over four hundred men between 1924 and 1972—it was possible to avoid detection, particularly with the creative use of the cityscape.

In theory, the public bathroom provided shelter from the glances of casual passersby as well as reasonable cause to have one's penis on display. Yet, compared to lavs, there were fewer arrests in Dublin in alleyways (which total

---

48. Broderick's fiction frames this book's Introduction and Conclusion, and his life and experiences as a bisexual man in Ireland are discussed in the Conclusion.

49. Kyriacco, who was living in the Dublin Workhouse at the time, was arrested in 1927 for committing an act of gross indecency with a teen. NAI, Dublin Circuit Court, State Files, 1C-90-35, docket 46, 26-Apr-27, the State v. Constantine Kyriacco. John Bodkin's case is discussed in Chapter 2.

50. Denton, "Open Secrets," 9.

51. Denton, 3.

Figure 1.2 Gross indecency arrest sites and/or alleged crime locations. Note the higher concentrations of arrest sites in particular areas of Dublin and its suburbs—Dublin City Center (88) and areas to the south of the River Liffey (11, 12, 13), Phoenix Park (14), and Howth (16). The Howth Railway Station was the site of a "ring" of men who had sex with men in the 1940s. In City Center, Beresford Place was the site of a summerlong Garda stakeout. The remainder are the cumulative arrest records for 1922–1972. Not all locations are noted in the criminal records, but this image is representative of the concentrations of activities in the city center.

16 percent of all arrests) or parks (6 percent of all arrests), where one was in danger of being stumbled upon by a patrolling Garda at any moment. The lav's sheltering walls (and, occasionally, roofs, though many Dublin public conveniences were open topped) also made a quick getaway more difficult and concentrated sexual activity in a single confined space that was known by the Gardaí to be frequented by men seeking such vices.

In the nineteenth century, "public conveniences" were built around Dublin because most houses did not have indoor plumbing, and the public toilets met the needs of a growing urban population. The public bathhouses were also important, particularly for the cramped tenement dwellers of the first half of the twentieth century. In addition, few Dubliners had cars, making numerous and easily accessible public toilets particularly useful. The public conveniences were either underground and paved in subway tile or aboveground redbrick or metal structures. They were well lit and ranged from basic amenities like urinal stalls and washbasins to paid privies, in which a customer paid a penny to enter a private cubicle with a sit-down toilet. Over the twentieth century, however, the need for public lavatories diminished. More people got indoor plumbing, particularly through the new housing units built to accommodate the displaced tenement occupants when the slum clearance projects were underway, and more shops, cafés, and pubs with their own toilets began to liberally dot the urban landscape. In the 1950s, at least seventy public toilets were running, though that number began to decline in the 1970s as the city administration sought to trim the budget, and the hundreds of toilet attendants were some of the first to go. By the late 1990s, all public conveniences had been closed and locked up permanently.[52] From the outset, public lavs were appropriated for a variety of purposes, from casual sex to drug use. City ordinances allowed the gardaí to fine lav users for a number of "immoral" activities, from obscene language, entering before someone who paid first, graffiti, and masturbation. All were punishable by up to a £5 fine.[53]

Comparatively speaking, public parks were not as dangerous in terms of the rate of detection, with just 6 percent of all arrests for 1922–1972 taking place in parks. It is very likely that Dublin's parks were used even more extensively by men seeking sex than the arrest records reflect. They were places where men knew they could find sex partners or bring sex partners picked up elsewhere, and if cautious, avoid detection altogether. The viability of parks for sex for both same-sex and different-sex couples is evident in both the ineffectiveness of policing efforts there, the cultural awareness of parks as sexual sites, and the visibility and invisibility that parks offered to individuals and couples seeking sexual privacy in public spaces. A hedge, an unattended shed, or a grassy ditch in one of the Georgian squares like St. Stephen's Green or the enormous Phoenix Park afforded couples discretion and semiprivacy. The sheer size of Phoenix Park, open to the public since the late eighteenth century, must have daunted the police forces both before and after independence. Though the park has its own on-site Garda station, there were only sixteen gross indecency cases between 1922 and 1972, which is best explained by the expansiveness of the park and the difficulty this posed for watching every nook and cranny it provided. Phoenix Park covers 1,750 acres of land and is enclosed by a seven-mile wall. In addition to a number of public conveniences, there were ditches (Figure 1.5), ample bushes, unattended sheds, and other structures, all spread out across the park. Between 1922 and 1972, at least sixteen men were arrested in Phoenix Park.[54]

52. Barry, "Hidden Dublin."
53. Barry.
54. NAI Dublin Circuit Court, State Files, File #1C-94-81 / Docket #30, 23-Sep-29, the State v. Francis McPartland; 1C-94-82/18, 27-Nov-29, the State v. Frank Eittett; 1C-04-83/28, 21-Jan-30, the State v. Walter Birks; 1C-95-5/21, 8-Aug-30, the State v. Patrick Moylan; 1C-94-89/61–64, 20-Jan-31, the State v. James Hand; 1C-94-89/61, 20-Jan-31, the State v. Michael Corr; 1C-94-92, 7-Jul-31, the State v. Thomas O'Reilly; 1C-94-94/57, 14-Oct-31, the State v. William Wilkie; 1C-95-126/11, 20-Jan-32, the State v. Caleb Wallace; 1D-44-28/67, 10-Apr-34, the State v.

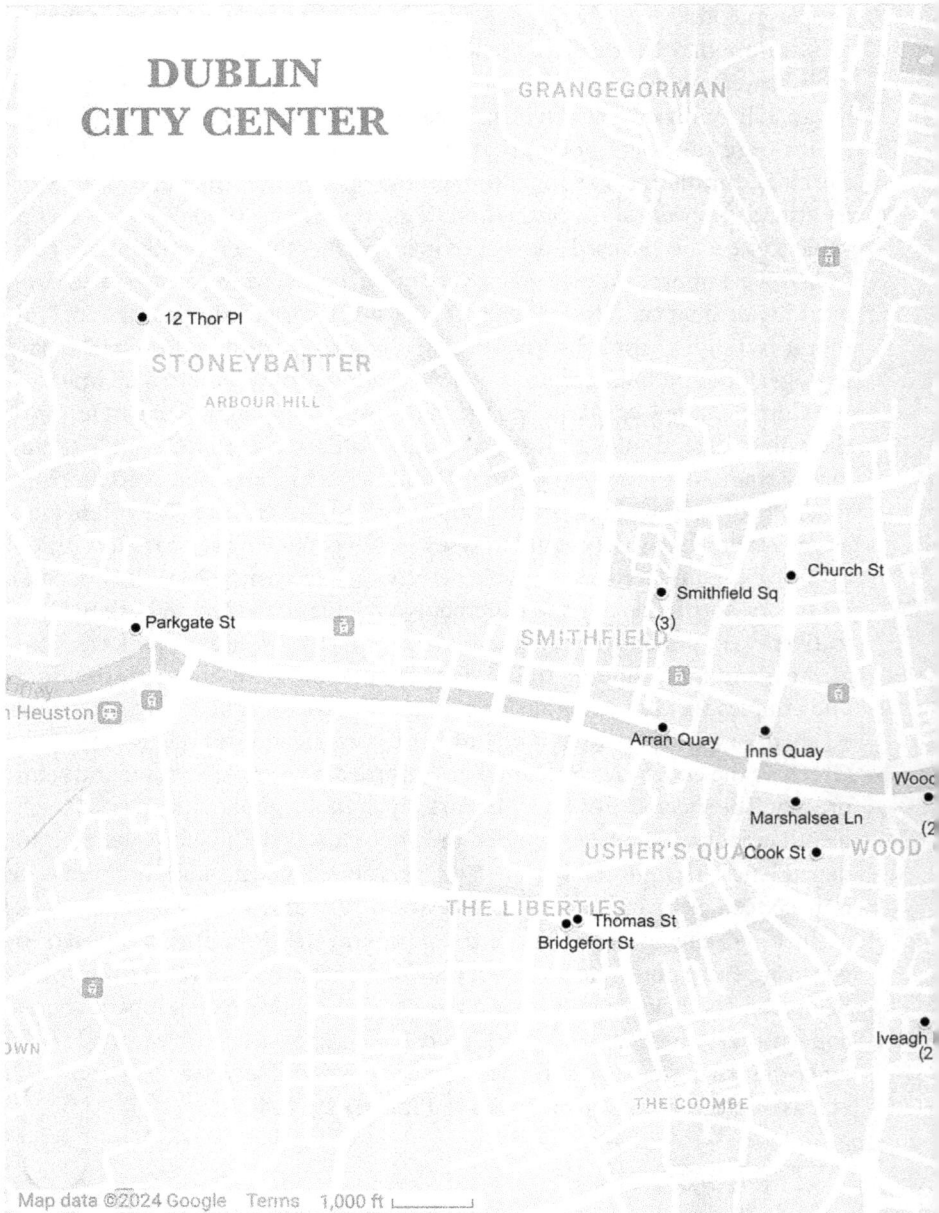

Figure 1.3 A closer look at the city center. *(Created with Google Maps.)*

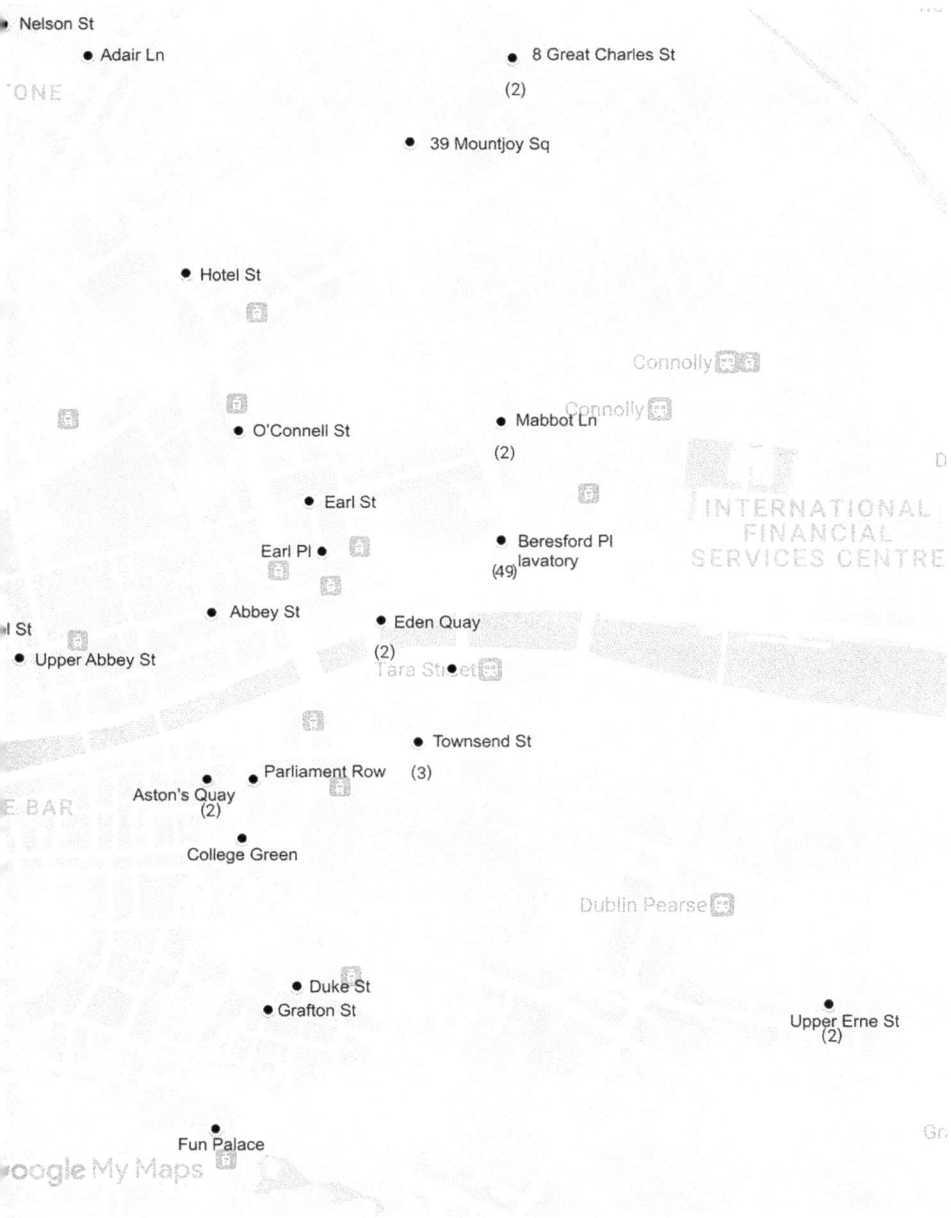

Nelson St

Adair Ln

8 Great Charles St
(2)

39 Mountjoy Sq

Hotel St

Connolly

Connolly

O'Connell St

Mabbot Ln
(2)

Earl St

Beresford Pl
lavatory
(49)

Earl Pl

INTERNATIONAL
FINANCIAL
SERVICES CENTRE

Abbey St

l St

Upper Abbey St

Eden Quay
(2)

Tara Street

Townsend St

Parliament Row   (3)

Aston's Quay
(2)

College Green

Dublin Pearse

Duke St

Grafton St

Upper Erne St
(2)

Fun Palace

Gr

Figure 1.4 Garda Photographic Division photo of a lavatory from above with a man inside. Photo taken to illustrate the Garda's view inside the lavatory from his perch above it. *(State Files, Dublin Circuit Court, 1D-44-30. Reproduced by kind permission of the Director of the National Archives.)*

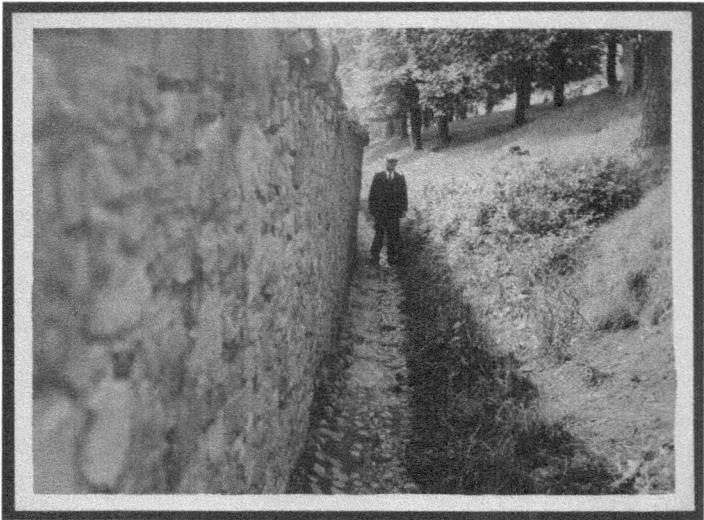

Figure 1.5 A Gardaí stands in a ditch in Phoenix Park to demonstrate the invisibility of men entangled there. *(National Archives of Ireland, State Files, Dublin Circuit Courts, 1D-28-124. Photo taken by Sgt. Michael P. Wall, Photographic Division, An Garda Síochána. Reproduced by kind permission of the Director of the National Archives.)*

When stumbled upon by patrolling Gardaí, different-sex couples were broken up and instructed to move along. When Garda Lawrence Pluck was on patrol on his bicycle, he saw a couple he took to be a man and woman "engaging in sexual intercourse," and he stopped to pull them apart. Yes, to pull them apart, in his words, *not* arrest them.[55] There is no evidence that different-sex couples were arrested at all in Dublin, though Phoenix Park was also known as a place where women sex workers plied their wares.[56] Gardaí often dealt with women sex workers summarily, meaning that they could arrest without a warrant and take offenders to be sentenced directly by a judge without a jury trial. Summary indictments usually entailed fines and briefer stints in prison, and left behind far sparser evidentiary records.[57] So, either Phoenix Park held so notorious a reputation after dark that different-sex couples—other than prostitutes and men seeking prostitutes—did not venture there, or the gardaí simply followed Pluck's example and broke those couples apart and sent them on their way. Conversely, in London, different-sex couples were not so lucky. According to Houlbrook, between 1918 and 1919, more different-sex couples were arrested for public indecency (having sex in public) in Hampstead Heath than same-sex couples.[58] Conversely in Ireland, if Pluck's method of dealing with them was the standard, couples who thought they were operating within the heteronormative sexual regime clearly practiced less caution than male couples, who hazarded arrest, imprisonment, and ruin with every sexual encounter.

Both lavatories and parks served as prime "cruising" ground for same-sex-desiring men. Broadly, however, Dublin was an immensely walkable city throughout the twentieth century, a factor that contributed to how dispersed same-sex sex was, more generally. While cruising, often on the way to or from a park, lav, pub, movie, or home, men walked the streets and occasionally

---

George Gaw; 1D-44-30/28, 3-Jul-34, the State v. Patrick Brennan; 1D-50-32/19, 13-Oct-50, the State v. Jeremiah Ryan; 1D-50-32/19, 13-Oct-50, the State v. William Mullen; V14-16-14/99, 3-Oct-62, the State v. Peter Collins. In this group there are also two from State Books, NAI State Books, Dublin Circuit Court, 1D-61-1, 18-Jan-37, the State v. John Byrne; and 1D-61-1/57, 18-Jan-37, the State v. John Redmond. There were also five cases in Phoenix Park that involved children under fourteen: four from NAI Dublin Circuit Court, State Files, 1C-94-88/33, 23-Mar-31, the State v. Patrick McGrath; 1D-27-12/68, 17-Apr-45, the State v. Michael Moore; 1D-33-112/23, 4-Jul-33, the State v. Alphonsus Keaney; 1D-44-31/69, 2-Oct-34, the State v. Thomas Dillon; and one from NAI State Books, Dublin Circuit Court, 1D-11-98/46, 18-Jan-39, the State v. Henry O'Brien.

55. It turned out the couple was actually two men, and the Garda was able to arrest the one he had grabbed hold of to pull them apart initially. NAI, Dublin Circuit Court, State Files, 1D-60-82, 14-Jan-38, the State v. Francis P. Supple.

56. Ferriter, *Occasions of Sin*, 225.

57. Denton, "Open Secrets."

58. Houlbrook, *Queer London*, 51.

picked up men they encountered out and about. Utilizing the passageways between hedges or fences offered men the thrill of taking someone's hand and leading them into a dark alley, listening for approaching footsteps on the cobblestone streets even as they fumbled about, unbuttoning trouser fronts and pressing closely together. Though arrests for same-sex sex crimes between 1922 and 1972 in alleyways account for almost 16 percent of all arrests, no single alleyway appears twice in the records. These were arrests of chance, or, much more rarely, the result of extensive police work by Gardaí committed to apprehending the perceived purveyors of vice in the city.

The stories I outline in the following chapters provide glimpses—fleeting, but there nonetheless—of a queer subculture in Dublin before the liberation movement. For historians who study same-sex desire in urban areas, many of the markers of that subculture will be unremarkable: networks of rent boys, queer language and alter egos, and public spaces used to seize brief moments of physical intimacy.[59] But historians still need to work on the history of Dublin's same-sex-desiring people, men *and* women. (Mea culpa: I am perpetuating the mancentric historiographical tradition because I've chained myself to these court records, from which women are absent.)

Dublin is a city, but it is *not* London or New York City. At midcentury, Dublin was home to just over five hundred thousand people, a fraction of the size of London or New York City in the same period.[60] But, like London and New York City, Dublin experienced waves of emigrants and (though less frequently) immigrants. Dublin City, in fact, experienced a very modest but consistent population growth from 1922 to the end of the century.[61] Still, while scholars like David Fitzpatrick and Sinéad Moynihan have charted the slow but important immigration into Dublin and other parts of Ireland, the flow was never enough to replace what was lost in the country overall.[62] A queer

59. For histories of urban queer subcultures in the nineteenth and twentieth centuries, see Maynard's various articles on Ontario; Chauncey, *Gay New York*; Houlbrook, *Queer London*; Boag, *Same-Sex Affairs*; Ross, *Public City/Public Sex*; Healy, *Homosexual Desire in Revolutionary Russia*; and Petri, *Places of Tenderness and Heat*.

60. Brady, *Dublin, 1930–1950*, 27. According to the London Data Store, in 1951, London had a population of 8,197,000 (available at https://data.london.gov.uk/dataset/historic-census -population) and, in 1950, New York City had about 7.8 million people (available at https://www 2.census.gov/library/publications/decennial/1950/pc-02/pc-2-47.pdf).

61. Brady, *Dublin, 1930–1950*, 27. According to the Office of Statistics, most rural counties in Ireland experienced population loss due to emigration across the twentieth century, though Dublin's population grew very modestly in that same period, largely due to receiving those emigrants. Available at https://www.cso.ie/en/releasesandpublications/ep/p-1916/1916irl/people /population/.

62. See Fitzpatrick, *The Americanisation of Ireland*; and Moynihan, *Ireland, Migration and Return*. It took most of the twentieth century for Ireland to return to a population level equivalent to that of before the Great Famine, despite large average family sizes. Between 1946 and 1951, for example, there were 66,000 annual births, and only 40,000 annual deaths. But

subculture emerged *despite* that brain and body drain. Same-sex-desiring men and women could've just emigrated and disappeared into one of those megacities. There were better economic opportunities for the emigrant elsewhere, and, even if all those cities were policing sexuality at a comparable rate, but with more resources and dedicated vice squads, it was much easier to move around in anonymity through the streets of London or New York City than Dublin, where the social rules of small-town Ireland still applied. Yet some, at least, stayed. Maybe they couldn't afford to go, maybe they felt ties to family too deeply, maybe they weren't as worried as they could've been, or maybe they couldn't conceive of uprooting their lives to start over somewhere new. In some ways, Justice Cahir Davitt was right when he declared that same-sex-desiring men were "prevalent in the city."[63] It probably wasn't the mundane utopia of John Broderick's fiction. We may never know just how robust Dublin's sexual subculture was—not, at least, with the scant evidence captured in the criminal records. But I hope this book goes a little way toward telling that history.

---

natural population growth was offset by migration; in the same period, an average of 24,000 people emigrated each year. Between 1951 and 1956, and average of 39,000 people emigrated each year, and, from 1956 to 1961, 42,000 emigrated each year. The census data for 1961 showed the lowest total population since 1871, with just 2.8 million people—over 100,000 fewer than there were in Ireland in 1951. See "Population: Average Annual Births, Deaths, Natural Increase and Estimated Net Migration for each Intercensal Period, 1926–2002," *Statistical Yearbook of Ireland 2002*, Ireland's Central Statistics Office, available at https://www.cso.ie/en/statistics/statisticalyearbookofireland/statisticalyearbookofireland/statisticalyearbookofireland2002 edition/.

63. "Vice Prevalent in Dublin," 13.

2

The Bait

When sentencing two men who were caught having sex in a car in Dublin in January 1931, a circuit court judge declared: "I regret, and I say it with the fullest sense of responsibility, that the vice you have been found guilty of is not uncommon in this city; but the citizens will be glad to know that the Gardaí are vigilant and watching, and that men inclined like you should know that the Gardaí are watching. The Courts will be eager to see that society is protected."[1] To this just, the onus of responsibility for dealing with Ireland's visible same-sex desiring men fell to the Garda.

When Ireland achieved independence in 1922, one of the first changes the new state made was the disbandment of the RIC and the creation of the Gardaí, or An Garda Síochána.[2] The RIC policed the Irish citizenry for over a century, meting out brutal punishments to those who dared to challenge English authority. Although most RIC officers were Irishmen, the organization was shaped by British rather than Irish interests. The majority of officers and leaders in the organization were Protestant, drawn from the "Anglo-Irish"

---

1. "Strong Comments by Judge—Two Men Sentenced—Outside the Pale of Civilisation," *Irish Independent*, 30 January 1931, 2.

2. The Civic Garda was created in 1922; the roll out of the new force took time, and in Dublin, in particular, the absorption of the DMP into the DMD took place in 1925. See Dukova, *Metropolitan Police and Colonial Legacy*, 135–139; and Conway, *Policing Twentieth Century Ireland*, 25–45.

population perceived by the Catholic majority as the arbiters of British imperialism in Ireland.[3]

The RIC did not focus on policing Irish sex. Irish sexual immorality was not destabilizing to the English rule of Ireland, and the English were quite confident in their mobilization of other perceived Irish failings—drunkenness, unruly wives and weak husbands, racial Otherness—to assert a paternalistic need for English oversight of Irish governance. Little effort was funneled into policing same-sex sex crimes, with investigations largely limited to those of adults sexually assaulting children under the age of twelve. Conversely, sexual morality *was* a key tool of Irish nationalism. In the nineteenth century, Irish members of parliament used homosexual scandals and English sodomy crime statistics to challenge England's moral authority to rule Ireland. Irish nationalist newspapers insisted that "gross indecency" was "the last crime an Irishman was likely to be guilty of" and published crime statistics that, by the grace of pure numbers rather than relativity, showed more sex crimes across the spectrum in London alone than in all of Ireland for any given year.[4] In the twentieth century, when Irish nationalism fused with Catholicism, Ireland's self-governance rested on its citizens' presumed sexual purity.[5] While policing sex may not have been a concern during the English rule of Ireland, Irish nationalists painted themselves into a corner. Sex *could* very well destabilize Irish rule of Ireland.

The Irish Free State was born out of a Catholic nationalist rhetoric of morality, and its leaders were quickly faced with a population that did not fit the mold of sexually pure Irish citizenship. Fervent belief in Ireland's sexual purity manifested in both informal and formal policing. As the historians James Smith and Maria Luddy have shown, Irish people locked away their daughters and sisters with alarming regularity for perceived sexual transgressions.[6] Gossip and rumor were powerful tools of shame, and the brunt of the assaults tended to impact Irish women more than men. For the most part, men were excluded from informal moral policing, so long as their trespasses remained

3. Conway, 25–45.

4. "Trial by Jury," *Freeman's Journal*, 23 September 1828, 2; for a discussion of Irish nationalist presses' use of homophobia to advance the nationalist movement, see Earls, "Unnatural Offenses of English Import," 396–424.

5. For a discussion of Catholicism and Irish citizenship in the twentieth century, see Ronit Lentin, "'Irishness,' the 1937 Constitution, and Citizenship: Gender and Ethnicity View," *Irish Journal of Sociology* 8 (1998): 5–24. For a history of Irish nationalism and Irish Catholicism, and where the two met and eventually merged, see Lawrence John MacCaffrey, "Irish Nationalism and Irish Catholicism: A Study in Cultural Identity," *Church History*, 42, no. 4 (Dec., 1973), 524–534; and Daniel J. O'Neil, "Irish Nationalism and Roman Catholicism: The Revolutionary Experience of Patrick Pearse (1879–1916), Horace Plunkett (1854–1932), and James Connolly (1868–1916)," *Canadian Review of Studies in Nationalism* 19, nos. 1–2, (1992): 59–78.

6. Smith, *Ireland's Magdalen Laundries*; and Luddy, *Prostitution and Irish Society*.

firmly in the realm of heterosexual sex. But priests and politicians alike repeated the mantra that same-sex desire was incompatible with Irishness, sending same-sex-desiring men like the Irish playwright Aodhán Madden into cycles of destructive self-loathing.[7] Same-sex-desiring men faced legal ramifications if caught, and they encountered the daily reminder that men like them were unwanted and under surveillance.

Ireland was by no means the only country to arrest and imprison men for having sex with men in the twentieth century. Sex between men, in public *or* private, was policed and illegal in England until 1967, in Scotland until 1980, in Northern Ireland until 1987, and in West Germany until 1994. In France, sex between men was technically decriminalized, but men were still harassed and arrested for things like loitering, public indecency, and indecent exposure: not technically laws that exclusively targeted men who had sex with men, but effectively used that way anyway.[8] In some places, like Romania, Poland, and the United States, men (and some women) were harassed or arrested because they were considered threats to state security during the Cold War.[9] Ireland saw itself as an equal to these European and North American countries.[10] In many ways, the nationalists who would found the Free State had been framing same-sex desire as something the English imported into Ireland.[11] While it would have been exciting and radical for those nationalists to really destroy the institutions of British imperialism in Ireland, like the court system, the laws, and the police force, it would have been hard for most of the Dáil members to imagine an Ireland that embraced a sexually liberated worldview. That said, some Dáil members were themselves in committed partnerships with members of the same sex or were close friends with those couples.[12] Mary McAuliffe is doing much fantastic work on the lesbians of the Irish revolution, which also highlights the ways the Free State was selective about how it pursued its postcolonial moral project.[13]

The increase in policing volume from the colonial period to the postcolonial period, and what that increase was intended to signal to Ireland's same-sex-desiring men, cannot be understated. In terms of population size, the Irish policing of sex between men was on par with much larger cities throughout

7. A. Madden, *Fear and Loathing in Dublin.*

8. See Ross, *Public City/Public Sex.*

9. O'Dwyer, *Coming Out of Communism*; and Johnson, *Lavender Scare.*

10. "Responsibility of Catholic Irishmen," *Donegal News* (1903–current), 26 October 1940, 5; "Address by President Kennedy," Seanad Éireann debate, 28 June 1963, available at https://www.oireachtas.ie/en/debates/debate/seanad/1963-06-28/2/.

11. See Earls, "Unnatural Offenses of English Import."

12. Kathleen Lynn served in the Teachta Dála (TD; the lower house of the Irish parliament) from 1923 to 1927. She lived with her life partner, Madeleine ffrench-Mullen, in Rathmines from 1903 until her death in 1955.

13. See McAuliffe, *Margaret Skinnider.*

Europe and North America.[14] But, in terms of the increase in policing, the shift in Ireland is only comparable to other states that wrested their independence from a colonial power.[15] This is particularly true in former British colonies.[16] The laws and judicial systems—even when incompatible with prior indigenous justice systems—were mostly preserved after independence, and the postcolonial states then increased the policing of sexuality, particularly of men who had sex with men and women who sold sex. In places like Nigeria, Cameroon, Jamaica, and Ireland, political and cultural rhetoric insisted that same-sex desire (and prostitution) were deviances imported to that place by the British. While, unironically, maintaining the British laws criminalizing same-sex sex, these states set about expunging the "scourge" of those imported sexual behaviors or identities. In some of these places, this is an ongoing state-enacted and socially acceptable violence.[17]

Where most European countries were trending toward the secular, particularly regarding laws governing things like sex and privacy, the Irish were taking a hard left back toward Christian ideology. Irish politicians and Catholic hierarchy affected an air of moral superiority in relation to the rest of Europe. This was so prior to independence in debates about Ireland's capability to self-govern and persisted after 1922. In a sermon in 1929, the Catholic priest P. J. Gannon said that "Europe is forgetting" the morality of Christianity, while "we Irishmen" would never forget.[18] The assertion of Ireland's moral superiority was repeated throughout the twentieth century, particularly with regard to Ireland's role as a producer of missionaries, priests, and nuns.[19] The evidence to the contrary—unwed mothers, rampant alcoholism, child neglect, prostitution, gambling, and "gross indecency"—was willfully ignored by Catholics or attributed to those urban centers (like Dublin), which were, by their very existence, anathema to Irishness.

At the state level, violence against same-sex-desiring people was horrible and ruined the lives of hundreds of Irish men. But it was also inconsistent.

---

14. See Chapter 1, "The City."

15. For examples of the legacy of colonial homophobia, see Wahab, "Homophobia as the State of Reason," 481–505; Lumsden, *Machos, Maricones, and Gays*; Ndjio, "Post-Colonial Histories of Sexuality."

16. See, e.g., Hoad, *African Intimacies*.

17. See, e.g., Winsome Marcia Chunnu, "Battyboy must die! Dancehall, Class and Religion in Jamaican Homophobia," *European Journal of Cultural Studies* 24, no. 1 (2020); Joseph Esin, "Homophobia Is Un-African: Critical Discussions on the Legacy of Imported Homophobia in Nigeria," Theses and Dissertations, University of Victoria, 2023; and Kalemba Kizito, "Bequeathed Legacies: Colonialism and State-Led Homophobia in Uganda," *Surveillance and Society* 15, nos. 3–4, (2017): 567–572.

18. "How Ireland Has Clung to the Faith," *Irish Independent*, 8 July 1929, 7.

19. E.g., "Responsibility of Catholic Irishmen," 5; "Ireland's Vocation," *Irish Independent*, 9 October 1933, 10; and "Striking Sermon in Dublin," *Strabane Chronicle*, 26 October 1940, 3.

The gardaí were given the impossible task of making Ireland *appear* like the chaste, moral, un-British utopia that its politicians and state arbiters promised. Actual policing was often haphazard, with some years seeing thirty, forty, or fifty men arrested and other years fewer than five. Yet the messaging that came from the state through judges and policing efforts was clear: men who desired sex with other men were not welcome in Ireland, and, more to the point, such desire was inherently not "Irish."

It fell to the newly created An Garda Síochána to combat the widespread visibility of the behaviors deemed un-Irish by the state. When the Free State was established, there was a near immediate shift in the policing of same-sex sex. From its inception, the Garda was tasked with clearing the streets of men seeking sex with other men. Gardaí walked the streets of Dublin in plainclothes hoping to catch cruising men. The Garda had a multitude of tactics for catching men having sex with men. One of the most controversial was when they used agents provocateurs, or men who used their own bodies as bait.[20] In some cases, gardaí participated in the very acts that landed other men in prison. Today these tactics would be illegal, defined as entrapment, and thus inadmissible in court, but, in the Free State, there were few precedents to stop the gardaí from using their own bodies as bait. But, while entrapment was successful in the earliest instances of gardaí employing it, it was still dangerous. As in the United Kingdom at the time, entrapment was an extreme measure.[21] The inherent danger of making one's body sexual bait reveals why it was used quite sparingly in the Garda, with only ten total cases between 1924 and 1936, before being abandoned entirely. Still, the employment of extreme measures speaks to the high stakes of policing same-sex sex.

The officers discussed in this chapter literally threw themselves into the work of finding and arresting same-sex-desiring men. But at what cost? While enforcing this vision of the Free State, the gardaí who baited men violated the acceptable norms of Irish masculinity. They transgressed to subvert. Without records of their own thoughts and feelings on their work in the 1920s and 1930s, we cannot know how they saw themselves, what their motivations were, or why they did what they did. By examining the conditions surrounding the early An Garda Síochána, and the details gleaned about these men from their courtroom testimonies and service records, we can piece together a sense of the gardaí who entrapped same-sex-desiring men in Dublin between 1927 and 1936. I argue that the use of entrapment in the early Irish state was born out of a desperation to realize a moral vision of Ireland, even as the acts themselves reveal how thin the veneer of Irish purity actually was.

---

20. Rey, "Parisian Homosexuals Create a Lifestyle," 179–191.

21. See Anna Livia and Kira Hall, *Queerly Phrased: Language, Gender, and Sexuality* (Oxford University Press, 1997), 337; Houlbrook, *Queer London*, 19–43; and Thane, *Unequal Britain*, 135.

To date, none of the scholarship on An Garda Síochána addresses the particular challenge of policing male same-sex sex. Many scholars have discussed the standards that Eoin O'Duffy and the early leaders of the force held for the Garda in terms of decorum, physicality, and moral aptitude. Liam McNiffe wrote a social history of the force from 1922 to 1952, which carefully calculated numerical data, including recruitment and retirement numbers, the representation of men from each of Ireland's counties in the new police force, and the distribution of gardaí throughout the twenty-six counties.[22] Former garda and then archivist Gregory Allen's work reflects his intimate knowledge of the Garda Museum archives and is as much a history of the individuals who shaped the force between 1922 and 1982 as a history of the force itself.[23] More recently, the legal scholar Vicky Conway published a book that looks at the history and development of policing in Ireland in the twentieth century with particular emphasis on social change, postcolonialism, and the Troubles of the 1970s and 1980s.[24] None of these accounts considers the precarious position of the Dublin gardaí who policed sex between men. In a state constructed around a postcolonial identity of Irish Catholic sexual purity, the gardaí instructed to dress in plainclothes and police male same-sex sex were put in morally dangerous but sexually exciting situations in the line of duty. From the perspective of the chain of command, all the way up to the commissioner of the Garda Eoin O'Duffy, it was necessary work. O'Duffy insisted that the new Civic Guard would be "entrusted [with] the task of demanding and insisting on respect for the law of the land, and the extermination of the type that is incapable or unwilling to assume the responsibilities of citizenship."[25] The city was teeming with sin, and it fell to the gardaí to run interference.[26] Inevitably, though, there were casualties in this kind of police work. Though they offered an incontrovertible body of proof—their own bodies—not all Irish juries were comfortable with the circumstances of the evidence. These experiences of the gardaí, both on the streets and in the courts of Dublin, are essential to understanding the nascent Irish state's investment in policing public sex and the realities of Irish "sexual purity."

One evening in early October 1927, Henry Coghlan cruised O'Connell Street, looking for men interested in a casual hookup. His search didn't take long. He stepped down into an O'Connell Street lavatory, and a man inside made eyes at him. There were plenty of empty stalls in the lav, but Coghlan didn't use one. Instead, he walked in and walked back out, brushing by the

---

22. McNiffe, *History of the Garda Síochána.*

23. Allen, *Garda Síochána.*

24. Conway, *Policing Twentieth Century Ireland.*

25. Allen, *Garda Síochàna,* 69. O'Duffy made the statement in 1926.

26. "A Correct Verdict," *Irish Times,* 7 February 1931, 6; "Another Case: Sentence of Seven Years," *Irish Independent,* 30 January 1931, 2.

man with whom he'd made eye contact. Coghlan went and stood in front of a nearby building under construction, seemingly admiring it. The man from the lav came and stood beside him. "That's a fine building they're putting up," the man, John Bodkin, said. "I believe it's going to be a hotel like the Gresham." Coghlan, who knew better, said he'd heard it would be shops on the bottom, not like the Gresham. Noticing the time, Coghlan told Bodkin that he had an appointment to keep, so he had to be off. The man said he'd walk with Coghlan, since he was heading in the direction of O'Connell Bridge. When they got to Abbey Street, Bodkin invited Coghlan into Mooney's, a nearby pub, for a drink. Coghlan said he couldn't, as he had that appointment at 6:00 P.M. Bodkin asked if they might meet up later that evening; Coghlan said he couldn't tonight, but that they could meet any other night. The man said he was going out of town, but that they could meet in a week's time, perhaps at Mooney's pub? Coghlan laughed and said no, "because if you turned up and I didn't, or I turned up and you didn't, it'd only be a case of a man drinking on his own," and what a lonely thing that would be.[27]

When Bodkin suggested the very spot in which they stood, Coghlan said yes, that would do nicely. They planned to meet again on October 11, at 7:00 P.M., on the corner of Abbey and O'Connell. When Coghlan offered his hand, the man from the lav grasped it and gave it a squeeze, saying, "I hope that there will be something doing." Coghlan only smiled and coyly replied, "You will have to wait and see." Bodkin headed off to the pub, and Coghlan continued on his way.[28]

The two met as arranged on October 11, 1927. Surprised that Coghlan had shown up, Bodkin said, "It's funny how one face knows another." When Coghlan asked where they ought to go, the man assured him that he knew of a "good place" at the back of the bank on Fleet Street, and they walked there together. As they walked, Bodkin told Coghlan of other good places around Dublin and of other men he'd gone with. "I met a very nice man from Ballsbridge about 3 weeks ago on O'Connell Bridge who asked me to go with him. I would have loved [to] but I had to get my bus home." As they walked down Parliament Row, Bodkin said to Coghlan, "You people have a great time here in the city. We can do nothing in the country, we are being watched everywhere."[29]

When they arrived at the "good place"—a public lavatory behind the bank—Bodkin led the way in. He struck a match, examining the stalls of the lav. The first was "dirty," but the next was clean enough. Bodkin then opened the lowest button on Coghlan's vest and all the buttons of his pants. He reached

---

27. NAI, Dublin Circuit Court, State Files, 1C-96-36, 13-Oct-1927, the State vs. John Bodkin, Deposition of Henry Coghlan.
28. Deposition of Henry Coghlan.
29. Deposition of Henry Coghlan.

down and gave Coghlan's penis "a squeeze." Bodkin pulled Coghlan close, caressed him, and then took off his own trousers and revealed his penis, saying, "Isn't that a fine big one? That may give you a horn. Look at that." Coghlan did look, but then stepped back, trousers still open, and told Bodkin that he was under arrest.[30]

Detective Officer Henry Coghlan was the first officer who left a record suggesting that he was instructed to bait a same-sex-desiring man into a crime. Coghlan had joined the DMP in 1922, when the DMP was still the DMD. Before he joined the Gardaí, though, he was just a young man trying to make his way in Ireland's largest city. Like many skilled and unskilled laborers, Coghlan worked as an "engineer" during and after World War I.[31] The war economy of 1914 to 1918 created a major demand for engineers, and the craft industries in Dublin drew from semiskilled and unskilled laborers, both women and men.[32] "Engineer" work ranged from laying telegraph cables to putting up temporary buildings—essentially, whatever the war effort needed. Since he joined the DMP after the war, instead of remaining in the skilled labor pool of the engineer union, Coghlan likely had no formal training in engineering and was one of the throngs of semi- and unskilled "engineers" for whom the industry had no need after the war. Like so many young men after him, Henry Coghlan may have joined the Garda because there was nowhere else for him to go.

After Irish independence, most, but not all, of the men who joined the Garda in the early 1920s were Catholic. Henry Coghlan was not. Like many families living in the "Pale"—or Anglo-Irish stronghold—of Dublin, Coghlan's family belonged to the Church of Ireland.[33] His parents married fairly late, a common occurrence at the time, when his mother, Mary Jane, was already thirty-one and his father, Robert, was thirty-four. They had five children, including twin boys, who all lived to adulthood, and one daughter who died as an infant. The seven of them lived in one of the outbuildings on the Canfort House estate, where Robert was the gardener for the Atkinsons. For a time, the shepherd for the Canfort farm also boarded with the Coghlans.

Though he might have stayed in Canfort and taken over gardening duties from his father, as a young man Henry struck out on his own. Shortly after World War I ended, the British granted all women over thirty the right to vote, and, in the 1919 khaki election, Ireland elected Sinn Feiners—the radical separatist party—to all the Irish seats of parliament. Sinn Fein refused

---

30. Deposition of Henry Coghlan.

31. Registered Number 12007, DMP general register, UCD Digital Archives, accessed on 9 August 2021, available at https://digital.ucd.ie/view/ucdlib:53465.

32. Pádraig Yeates, "Craft Workers during the Irish Revolution, 1919–22," *Saothar* 33 (2008): 37–54.

33. The Church of Ireland is an autonomous province of the Anglican Communion.

to take their seats in London, instead forming their own government in Dublin and forcing the British to respond. The next eighteen months were a brutal war for Ireland's independence, with the RIC and DMP embroiled in the fight against the IRA, right up to the truce and Treaty of 1921. We can't be certain if he fought in the War of Independence, but we can be sure that he didn't fight for the British, because in 1921 Henry Coghlan joined the Criminal Investigation Department (CID) in Dublin.[34] The CID was created by Michael Collins as an armed, plainclothes, counterinsurgency police unit during the Civil War. The CID was known for its brutal interrogation tactics and for murdering anti-Treatyite prisoners and suspected Republicans.[35] For the dozens of CID agents who were then absorbed into the DMP/DMD/Garda, "extreme" policing probably felt like the standard that one simply strove for. Coghlan served for a year and two months in the CID. With wartime engineering work dried up and likely no interest in returning to his family's country home in the midlands, Coghlan joined the DMP. Like many of the CID men who transitioned over to the Garda, he came with a recommendation from his superior officer, who also joined the chain of command at Coghlan's station in Dublin. It was no longer his job to catch rogue Republicans; thereafter, Coghlan was a member of the "police force for the people."[36]

Like Coghlan, most of the gardaí who made themselves bait in the gross indecency trap joined the force before the DMP merged with the Garda. Of the nine men involved in entrapment cases, six were hired between 1920 and 1924. This was a particularly tumultuous time to join, as Dublin was the center of much of the War of Independence and Civil War fighting. The DMP was left intact when the Garda was initially formed, in 1922, and was then amalgamated with the Garda in 1925.[37] As noted, the Garda was intended to be a "police force for the people," distinct from the former RIC. From their beginning in the early nineteenth century, the RIC was a tool of colonial control, aiding British soldiers in crushing Irish rebellions, following orders to evict rural tenant farmer families from their homes, and enforcing the laws disenfranchising Irishmen and -women passed by Parliament in London. The

---

34. Since most CID members were drawn from the pro-Treaty IRA, it's possible that he fought for Michael Collins.

35. The Irish Civil War was fought over the signing of the Anglo-Irish Treaty, which ended the Irish War of Independence and granted Ireland independence with the caveat that every county in Ireland had to vote whether it wanted to stay in the Union with Britain or wanted to join the Free State. This divided the island into the twenty-six counties who voted to join the Free State and the six northeast counties—collectively known as "Ulster"—that remained in the United Kingdom. Some members of the IRA and Sinn Fein (the nationalist political party that launched the War of Independence) felt this was a betrayal of the Catholics and nationalists in the north. Thus, they walked out of the Dáil and instigated the Civil War.

36. McNiffe, *History of the Garda Síochána*, 9–10.

37. McNiffe, 9–10, 12.

Garda was supposed to be different. In 1925, "[District Justice Kenneth Reddin] wanted it understood that the days when a police officer might treat an ordinary citizen as an inferior animal had definitely ceased. The police were paid and kept and run by the people and they were the servants of the [Irish] people," rather than by the British government.[38] In some important ways, they were different. The criminologist Vicky Conway argues that the omnipresent British police and policing in Ireland is central to understanding Ireland as a colony of Britain.[39] Twelve hundred British barracks were spread throughout Ireland, the police forces that were sent to the rest of the empire were trained in Ireland, and there was a popular belief that the British were always watching the Irish. Referring to the RIC, Irish member of parliament John Dillon asserted, in 1902, "The police in Ireland are not guardians of the peace as their position is understood in England or Scotland. They are simply a force kept together in military strength for political purposes."[40] After two short but devastating and traumatic wars, the Garda was created to fill the void of the RIC after it was dissolved, and to support the independent Irish state. In its early years, the Garda was intended to diverge dramatically from the RIC; they were given new uniforms, established as an unarmed force, and recruited from a population that was already loyal to the independent Irish state.[41]

To ensure that the Garda could be a "police force for the people," the new gardaí were drawn up from the following groups of men, in order of importance:

(a) IRA as well as Irish Republican Police; (b) men dismissed or resigned from the RIC or DMP because of conscientious or patriotic motives; (c) the civilian population; (d) [and if absolutely needed] disbanded RIC and DMP members. The new policeman had to take an oath in which he would swear among other things not to join any political party or secret society.[42]

The gardaí recruited from 1922 to 1932 met those recruitment expectations; 55 percent were drawn from the former IRA membership, 23 percent were civilians with no military or police background, and less than 5 percent were former RIC or British army.[43] Yet, while the gardaí, the uniforms, and the language surrounding the new force were new, the organizational structure of the Garda greatly resembled the RIC because (for practical reasons) the or-

38. "Civic Guard Sergeant Sued," *Drogheda Independent*, 17 October 1925, 5.
39. Conway, *Policing Twentieth Century Ireland*, 25.
40. "The Over-worked R.I.C.," *Connaught Telegraph*, 19 July 1902, 4.
41. "Brisk Recruiting," *Longford Leader*, 21 October 1922, 6.
42. McNiffe, *History of the Garda Síochána*, 12.
43. McNiffe, 34.

ganizing committee was primarily former RIC members and officers.[44] The Garda occupied eight hundred of the old barracks, with an average of six gardaí assigned to each station, and followed similar training and policing procedures.[45] Conway suggests that the changes made were symbolic at best and not particularly radical. Yet the face of the Irish police force changed, and that was significant for creating a new relationship with the Irish people. Further, during the Civil War, one of the most important changes was implemented: the disarming of the Irish police force. The only exception was the CID, which disbanded in 1923 after the Civil War hostilities ended. Thereafter, the police force in Ireland was unarmed. There would no longer be a militant force handling Ireland's domestic issues, a significant divergence from the colonial model and the Royal Ulster Constabulary.[46]

Domestic issues, however, posed a problem for the state. The revolution was a political one, not the social one of the 1916 Easter Rising.[47] Poverty and suffering were rampant in the young state, unemployment was high, and the majority of crimes, including larceny and public drunkenness, were poverty related.[48] Though thousands of Irish men and women were able to get work to feed the war machine between 1914 and 1920, the postwar period had no need for those industries and the realities of a stagnated Irish economy resumed. In 1920 alone, 15,531 people emigrated, on trend with the drain of young people that Ireland had been experiencing since the Great Famine. Between 1851 and 1920, 4,338,199 people emigrated, about equal numbers of men and women, which made up an estimated 83.2 percent of the average population of the country.[49] Historian Joseph Lee suggests that this "population problem . . . probably contributed to political stabilisation" after 1922; yet, for the people who didn't emigrate, life wasn't the utopia that independence promised.[50]

Cumann na nGaedheal, the party that formed itself out of the first government of the Free State, was tightfisted and reluctant to see poverty-related criminality as a social problem.[51] Sex crimes, on the other hand, were a major concern. The Free State coalesced around what it was against—sex and Englishness—rather than what it stood for. With much of the original social and labor-based organizing of the 1912–1916 revolutionaries set aside in favor

44. Conway, *Policing Twentieth Century Ireland*, 27; McNiffe, 34.
45. McNiffe, 13; Conway, 28.
46. Conway, 46.
47. Ferriter, *Transformation of Ireland*, 298.
48. Lee, *Ireland 1912–1985*, 126–127.
49. *Emigration Statistics of Ireland for the Year 1920*, House of Commons Parliamentary Papers Online, ProQuest Information and Learning Company.
50. Lee, *Ireland 1912–1985*, 71.
51. Ferriter, *Transformation of Ireland*, 292–297.

of political stability, the policing of sexuality became all the more key. Anthony Keating, Mary G. Valiulis, Morgan Denton, and many others have shown that the thrust of policing focused on controlling women.[52] Through legislation that deprived women of economic independence and bodily autonomy, and both formal and informal networks of policing to control female sexuality, the Free State meted out harsh measures to ensure Irish women knew their place and stayed there. Her place, in the home, as a mother to many happy yet impoverished Irish children, was further enshrined in the 1937 Constitution. But the state's concern with sex did not stop with women. According to Keating, the Free State suppressed the 1926 Report of the Committee on Venereal Disease, which "provided evidence that the spread of sexually transmitted disease was a phenomenon that correlated with the movement of Free State troops around the country."[53] Ferriter's *Occasions of Sin* reveals that the Free State, in coalition with the Catholic hierarchy of Ireland, launched a crusade against same-sex desire as well.[54] Sex was shrouded in shame, or, as the sociologist Tom Inglis called it, the "habitus and ethos" of Catholic morality.[55]

The labor that Coghlan undertook when he cruised O'Connell and then met up with Bodkin, all while in plainclothes and effectively inviting the man to make a sexual advance, was an example of a recent development in police work: investigation. During the nineteenth century, there was little organized investigative police work or collection of evidence and production of information to be utilized in a prosecution effort. Scholars of policing describe the period of 1800–1880 as one in which investigative policing was spearheaded by individual detectives. From 1880 onward, as policing organizations grew and bureaucratized, they established specialized branches dedicated to investigative policing.[56] This reform and growth period stretched from around the 1880s to the 1930s, which was a significant point in time for the fledgling Garda of independent Ireland. According to Brendon Murphy, "Crimes involving willing or mutually implicated parties, such as white collar crimes, corruption, consensual sex offences and drug-trafficking . . . are normally conducted in secret, and accordingly specific methodologies have evolved in order to investigate them. These methodologies are often undercover, and typically involve deception."[57] From plainclothes detectives cruising in unmarked

52. Denton, "Open Secrets"; Keating, "Sexual Crime in the Irish Free State 1922–33," 135–155; Keating, "Policing Culture, Gender, and Crime in the Irish Free State," 87–146; Finnane, "Carrigan Committee," 519–356; McAvoy, "Sexual Crime and Irish Women's Campaigns for a Criminal Law Amendment Act," 84–99.

53. Keating, "Policing Culture, Gender, and Crime," 90.

54. Ferriter, *Occasions of Sin*, 100–214.

55. Inglis, *Moral Monopoly*.

56. B. Murphy, "Deceptive Apparatus," 223–244, 226.

57. B. Murphy, 228.

cars to deep undercover agents planted in criminal organizations, the intelligence-gathering potential of what Murphy terms "authorized deception" and "authorized crime" is as essential to solving criminal activity today as it was in 1927. While—as in the case of Henry Coghlan and John Bodkin— this line of policing could lead an officer into morally suspect territory, clandestine surveillance and undercover work was essential to Irish policing, particularly the policing of sex crimes, from at least 1927.

The encounter between Coghlan and Bodkin was recounted by both men in depositions for Bodkin's gross indecency trial in October 1927. Court transcripts show that after their first meeting, Coghlan returned to the College Street Station, where he received "special instructions" from Inspector Patrick O'Connell to meet up with Bodkin as arranged on October 11. Coghlan did not reveal the details of those special orders in his deposition. Did Inspector O'Connell tell Coghlan to specially bait Bodkin into committing a sex crime? Did he give Coghlan a blank check and instruct him to do whatever was necessary to arrest Bodkin? Or did he just trust his officer to do the right thing and affirm Coghlan's hunch that there was something amiss about this character that warranted following up? Though he didn't elaborate on what directions his superior officer gave him, Bodkin's lawyer asked Coghlan questions that were clearly intended to insinuate that Coghlan had led Bodkin on and incited the sexual encounter. Refuting Bodkin's claims, Coghlan insisted that he hadn't told Bodkin they'd pick up boys behind the bank for a few pence, nor did he put his own arms around Bodkin during their intimate lavatory embrace. He also insisted that he didn't make any kind of invitation for anal sex or suggest Bodkin remove his own trousers. Unsurprisingly, Bodkin's recollection of the evening was less one sided than Coghlan's.

Brendon Murphy notes that because sex-related crimes tend to be committed in private or concealed ways, undercover agents were the best source of information for criminal cases.[58] When the crime is the sex act itself, though, the role of the undercover agent can be tricky. How does one secure a body of evidence for a sex crime, if it is the act itself that is the crime? Between 1930 and 1967, in Britain, the preferred method of detection was surveillance of popular public sex spots. Similar methods were preferred in most U.S. states well into the 1980s. In Ireland, where same-sex sex was illegal until 1993, surveillance of popular public sex spots was most employed after 1935. But, as Coghlan demonstrated on October 11, 1927, police officers could and did employ their own bodies as sites of criminal activity, thereby creating their own body of evidence.

---

58. B. Murphy, 223–244.

The use of authorized deception to gather evidence need not always involve the committing of authorized crime. The historian Michel Rey has shown how agents provocateurs were sent into the streets and taverns of eighteenth-century France to enter into the homosexual subculture of Paris, but that didn't necessarily require inciting members of the subculture to sex crimes.[59] Indeed, as William Peniston shows, by the Napoleonic period, the sex act itself was not necessarily illegal, but the police still saw same-sex-desiring men as subversive to social norms and thereby in need of close scrutiny. And yet, in some cases, even though the courts were unlikely to send homosexual men to prison, French police in the late nineteenth century still used entrapment tactics in public lavatories as grounds to harass, interrogate, and arrest the French same-sex-desiring men.[60]

Much like the fledgling Irish Free State's Civic Garda, the London Metropolitan Police experimented with undercover officers given special orders to investigate same-sex sex offenders. Between 1918 and 1935, in London, plainclothes officers were instructed to infiltrate queer pubs and clubs and bait men into indecent assault in public urinals. This was an effective policing tactic but proved a moral quandary. Here they were sending their officers into situations where they were expected to fit in with a queer crowd and where they might feel pressured or encouraged to engage in sex acts themselves. Superior officers tried making sure that the men who went undercover didn't stay in that job for too long or get reassigned to that unit too often. By the 1930s, this was untenable. There weren't enough officers to maintain the constant shift, and too many men felt uncomfortable with the orders. The unit in charge of infiltrating gay clubs was dissolved by 1935.[61]

Starting with Coghlan's entrapment of the man in the lav, entrapment was a tactic of Irish policing of same-sex-desiring men as early as 1927. These entrapments were not casual brushups in the lavatory. They involved gardaí inviting or allowing the mark to kiss, unbutton, or stroke the garda's body. In the process, the bodies of the gardaí were made evidence for prosecution. These operations often involved several arranged meetings with a suspect after a garda displayed the signals and body language of a sexual invitation—an elbow rub at the urinal, or the display of an erect penis—and even the committal of "acts of gross indecency" by the gardaí themselves. This was true for Henry Coghlan in October 1927. While he described his encounters with Bodkin in a methodical manner, in his own words he presented a scenario in which he allowed a man to undress him and caress his penis. Coghlan didn't

59. Rey, "Parisian Homosexuals Create a Lifestyle," 179–191.
60. Peniston, *Pederasts and Others*, 25–26.
61. Houlbrook, *Queer London*, 26–31.

stop Bodkin from opening his trousers, fondling his penis, or intimately embracing him. He didn't stop Bodkin until Bodkin presented his own penis.

It's hard not to wonder if Coghlan permitted the ruse to go on so long because of his own interest in the exchange. What pleasure, what thrill did he feel as this strange man touched him in the semiprivacy of a lavatory stall? What shame or embarrassment did he feel as he described this for the court representative who took his deposition? Did he feel powerful in that vulnerable moment because he knew it was a ruse? Did he want to pursue this moment to its logical, orgasmic conclusion, thus making him regret telling his superior officer about Bodkin at all? Was he disgusted, aroused, or somehow detached completely from the experience? In recounting the events of October 11, 1927, he did not convey his feelings or possible inner turmoil. He presented information with the affect of a man just doing his job, but, surely, he knew that what he'd done was unusual.

Arguably, the gross indecency laws were too vague to say what would have been "far enough" for Coghlan to arrest Bodkin with sufficient evidence. Prior to Bodkin's case, only a few of Dublin's gardaí had stumbled on men having sex with each other in public. The pre-1922 DMP did not go looking for trouble, as it were. With very few exceptions, before 1922, same-sex sex crimes were brought to the authority's attention by third parties, usually a concerned parent or, in the case of a couple of soldiers, their commanding officer. Under the Garda commissioner O'Duffy, however, that kind of passive police work was not enough. O'Duffy envisioned the Garda playing a central role in the shaping of the nation's social order and took a particular interest in sexual crime.[62] As such, O'Duffy had the Garda dedicate considerable resources to policing sex. They drove streetwalking sex workers underground and, for the first time in Irish history, conducted extensive campaigns to seek out and arrest men having sex with other men.[63] During O'Duffy's term as commissioner, from 1923 to 1931, 145 men were prosecuted for gross indecency or sodomy in Dublin. Under his leadership, the Garda were the first Irish police force to utilize investigative, undercover, and—based on Coghlan's experience—authorized crime as a means to detect and arrest gross indecency offenders.[64]

Why, of all the gardaí stationed in Dublin, was Coghlan the one instructed to bait a man into a gross indecency offense? It was his first recorded arrest of a gross indecency offender and, as far as I have been able to discern, his last. Neither of the superior officers who vouched for him in the trial were involved with gross indecency cases after Coghlan's. He had undercover experience from his year with the CID, but infiltrating anti-Treaty rings was un-

---

62. McGarry, *Eoin O'Duffy*, 116–140.
63. See Luddy, *Prostitution and Irish Society*; and Denton, "Open Secrets."
64. McGarry, *Eoin O'Duffy*, 91.

doubtedly a different kind of work. In some ways, he was unlike his fellow detectives in the DMD. In 1927, he was twenty-nine years old and still unmarried. He finally married a woman, Annie Sheridan, in 1937, but the two never had children, even though she was twelve years his junior. He was an Anglican in a predominantly Catholic organization. He never rose in the ranks of the Garda and was discharged in 1947 as "medically unfit," almost five years before the other men recruited with him would have retired.[65] Whatever his "medical" issue, however, it wasn't terminal; he died at eighty, considerably older than the average life expectancy of Irish men at that time.[66] Perhaps his oddities were what made him a useful tool for this experiment, and, at least in his case, he was successful.

On the night of October 11, when Coghlan finally revealed himself as a garda, Bodkin reportedly said, "In the name of the Blessed Virgin and St. Joseph, let me off! Are you going to ruin me? I am a business man, and there's no place for me now, only the workhouse." Coghlan told Bodkin that no, he would not allow the man to go. Distraught, Bodkin lay on the ground, pleading with the officer. Coghlan told him that it was no use, to "stop his fooling and come away."[67] The judge sentenced John Bodkin to twelve months of prison time, with hard labor. Curiously, he was not immediately carted off to Mountjoy. He was able to negotiate deportation rather than spending twelve months in prison, as he'd had surgery for cancer recently. His friend who lived in town, Thomas Rowen, wrote to the judge and then the minister for justice, seeking clemency on Bodkin's behalf on account of the man's "infirmity." Shortly after avoiding being imprisoned, Rowen wrote again on Bodkin's behalf, asking to have the exile removed from the sentence because Bodkin's health was at risk from the hardships of travel.[68]

Only one other officer successfully baited a man with sex in 1927. Detective Officer Stephen McWilliams picked up Arthur Woods less than a week after Coghlan baited Bodkin. McWilliams alleged that the defendant touched his penis but that McWilliams turned away and then led Woods back to Rathmines Garda Station where he arrested and charged Woods with attempting to procure an act of gross indecency. The judge who stood in the Woods case commended McWilliams for showing "particularly keen intelligence in doing his duty. It was men like him who succeeded in freeing this country of

---

65. The details of his dismissal are not included in his file in the DMP general register: Registered Number 12007, DMP Personnel Registers, UCD Digital Archives.

66. Maev Ann Wren, "Irish Life Expectancy below EU Average, Study Shows," *Irish Times*, 24 May 2001, accessed on 12 August 2021, available at https://www.irishtimes.com/news/irish-life-expectancy-below-eu-average-study-shows-1.309456.

67. NAI, Dublin Circuit Court, State Files, 1C-96-36, 13-Oct-1927, the State v. John Bodkin, Deposition of Henry Coghlan.

68. NAI, Department of Justice, ref. no. 2019-85-299, "John Bodkin's Deportation."

certain classes of crime and making it a country worth living in. He wished the constable's conduct to be brought to the notice of his superiors."[69]

The representatives of the Irish state—the gardaí, the prosecutors, the judges—were invested in obscuring the presence of homosexuality in Ireland, while simultaneously striking fear into the heart of same-sex-desiring men and destroying the lives of those who failed to take the warning to heart. Woods, aged fifty and retired from the British Army, was found guilty, and the judge sentenced him to twelve months imprisonment with hard labor. During the trial, the state solicitor said that "the crime of which the accused was found guilty was like a foul sewer running through a city in every direction. He was inclined to say that it was the FACILITIES OFFERED for the commission of the crime here that brought the accused and people like him to the country."[70] Though Woods was an Irishman, he lived full time in Britain and only visited home once a year. The reporters, prosecutor, and judge were clear about Woods's foreignness: even though he might've been born an Irishman, he'd aligned himself with the British, he lived in Britain, and he only came to the Free State to impose his immoral ways on the Irish.[71]

There were no other entrapments in Dublin until 1930. Perhaps the tactic was too distasteful for the gardaí and their supervisors, and they left well enough alone until a new band of true believers came along and fulfilled their duty to the state. Perhaps, however (and these need not be mutually exclusive), these first two encounters were investigative missions that just got a little out of hand. Coghlan and McWilliams teased out some significant details in their undercover conversations with Bodkin and Woods, respectively. Coghlan discovered several sites around the city that were visited by men seeking sex with other men. He practiced a behavior—walking into a public lavatory and walking back out without relieving himself and making eye contact with another man in the lav—that would become a useful marker for later gardaí to identify potential offenders in stakeout operations. When Detective McWilliams asked Woods how he picked men, Woods replied that it "depended how the conversation was opened and carried on, and that he was generally lucky to find the right fellow." Woods told McWilliams all about his sexual adventures in the Navy, where it was common for men to commit sodomy with one another as well as something he called "gammaroughing." McWilliams and Coghlan pursued these men over several days or weeks to learn their habits, their haunts, and their language. Perhaps they crossed the

69. "An Appalling Crime: A Visitor's Grave Offence," *Irish Independent*, 26 November 1927, 10.

70. "Like a Foul Sewer: Civic Gardaí Who Are Making Dublin Cleaner," *Evening Herald*, 25 November 1927, 2. Emphasis in original.

71. "Like a Foul Sewer," 2.

line into "too far" by accident, but the results were positive, and the intelligence gathered would serve the Garda in the decades to come.

There can be no doubt that the Garda commissioner O'Duffy pressured the police force to drive the same-sex-desiring men off the streets. In 1930, Commissioner O'Duffy delivered a report to a government commission investigating sex crimes in Ireland. The report showed an increase in all sex crimes from 1924 to 1929. In 1924, for example, there were a total of thirteen prosecutions and eleven convictions for sodomy and indecent assaults on males for all of Ireland.[72] In 1928, there were 41 prosecutions and 34 convictions for same-sex sex crimes involving males. In 1924, there were 98 total prosecutions for all sex crimes, including "defilement, carnal knowledge, or rape of girls," "indecent assault on girls," "incest," "sodomy," "indecent assault on boys or men," "bestiality," and "other." By 1929, that number had doubled to 196 prosecutions.[73] Of course, the report was not evidencing an increase in those sexual activities but, rather, an increase in policing. That shift can only be attributable to O'Duffy's leadership. The Garda was a nationalized police force, with O'Duffy at the helm. Significantly, three of the ten entrapment cases were in 1931, and, in total, the DMD arrested and tried forty men for gross indecency crimes that year, more than any year prior.

While six of the gardaí who entrapped same-sex-desiring men were members of the DMP before it became the DMD of the Garda, three were hired on during the major period of recruitment to replace the disbanded RIC. When the RIC pulled out of Ireland in 1922, there were just over 380 men to tend to the policing of all of Ireland. In the next decade, over 8,000 were recruited and trained.[74] Per O'Duffy's guiding vision, the gardaí should embody the ideal Irish Catholic nationalist man. The recruiting notice in October 1922 read:

Conditions—

Candidates are to be unmarried and between 19 and 27 years of age. Minimum height 5 feet 9 inches. Minimum chest measurement 36 inches.

Candidates will be examined in Reading, Writing from Dictation, and Arithmetic—first four rules simple and compound. They will also be required to write a short composition or letter on a sample subject.

72. Notably, four of these were in Dublin. As one might expect, Dublin, which was home to about one-sixth of the Free State population, was more heavily policed and more heavily represented in these kinds of crime statistics analyses.

73. NAI, Department of Justice, H247.41A, Evidence from Eoin O'Duffy to the Carrigan Committee.

74. Conway, *Policing Twentieth Century Ireland*, 29; McNiffe, *History of the Garda Síochána*, 39.

Candidates should obtain and be prepared to forward, when required, their Registrar's Certificate of Birth, as well as Testimonials from their Clergymen and the Divisional, or, in his absence, the Brigade Commandant. They will be medically examined at the Superintendent's Office, and will pay the doctor's fee for the same.[75]

This ad, and subsequent ads in the next three decades, outlined the characteristics demanded of aspiring recruits. Candidates who could speak and write Irish were exempted from some of the core requirements, because they were needed to serve the rural Gaeltacht communities.[76] A total of 8,230 joined the Garda between 1922 and 1932, and an overwhelming number of them, 98.7 percent, were Catholic.[77] O'Duffy "frequently reminded his force that they were not merely men carrying out an ordinary job, but policemen doing a Christian duty."[78] The new Garda was a pivotal institution in independent Ireland, and its overwhelming Catholic makeup evidenced the significance of Catholicism—not just Christianity—to defining Irishness as different from Britishness. In this postcolonial state, difference was essential to autonomy.

Ideological and religiocultural assimilation was just the beginning. Recruits were generally unmarried to ensure their impartiality in upholding the law, although they could get special dispensation to marry women approved of by their superior officers.[79] Once in the force, proper comportment included a priestlike chastity. Beyond the justification that these men were expected to have no entanglements when they joined—which was why they were also placed in districts far from home, where they would have no loyalties to friends or family—this mirrors expectations identified in Joseph Nugent's discussion of the priest as an Irish masculine ideal.[80] In the same way that the priest was expected to be celibate in his service to God, the garda was in service to the state, and moral behavior was not just expected; it was necessary. These men of "good character" were charged with setting and then meeting the standard of that idealized Irish manliness.

But perhaps most importantly, recruits and then officers had to meet certain standards of physical fitness. While 5 ft., 9 in. wasn't tall nor was a 36 in. chest measurement broad by global standards in 1924, it was a clear communication that taking up a minimum amount of physical space was im-

75. "Notice," *Irish Independent*, 4 October 1922, 3.

76. The Irish Catholic and nationalist moral order referred to here is discussed at length in the Introduction to this book.

77. McNiffe, *History of the Garda Síochána*, 39–51.

78. McNiffe, 138.

79. Conway, *Policing Twentieth Century Ireland*, 31.

80. Joseph Nugent, "The Sword and the Prayerbook: Ideals of Authentic Irish Manliness," *Victorian Studies* 50, no. 4 (2008): 587–613.

portant to policing. Most of the men hired between 1920 and 1932 met or exceeded those minimums by several inches. Once in the force, physical fitness was an integrated aspect of garda training and everyday life. The Garda Gaelic Athletic Association was founded in 1922, with members competing in hurling, Gaelic football, swimming, javelin, and other athletics. The official Garda teams were often praised in the newspapers for their excellent performances in matches.[81] These men were to embody both the health and the vitality discussed in Patrick McDevitt's work on "muscular Catholicism" and the chaste and Catholic respectability noted by Nugent. These sometimes-competing ideals were grounded in a romantic nationalist vision of Ireland.[82]

As the Civic Guard grew in numbers and efficiency, and O'Duffy imposed his martial masculinity on their ranks, they sought out and arrested more men having sex with other men. Still, for any members of the Carrigan Committee who may have believed that the British were the sole source of immorality in Ireland, as politicians and the nationalist media had claimed for over a century, their finl report proved otherwise. O'Duffy tasked himself with forging a moral nation and pressed the Carrigan Committee to recommend major overhauls to the criminal justice system. He believed that the laws governing same-sex sex, rape, abandonment, and other sex crimes were insufficient. He asserted that the existing laws were English and had no real application to Ireland. "The present state of the law," he said, "is disgraceful in a Christian country, and the whole question of morality crimes should be now dealt with from an Irish point of view."[83]

Without the means to truly eradicate the sex crimes that were supposed to disappear with the British, the Free State—through O'Duffy—took pains to sweep it under the rug. Throughout the twentieth century, the public was kept none the wiser with strictly coded news reports of all sex crimes, including same-sex sex. It was only ever an "appalling crime," or "a vice in Dublin," or the technically correct but eternally vague "act of gross indecency."[84] Without speaking openly about sex, the *Irish Times* quoted judges lecturing defendants on the ways they'd "defiled their bodies and debased their minds. They . . . sinned against the law of man and the law of nature, and had brought permanent shame on their families."[85] But, with few exceptions (and I dis-

---

81. Conway, *Policing Twentieth Century Ireland*, 31.

82. McDevitt, "Muscular Catholicism," 262–284; and Nugent, "The Sword and the Prayerbook," 587–613.

83. NAI, Department of Justice, H247.41A, Evidence from Eoin O'Duffy to the Carrigan Committee.

84. "An Appalling Crime," 11.

85. "An Appalling Crime," 10; "Judge and Vice in Dublin: Three Men Sentenced," *Irish Times*, 7 February 1931, 6.

cuss one exception in the next two chapters), the majority of policing focused on the men like John Bodkin and Arthur Woods who sought sexual partners in public and semipublic spaces. With the reality of just how widespread same-sex desire was in Ireland—well beyond what the nationalists imagined there could be once the English left—the optics were unacceptable. So, it fell to O'Duffy to keep the streets clean of the sex workers and the queer men, lest the truth of Ireland's shame be revealed.

O'Duffy was wildly disliked by his colleagues in the Free State, and, when de Valera and Fianna Fáil came to power in 1932, he was relieved of his role as commissioner. He went on to establish Ireland's very own fascist organization, the Blue Shirts, modeled after Mussolini's Black Shirts.[86] He never married but reportedly attended the wild parties thrown by the camp founder of the Gate Theatre, Micheál Mac Liammóir. Mac Liammóir allegedly told several people that O'Duffy was, indeed, a homosexual, though in his published writings he only referred to O'Duffy as "my dear friend."[87] According to the journalist Mary Kenny, O'Duffy would pick Mac Liammóir up after a Gate production in a private car and would attend Mac Liammóir's parties.[88] If the rumors were true, though, O'Duffy managed to keep a tight lid on his own sexual adventures, even as his officers picked up and booked Dublin's cruising queer population. Like most of Ireland's elite queer men and women, O'Duffy had the power and privilege to keep his private life private because his liaisons took place behind brightly colored doors in posh neighborhoods rather than in the public lavs off O'Connell Street.

A surge of arrests in 1931 may reflect O'Duffy's response to the suppressed Carrigan Report. No one outside the government saw the Carrigan Committee's findings until the 1980s. Rather than come to terms with the fact that Ireland was not the pure beacon of sexual morality that its priests and politicians claimed—claims that were undermined daily by the coded reports of sex crimes up for trial in the newspapers—the Irish state suppressed the collected data and chugged along under the facade of Irish Catholic nationalist ideology. Though most arrests were the result of police surveillance of public lavatories or third parties bringing evidence to the Garda, three of the arrests that year were made by officers using their own bodies as bait. There's no publicly available record of the superior officers of the DMD issuing specific orders to surveil or entrap same-sex-desiring men. Historians have yet to find such an initiative outlined or even mentioned in the records left behind by O'Duffy himself. The only evidence we have yet is the testi-

86. "GEN. O'DUFFY RESIGNS: Blueshirts' Leader IRISH POLITICAL BOMBSHELL," *The Manchester Guardian*, 24 September 1934, 10.
87. McGarry, *Eoin O'Duffy*, 163–168.
88. Kenny, *The Way We Were*, 76–77.

mony of officers like Coghlan, who asserted that they were acting on "special instructions."[89] In the wake of what O'Duffy likely perceived as a failure of the Carrigan Commission, the commissioner may have attempted to take matters into his own hands.

Surely, some of the gardaí who went the extra mile were ladder climbers. Some were, undoubtedly, taken in by O'Duffy's vision. It's hard to tell what sort James H. Beggs was. One thing is certain: he was English. He was born in Bradford, Yorkshire, in 1884, but he and his entire family were living in Waterford by 1901. His father was a tailor's cutter, his eldest sister a draper's assistant, and yet another sister a photographer's assistant. As a seventeen-year-old boy, and the eldest son, he worked as a clerk and copyist. At twenty-one, he joined the RIC, in 1905. Curiously, he told the recruiter that he was Catholic when he applied; according to the 1901 census, everyone else in his large family (he had five sisters and one brother) were Presbyterian.[90] Though Catholicism was always more widespread in Ireland than Protestantism, the early separatist and Home Rule movements weren't particularly sectarian, so it would be too cynical to imagine he converted to stay ahead of political machinations. Maybe he converted in earnest. Maybe not.

Either way, Beggs became a cog in O'Duffy's sex-policing machine. He managed to keep his job as a staff sergeant after the disbandment of the RIC and absorption of the DMP. From there, he rose through the ranks of the Dublin branch of the Garda to become the inspector by 1930. Whether he was a true believer in the Irish nationalist rhetoric and O'Duffy's vision or not, he played the game well. He was visibly active in the standardization of physical fitness in the force, serving as president of the Dublin Met's swim club (see Figure 2.1). Most important, he personally oversaw a major months long investigation of a suspected male brothel in Dublin, and supervised Detectives Michael Kearney and William Davis in their 1931 undercover work.[91] As he did these good works, he earned commendations from the circuit court judge Cahir Davitt, son of the famous Fenian Michael Davitt, for his work in rooting out the "vice" that was rampant in the city.[92] Of course, whether Beggs believed or not doesn't really matter in the end. His detectives watched for and baited same-sex-desiring men. O'Duffy's work got done, one way or another. Men like O'Duffy and Beggs kept their own hands clean while sending their officers into public lavatories to find a body of proof for conviction.

89. NAI, Dublin Circuit Court, State Files, 1C-96-36, Deposition of Henry Coghlan.
90. The Beggs family were the only of their name in Waterford in 1901. See the NAI, Census 1901, available at https://www.census.nationalarchives.ie/.
91. NAI, State Files, 1C-94-89, 21-Jan-1931, the State v. James Hand, Frank North.
92. "Vice Prevalent in Dublin," Irish Times, 13 February 1931, 13.

Figure 2.1 The Garda Swimming Club, Dublin Metropolitan Club. Inspector James Beggs served as the club's president. (The Garda Review, *July 1928, p. 748. Courtesy of the University of Limerick Digital Library.* © *An Garda Síochána and the Glucksman Library, University of Limerick.)*

O'Duffy's influence on the young men who joined the Garda Síochána cannot be understated. Like any good fascist, he cultivated a (homoerotic) cult of personality. Also like any good fascist, O'Duffy was a walking contradiction. Ferriter, in a talk given at the University College Dublin, said that there was very much the "public" and the "private" O'Duffy. Ferriter referred specifically to O'Duffy's insistence that gardaí not drink alcohol while he himself was an alcoholic, or his insistence that athleticism be central to the force even as he smoked fifty cigarettes a day.[93] But his men followed him. Many resigned after he was forced to leave the Garda, and as shown by the efforts of James Beggs, Michael Kearney, William Davis, and half a dozen other gardaí who actively sought out same-sex-desiring men to arrest between 1930 and 1932, many were willing to do whatever was necessary to polish the facade of Irish purity.

Curiously, though, most of the men who engaged in these morally suspect tactics joined the force before the Garda was created and before O'Duffy cultivated his cult of personality. Still, their considerable dedication of time and resources to policing sex suggests that the party line carried forward and backward: to join the team you had to do your part, and to stick around you

---

93. Diarmaid Ferriter: Launch of DMP and Garda Personnel Registers, University College Dublin, 29 January 2018, available at https://soundcloud.com/real-smart-media/diarmaid-ferriter-launch-of-dmp-and-garda-personnel-registers.

had to do your part. But not all the baiting in 1931 was successful. In May, Detective Redmond Shea encountered Richard Clarke in a lavatory. Clarke allegedly exposed himself to the garda, then felt the fabric of the garda's pants. Shea claimed that, as they were leaving the lav together, Clarke had been fondling himself through his pockets the entire time. They went together to a shed, where Clarke put his hands down Shea's pants, but were shortly interrupted by another man who came in. Clarke and Shea arranged to meet the next day at another public lavatory. Shea claimed that he prevented Clarke from attempting to bring him to arousal during their rendezvous. When Clarke asked Shea to "handle" Clarke's penis, Shea said no. It was only then, on the second day of much fondling, that Shea arrested Clarke. In court, Inspector Tim O'Neill, who supervised several other gross indecency investigations in the late 1920s and early 1930s, testified that he was in the room at the Garda station when Clarke was being questioned. Clarke claimed that nothing happened between him and the garda and stuck to his story in the interrogation room and in the courtroom. No other gardaí could verify Shea's version of events. The jury found Richard Clarke not guilty.[94]

In June, and just a few days before the quarterly circuit court session that would hear more than half of 1931's gross indecency trials, garda Patrick Burns and his partner, John McCloskey, arrested Patrick Byrnes. Detective Burns and McCloskey were responsible for arresting at least five men for gross indecency in 1931. In the Byrnes case, Detective Burns intentionally brushed elbows with the defendant in the public lavatory at St. Stephen's Green. Detective Burns then led Byrnes to a secluded alley, where Byrnes felt Detective Burns's penis through his trousers. It was only a few moments more before McCloskey showed up to help arrest Byrnes. With McCloskey's corroborating testimony, Byrnes was found guilty and sentenced to twelve months in prison with hard labor.[95]

Though O'Duffy left, the core of what he was trying to do—suppress the visible elements of sex in Ireland—was carried on by the Garda and the new government. Still, Fianna Fáil, terrified that those loyal to O'Duffy would rise up against the new government, hired hundreds of new recruits in 1933 who would be loyal to de Valera rather than O'Duffy. Political loyalty, though, was not a marker of moral or effective policing. One Fianna Fáil recruit, Thomas Curass, found trouble as soon as he hit the beat. In July 1933, not even a full year out of training, he arrested Magnus Robertson on gross indecency charges. Curass alleged that, while dressed in plainclothes, he encountered

94. NAI, Dublin Circuit Court, State Files, 1C-94-92, docket 35, 7-Jul-31, the State v. Richard Clarke.

95. NAI, Dublin Circuit Court, State Files, 1C-94-92, docket 39, 7-Jul-31, the State v. Patrick Byrne.

Robertson on the street and struck up a conversation. It turned to women, to which Robertson supposedly said that "he preferred a man . . . when he was excited," and that he knew a fourteen-year-old boy who would do it for three pounds. Curass told Robertson that he would cost a lot more—ten quid at least—and Robertson allegedly whipped out his checkbook, intent on paying the man for sex then and there. Robertson, on the other hand, claimed that they'd had a nice conversation, that Curass had said he needed a pound, and Robertson said he only had a tenner but would give it to him anyway. The ten-pound note was taken into evidence when Curass arrested and charged Robertson.[96] Like Redmond Shea's bungle two years earlier, Robertson was allowed to walk. The state turned up a nolle prosequi, unwilling to pursue a case with such tenuous evidence. Though not necessarily connected to his failure to employ effective tactics in policing same-sex-desiring men, Curass only lasted another three years in the DMD.[97]

Baiting same-sex-desiring men was morally dangerous work. More problematically, it wasn't all that effective. In cases where the bodies of the gardaí were the evidence of gross indecency, the prosecution only had a 50 percent conviction rate. It should be no surprise then that it was ultimately abandoned by the Garda after 1936. The last garda to admit to baiting was Officer Michael Kearney.[98] He joined the force already married, a thirty-year-old laborer from rural Meath.[99] His father was not around when he was growing up, and he lived with his mother, uncle, and two siblings.[100] He moved to Dublin with a letter of recommendation from his priest and joined the DMP in 1920.[101] He served thirty-one years with the Garda, and, though he was never promoted, leadership asked him to stay past what would have been a typical retirement date when the garda was in desperate need of officers without a willing

---

96. NAI, Dublin Circuit Court, State Files, 1D-44-30, docket 30, 3-Jul-33, the State v. Magnus Robertson.

97. Thomas Curass was English, born in Boroughbridge, York. Shortly after the 1911 census was taken, he (and possibly his family) moved to Ireland from England. Though he found employment as a bottle worker, within months of arriving he was arrested and sent to Mountjoy Prison for breaking into a shop and stealing sweets in Dublin. Mountjoy Prison Register, p. 157, line 29. Available at https://digital.ucd.ie/view/ucdlib:43945.

98. DMP and Civic Guard (Garda Síochána) Personnel Registers, 1837–1925, held by Garda Museum and Archives, digital content by University College Dublin, published by UCD Library, University College Dublin. Michael Kearney is Warrant Number 11721, p. 253. Available at https://digital.ucd.ie/view/ucdlib:53467.

99. Michael Kearney, son of Daniel and Ellen Kearney of Castletown, County Meath, born September 5, 1891. Church Records, available at https://civilrecords.irishgenealogy.ie/.

100. In the 1901 Census, Kerney lived with his mother and his mother's brother, plus three siblings. By 1911, the Census reports that the uncle was gone (probably passed away), and mother was head of household. His mother is listed as "married," rather than widowed, which suggests an absent husband rather than a dead one.

101. DMP register book, p. 253.

or able population to fill the positions.[102] He died young, at sixty-six, not long after retiring.[103] By the time he started thrusting his own body into sting operations, Michael Kearney had already been surveilling same-sex-desiring men for over six years. He and his partner, William Davis, observed James Jones and Frederick Newman engaging in sex acts in a public lavatory in 1930. Kearney and Davis, and their superiors, Tim O'Neill and James Beggs, respectively, were exceptional in that they were involved with more gross indecency cases than any other gardaí in the 1930s. Kearney and Davis alone arrested at least ten men between 1929 and 1936.[104]

Despite considerable success with observation and stakeouts, in 1936, Kearney decided to throw himself into the work of policing same-sex-desiring men. In October, he was successful. With Davis's corroborating evidence, he was able to get Edward Chandler convicted and sentenced to six months imprisonment with hard labor. But, later that same year, the same approach was not successful. In the courtroom, Robert Potterton turned the language of sexual predation against Kearney:

> [DO Kearney] seemed to be standing very close to me. I got the suspicion that there was . . . something wrong with him. . . . I then turned round to go out . . . the Gda turned round while we were standing almost face to face and very close to one another. I immediately noticed that he had not buttoned his trousers and his clothes were in the same position as if he was going to make water still. I felt his private part touching against my hand.[105]

It was Kearney's word versus the defendant's. Davis was unable to say whether the defendant had actually grabbed Kearney's penis, or if Kearney had, indeed, pressed his penis against Potterton's hand. The case was thrown out. As in 1933 when Magnus Robertson outlined Officer Thomas Curass's role in the exchange of money, the officer had no supporting witness.[106] Entrapment was more than an extreme approach to policing gross indecency; it was simply unreliable.

---

102. DMP register book, p. 253.

103. DMP register book, p. 253.

104. NAI, Dublin Circuit Court, State Files. In my years of working with these court records, one of my data collection points has been to identify, whenever possible, which gardaí were involved with each case. I have that data for 1924–1955.

105. NAI, State Files, City and County of Dublin, 1D-55-73, docket 8, 11-Dec-1936, the State v. Robert Potterton.

106. NAI, State Files, City and County of Dublin, 1D-44-30, docket 30, 22-May-1934, the State v. Magnus Robertson.

Gardaí whose bodies were made evidence in these cases were put in precarious positions. Some, like Michael Kearney, obviously thought they knew
how best to play the field. Kearney had seen both what evidence convinced
juries and what tactics were likely to get a case thrown out. Already by 1936,
the gardaí who presented their bodies as evidence only won their cases half
the time. Why, then, did this forty-six-year-old man thrust his body into the
mix? Maybe he was moved by the residual anti-sex fervor that was introduced
by O'Duffy and, at least rhetorically, maintained by Fianna Fáil. Maybe he
was given "special instructions," though it seems unlikely as no supervising
officers gave testimony in his case to shore up his moral high ground. Maybe, after years of watching men have sex with men in public lavatories, he
wanted to feel those feelings himself. We simply cannot know.

Even without written records, it seems clear that O'Duffy created a culture in the Garda that inspired these kinds of reckless moves: the contradic-
tory practice of committing an act of gross indecency to catch a gross indecency offender. But that obsession was not necessarily shared by all state
officials across the board. Even as judges and state solicitors lamented the
vice that seemed to overrun Dublin, few were willing to simply take a garda
at his word if and when conditions were unseemly.[107] Judges and juries were
put in the uncomfortable position of passing judgment on defendants when
the officers were all too often also implicated in the acts.

Though he slipped into the world of same-sex desire briefly in 1936, Kearney—like Coghlan, Davis, and the others—successfully extricated himself
before causing too much self-harm or career-ending damage. Unlike the victims of their attentions, no gardaí experienced the harsh repercussions of getting caught engaging in sex with other men. Whether they were tormented
by their own desires in their intervening years, we may never know. In the
end, their work paid off. The intelligence gathered in these undercover operations proved essential to policing same-sex sex from 1936 on. Their suc-
cesses and failures in court set a standard for future Gardaí to replicate and
scale. And their efforts—whether motivated by bureaucratic people-pleas-
ing, desire, or belief in the homophobic habitus and ethos of the Free State—
facilitated the oppression of same-sex-desiring men for decades to come.

---

107. "Vice Prevalent in Dublin," 13; "Strong Comments by Judge—Two Men Sentenced—
'Outside the Pale of Civilisation,'" *Irish Independent*, 30 January 1931, 2.

3

The Cabbie

In many ways, James Hand was a fortunate man.[1] He owned his own horse and hackney carriage and was able to support himself as a cabbie for hire in Dublin city center.[2] In 1930s Dublin, this was no small feat. According to historian Mary Daly, emigration was essential to keeping the Irish economy in balance. By 1930, the United States—the preferred destination of most emigrants—had cut their available visas for the Irish in half and regularly fell under that quota.[3] As Joseph Lee notes, even with the constant flow of emigration, the late 1920s unemployment rates were high. The 1926 census

---

1. "James Hand" was, unfortunately, a very common name in twentieth-century Ireland. The court records do not provide an age, a middle name or initial, or any specific biographical details about this James Hand other than his horse and hackney cab business and his residence before he was arrested. I guesstimated, based on the ages of Michael Corr and Frank North, that James was between thirty and forty-five at the time of his arrest—close to Frank's age of thirty-two but possibly as old or older than Michael Corr (forty-three). That would mean he was born sometime between 1885 and 1905. Fifty James Hands were born in Ireland between 1885 and 1905, including three in Dublin North and two in Dublin South. Only one James Hand in the 1911 census was a car driver—son of James Sr. and Elizabeth Hand. Based on the fact that this James and Elizabeth Hand lived exclusively in Dublin North neighborhoods throughout their publicly recorded lives—and Thor Place is also there—and the absence of any other James Hand who worked as a cab driver, I think it's safe to assume that he is that James Hand. Available at http://www.census.nationalarchives.ie/.

2. "Further Charges," *Evening Herald*, 12 February 1931, 4.

3. Mary Daly, "The Irish Free State and the Great Depression of the 1930s: The Interaction of the Global and the Local," *Irish Economic and Social History* 38 (2011): 19–36.

data reveal an 11.9 percent unemployment rate, though the Irish government only reported an official 6 percent rate.[4] When emigration wasn't an option, unemployed men moved to the city to find work. Few were successful. Dublin and the rest of urban Ireland was underdeveloped in industry, and the economy was predominantly agricultural for much of the early decades of the Free State.[5] Hand's means of self-employment was thus his good fortune indeed. For those who were able to find work, transport work like cabbie driving was the most common in Dublin. People working in transport accounted for 10 percent of the total workforce in the 1930s. While those census figures included various work including postal sorting and delivery, porters, and messengers, it also included men like Hand, working directly in the transportation of people and goods around the city.[6]

In 1931, Hand was well established in Dublin. At forty-one years old, he lived alone in a comfortable terraced cottage at Twelve Thor Place, in the Stoneybatter neighborhood.[7] Stoneybatter and the adjoining Arbour Hill had been inhabited since at least the fifteenth century, according to archaeological records, and were the area of the city where Danish migrants built their homes after establishing Dublin as a trading port.[8] Though close to the Arbour Hill Cemetery, where the executed leaders of the Easter Rising were buried in a mass grave, Thor Place was relatively unscathed during the urban warfare of the War of Independence and Civil War. Dublin in the 1930s underwent incredible physical transformation, but the Dublin Corporation could not keep up with the housing demands of the city's population. Most of Dublin's grand Georgian architecture had fallen into disrepair, and tenements packed multiple families into too-small subdivided houses. Half of the city's population increase from 1930 to 1950 was "in-migration" from other parts of Ireland.[9] One-third of Dublin's population lived in overcrowded conditions in the 1930s, and only one in twelve people lived alone in Ireland in 1926.[10] Though Thor Place was decidedly working class, it was located just a stone's throw from the posher homes of the Stoneybatter neighborhood. That his

4. Lee, *Ireland 1912–1985*, 126.

5. Brady, *Dublin, 1930–1950*, 31.

6. Brady, 31.

7. "Further Charges," 4. Yes, this is the same Stoneybatter neighborhood centered in Tana French's excellent novel *The Trespasser!*

8. "Explore the History of Collins Barracks," National Museum of Ireland, museum.ie, accessed 10 August 2023, available at https://www.museum.ie/en-IE/Museums/Decorative-Arts -History/Visitor-Information/About-The-Museum/History-Architecture.

9. Brady, *Dublin, 1930–1950*, 45.

10. Brady, 51; Maria Luddy, "Marriage, Sexuality, and the Law in Ireland," in *The Cambridge Social History of Modern Ireland*, edited by Eugenio F. Biagini and Mary E. Daly (Cambridge: Cambridge University Press, 2017), 344.

self-employment afforded him a place to himself, even if it was in a working-class neighborhood, set Hand apart from many of his contemporaries.[11]

Hand's family had deep roots in North Dublin. He was the only surviving son of James and Elizabeth Hand, working-class people who lived on the outskirts of the Stoneybatter neighborhood most of their married lives.[12] They were eighteen when they married—young by today's standards but even more so for a period in Irish history when people typically didn't marry until their late twenties or thirties.[13] They were both North Dubliners through and through, born there, raised their family there, and died there. They had four children survive to adulthood, James Jr. the youngest, but Elizabeth suffered through fourteen pregnancies to get those four. She worked in domestic service for most of her life. James Sr. was an unskilled laborer who moved from job to job to do whatever work he could to provide for his family. When he and Elizabeth married, he was doing some painting. When his daughter Kate was born, he was a wine porter. When his son James was born, he was a laborer. But sometime between 1901 and 1911, he got himself a horse and hackney cab and started up a steady career as a cabbie. He was probably still driving in 1915 when he passed, taken by an untreated cancer.[14]

In 1911, twenty-one-year-old James Jr. lived with his parents, two of his sisters (Catherine and Mary) and his unmarried aunt, Mary Sherwin, who was his mother's sister. He worked as a cab driver, presumably with his fa-

---

11. Today, Stoneybatter is considered Dublin's "hipster" neighborhood. See Michael Freeman, "Your Guide to Stoneybatter: Dublin's Inner-City Village with Hipsters and a Lot of Heart," TheJournal.ie, 6 July 2018, available at https://www.thejournal.ie/stoneybatter-neighbourhood-guide-2-4112038-Jul2018/.

12. They're probably the James Sr. and Elizabeth Hand who married in 1872, though, at the time James's profession was listed as "painter." It's possible he *was* painting buildings at the time; most years his profession is listed as "laborer." It wasn't until the 1910s that he got himself a horse and carriage and became a cabman. In 1911, James Jr. was also working as a "cabman"; it's unclear from the sources if he had his own horse and hackney cab, or if he and his father took shifts with the one set. It seems unlikely that he still had the same horse twenty years later, but if he kept it in good working order, he may well have had the same hackney carriage. Civil Records of Ireland, Marriages, Dublin North, group registration ID 2781676, irishgeneaology.ie.

13. According to Maria Luddy, marriage patterns were deeply impacted by the famine era; in 1911, 12 percent of men aged forty-five to fifty-four had never married, and 25 percent of women in that same age category never married. These statistics are for the country as a whole, including rural areas, where primogeniture and other factors impacted marriage rates as well. It is possible that marriage statistics were less impacted in Dublin because households simply needed multiple incomes to survive. "Sexuality, and the Law in Ireland," in *The Cambridge Social History of Modern Ireland*, ed. Eugenio F. Biagini and Mary E. Daly, (Cambridge University Press, 2017), 344–346.

14. NAI, 1911 Census, North Dublin, available at http://www.census.nationalarchives.ie/pages/1911/Dublin/Glasnevin/St__David_s_Terrace__Blackhorse_Lane/16572/.

ther.[15] His older sister Ellen had long since moved out and had her own family a few streets away.[16] Ellen and her husband's home in 1911 was at 15.1 St. David's Terrace, Blackhorse Lane, in Glasnevin, just northwest of Stoneybatter where our James Hand would rent a house on Thor Place; theirs was a terraced two-story house, which they shared with another family, the Fletchers. James Jr. worked with his father, up until his father's death, and then struck out on his own, taking the cab and horse to support himself.[17] Thanks to his parents' endless toil on behalf of him and his sisters, James Hand Jr. was given something that looked a lot like a better life than that of his parents, who both died young: James Sr. at sixty-one, and Elizabeth at sixty-seven.[18]

In his social life, too, Hand was fortunate. Though he was a notorious gossip, a habit that got him into trouble more than once, he was well known and liked in his social circles.[19] Significantly, he was able to surround himself with men like him: men who desired other men. He found those men in the pubs, through coded correspondence, and on the streets of Dublin. He helped other men find companionship in a city otherwise unwelcoming of their desires. He gave love and received love in return.[20]

But Hand also lived in a state very much in the throes of postcolonial self-determination, one growing in hostility to visible immorality. In the early 1930s, hundreds of women were imprisoned in Magdalene laundries or Mother and Baby Homes for perceived sexual indiscretions or crimes like "concealing a birth," as hundreds of sex workers were forced by patrolling Gardaí to take their work off the streets and into (the arguably more dangerous conditions of) brothels, and nearly fifty men were arrested for crimes of "gross indecency."[21] In a city where judges deemed his love a "scourge," "filthy, unnatural, and detestable," and a "disgusting offence," and where juries con-

15. Ellen and her husband Michael Brohoonan had three children already by 1911: NAI, 1911 Census of Ireland, available at http://www.census.nationalarchives.ie/pages/1911/Dublin /North_Dock/Seville_Place_Cottages__Third_Ave_/19110/.

16. Within a few years of the 1911 census, however, Elizabeth and James Sr. would move in with Ellen. That is where they would both die.

17. NAI, 1911 Census, North Dublin, http://www.census.nationalarchives.ie/pages/1911 /Dublin/Glasnevin/St__David_s_Terrace__Blackhorse_Lane/16572/.

18. Both died from bone-related health complications: James Sr. had a "carcinoma" on his humorous, and Elizabeth broke her femur and probably got an infection that led to heart failure. Obviously, I don't have medical training myself, but I'd speculate that both suffered from osteoporosis brought on by malnutrition and hard lives.

19. NAI, State Files, 1C-94-89, 21-Jan-1931, the State v. James Hand, Frank North, Michael Corr, Statement of Edward Payton.

20. The State v. James Hand, Frank North, Michael Corr.

21. Smith, *Ireland's Magdalene Laundries*, 44–82; Denton, "Open Secrets," chap. 4; Luddy, "Marriage, Sexuality, and the Law in Ireland."

victed men like him for public displays of intimacy, Hand's good fortune was tenuous at best.[22]

Like most of the men in this book, I found James Hand in the Dublin Circuit Court State Files.[23] In 1931, his good luck ran out, and he was arrested for an act of gross indecency in Phoenix Park. As a result of his arrest, he was evicted from his home. I don't know what happened to his horse and carriage, in the three years of his imprisonment, or if he got them back when he got out. At least, though, his friends didn't abandon him entirely. His lover-turned-codefendant, Michael Corr, never turned witness against him. It is likely, based on the timeline of his friend Frank North's first questioning by the Garda and Hand's choice to seek companionship in the brisk winter night rather than at home, that North warned him that the gardaí were watching his house. He came under police scrutiny because of the loose lips of another friend, Edward Payton. But Payton told the courtroom in January 1931 that he wished he'd never gone to the gardaí, and he regretted the whole sordid affair.[24] Hand's life may have been upended, but he lived his life knowing full well the possible consequences of his sexual partners, camp persona, and matchmaking. The version of his story that I tell here, reconstructed though it is from scraps, painful moments, and dead ends, provides insights into the history of men who had sex with men in Dublin as well as the Irish state's response to them.

Men like Hand were not content to disappear, despite the nascent Irish state's efforts to eradicate the visible signs of sexual "immorality." Instead, they carved out spaces to meet, laugh, and make love in Dublin, turning urban renewal projects like slum clearance and the establishment of public parks into sexual and social opportunities. And though Hand was, ultimately, arrested because a friend outed him to the Garda, his story actually highlights the limits of Ireland's postcolonial moral order. While Ireland shared a cultural antipathy toward same-sex desire with the Americans and British, policing in Dublin was tied to ideological and postcolonial state-building goals. In Chapter 2, I discussed some of the limitations that the Garda faced when developing strategies for addressing the visibility of same-sex-desiring men in the capital city. Ironically, Hand's arrest at the prompting of an informant is so unusual in the court records that it highlights how uncooperative the general population of Dublin was in aiding the efforts of the gardaí to police sexuality.

---

22. "Further Charges," 4; "Serious Charges," *Evening Herald*, 12 February 1931, 4; "Wiping Out a Scourge," *Irish Times*, 28 February 1931, 3.
23. The State v. James Hand, Frank North, Michael Corr.
24. The State v. James Hand, Frank North, Michael Corr, Testimony of Edward Payton.

Arrest was always more likely in Dublin than in most other areas of the Free State. When fascists like O'Duffy were at the helm of the Garda, and company men like Beggs were on the case, chances were at their highest. Beggs was the inspector responsible for organizing a yearlong surveillance operation of Hand's home at Twelve Thor Place. Hand had the great misfortune of living right at the nexus of fascist police leadership and eager followers seeking to crack down on perceived immoralities. The year after O'Duffy delivered a report on sex crime statistics to the Carrigan Committee, the Garda pursued one of their most vigorous campaigns against men who were having sex with other men in Dublin. In 1931, forty men were arrested and tried at the Dublin Circuit Court, among them James Hand, Frank North, and Michael Corr. Compared to just eight in 1930, and five in 1932, it's readily apparent that Hand was in the right place but at the wrong time.

For most years, and most of the time, Dublin was the right place for queer men. It was home to robust theater, arts, and musical communities, which catered to men (and women) with means and interest. Like Mac Liammóir and Edwards, the right social circles permitted same-sex-desiring people to live together openly.[25] Starting in the 1930s, the Dublin Corporation increasingly expanded public access to the walled gardens and parks, beautiful spaces by day that provided ample cover for amorous couples by night.[26] A mixture of grand Victorian public toilets and simple partitioned urinals continued to operate from the start of the Free State throughout the 1970s and 1980s and were sites that both local and visiting men—and occasionally gardaí as well—cruised in the evenings. The 1930s and 1940s brought in movie theaters; the silver screen was a draw for most Irish people, and the dark theaters and elbow-to-elbow seating provided cover for all kinds of sexual activity, both wanted and uninvited.[27] Pubs continued to serve as a homosocial space for men throughout the twentieth century, with some even catering to the "musical" (code for same-sex-desiring) crowd.[28] For some, Dublin was a city of opportunity. For others, it was a city of dangers. Sometimes it was both.

Hand wasn't a man who let fear of consequences rule his life. On January 6, 1931, he was out with friends, taking a stroll through Phoenix Park with a

---

25. Though generally understudied, there were several well-known revolutionary women who built lives together in Dublin. Mary McAuliffe has produced recent work on Margaret Skinnider and her life partner Nora O'Keefe and is currently working on a book about Kathleen Lynn and her life partner Madeleine ffrench-Mullen. See McAuliffe, *Margaret Skinnider*.

26. See Brady, *Dublin, 1930–1950*, 122–124.

27. The first cinema in Ireland, the Volta, was opened at Forty-Five Mary Street, Dublin, in 1909, by the novelist James Joyce. Peter McCann and Martin Kelly were arrested in 1931 after they were caught canoodling in a movie theater. NAI, Dublin Circuit Court, State Files, 1C-94-92, 7- Jul-1931, the State v. Peter McCann and Martin Kelly.

28. Sam McGrath, forthcoming chapter in *The Irish Pub: Invention and Re-Invention* (Cork University Press).

few bottles of stout. They stopped in an unlocked park shed to drink their beer. One of Hand's friends said, "Why Mary Hand, you should be tight," to which Hand replied, "Ask my cunt, I am as wide as a gate!" They all laughed, and most of the party moved on, laughing and drinking. Hand and Michael Corr remained in the shed.[29] Corr, a railway engine cleaner from Dun Laoghaire, stood close to Hand in the shed, taking a long drink from his bottle of stout. Alone at last, Hand asked Corr how long he'd been in "the game." Corr replied that he'd been at it for years. They spoke in low voices, unaware that a garda was concealed on the other side of the wall listening to their every word.[30]

Hand knew he was taking a chance when he pressed Corr up against the wall of that shed, some one hundred feet from the Phoenix Park Garda depot. That knowledge seemed part of their foreplay. After Hand asked Corr, "Do you mind if I feel you?" and Corr said, "I do not mind," each opened the other's trousers. Hand whispered, "If we were caught now . . ." and Corr said, "I believe this place is full of detectives." Hand replied, "I know two of those bobbies." We can only speculate on the tone of this conversation, recorded and repeated as it was in courtroom testimony by the garda who was hiding on the other side of the shed wall. Did they whisper these words fearfully? Lustily? Was the danger thrilling, making their hearts race and their bodies tremble? When Hand claimed he knew two of the gardaí, did he mean he knew the specific gardaí who typically patrolled Phoenix Park, or was he suggesting that he was friendly with some other gardaí on the Dublin force? Was he saying it derisively or dismissively? Is this even what they said, or is this conversation a fabrication of the garda? While there is much that we can learn from the official records of state apparatuses, uncertainty is never far.

Though not a daily occurrence, same-sex-desiring men in the know—and from the context of this case, Hand seemed to be "in the know" more than most—would have been aware of the consequences for getting caught having sex with another man. In 1929, fifteen men were arrested for gross indecency, and at least two had their names splashed across the Dublin-based *Independent*.

> Reginald O'Brien, dentist's assistant, Manders Tee., Ranelagh, and Thomas O'Brien, window cleaner, Dorset St., were returned for trial, charged by Insp. Dunleav with behaving indecently at Upper Hatch St. near Harcourt St. John Donagh, Bremore, was at Balbriggan sentenced to one month's hard labor on a charge of indecent behavior.[31]

---

29. The State v. James Hand, Frank North, Michael Corr, Deposition of Garda William Davis.
30. Deposition of Garda William Davis.
31. "Dublin and District," *Irish Independent*, 27 March 1929, 8.

Judge Davitt sentenced Victor Furley, who pleaded guilty to a large number of counts of gross indecency, to fifteen years' penal servitude, and in commending Det. Officers Madden and Cryan, who had assisted in bringing the accused to justice, said it was revolting that police officers and Irishmen should have to be employed in detecting such crimes.[32]

With a range of potential sentences from one month to, horrifyingly, fifteen years, a cautious and vigilant reader might've thought twice before heading out to cruise public toilets. Maybe Hand didn't read the *Independent*. Maybe he did, but chose to live and love his own way regardless. Hand, whom friends and acquaintances described as always on the move, who knew Dublin well as he carted paying customers to and fro, probably felt safe in his city. In 1931, gardaí were still figuring out their tactics for policing same-sex-desiring men; there weren't yet specific zones that were consistently policed. Undoubtedly, some did see those little notices in the paper and were deterred from seeking companionship. In Hand's case, the danger that he and Corr whispered about as they pressed together in the shed was not enough to stop them. Hand may have had reason to believe that the park shed was safer to bring a man to than his cottage on Thor Place. Or, perhaps, he simply wasn't content to be driven into hiding.

Despite the danger, they unbuttoned the front of their trousers and held each other close. When Corr invited Hand to "put it between my legs," Hand eagerly complied, saying, "It will help to rise you." Their passionate embrace began to shake the shed wall against which Corr was leaning. And that's when the peeping garda popped out from behind the wall, flashing a torch on the two men. They jumped back from each other, trousers open and penises exposed, automatically declaring that they "weren't doing anything." Garda William Davis called for his partner, and they took Hand and Corr to the station.[33]

After they were separated into interrogation rooms, the real hammer dropped.[34] Hand learned that the gardaí were literally out to get him, because of information they got from his friend Payton a full year ago. Hand was charged with committing an act of gross indecency in Phoenix Park, in January 1931, and with being "party to the commission of" an act of gross indecency, in 1930—effectively, what the judge in his case later called, "conducting a male brothel."[35] The gardaí, at Inspector Begg's direction, informed Hand that they'd both been watching his house for twelve months and had mul-

---

32. "Dublin and District," *Irish Independent*, 26 October 1929, 10.
33. The State v. James Hand, Frank North, Michael Corr, Deposition of Garda William Davis.
34. Deposition of Garda William Davis.
35. "Serious Charges," 4; "Wiping Out a Scourge," 3.

tiple witnesses ready to attest that he'd been using his house for "immoral purposes."[36]

Hand regularly used his home at Twelve Thor Place to entertain. Sometimes he facilitated meetings between his friends and rent boys. Many people knew about Hand's activities in his home, including Payton, and seemed not to care. But Hand's wagging tongue changed that. According to Payton, Hand spread some rumors about the alleged sexual indiscretions of Payton and his sister—which Hand insisted were just jokes and not to be taken seriously—but Payton was sensitive. After several weeks of quarreling, Payton went to the gardaí and informed on Hand. He told Inspector Beggs that Hand was using his residence for "immoral purposes." Beggs took that information and then started watching Hand in his home for the better part of a year, noting and gathering evidence from the young men who came and went. The legwork that went into apprehending Hand suggests just how seriously Beggs and his supervisors took the threat Hand posed to society. When he was caught with Corr in Phoenix Park in January 1931, Beggs had more than one charge to pin on Hand.

Curiously, Hand's case is one of only a handful in which someone reported suspected homosexual activity to the gardaí. In a city where same-sex-desiring men shared the public spaces with other Dubliners, one might expect that neighbors or just random bystanders might see something and say something. Yet there were very few examples in the court records of consenting adult men who were brought to the attention of the garda.[37] Of the ninety-four cases of gross indecency in a public lavatory, for example, only two were the result of a man who was propositioned and outraged by the sexual advance.[38] This is a strange absence in the records, because public lavatories were a hotbed of sexual activity in the 1930s, 1940s, and 1950s, and one of the most common places a man was likely to be caught. The role of Hand's friend Payton in this case makes it a particularly unusual one, even as the circumstances of Hand's actual arrest—in an intimate embrace with another man in Phoenix Park—were quite the norm for gross indecency arrests.

---

36. The State v. James Hand, Frank North, Michael Corr, Statement of Edward Payton.

37. In cases of men seeking sex from other men or boys over age seventeen (juvenile-adults): I've only found three cases of three hundred in which a neighbor, friend, or bystander informed to the gardaí and that led to an arrest for gross indecency.

38. 1924–1972. The crime location is not always identified clearly in the court records. Of the ninety-five, six cases involved boys under fourteen. The two cases in which an adult made an unwanted pass at a non-Garda in a lav are: NAI, State Files, 1C-94-84, docket 17, 6-May-1930, the State v. James Jones; NAI, State Files, 1D-27-12, docket 48, 11-Jan-1945, the State v. John Smith. There are a handful of other cases of unwanted advances where the location of the crime was not indicated in the court records or the location was not a lavatory.

The absence of denunciations in the gross indecency records is peculiar. There were certainly those who took it upon themselves to enforce the Catholic-nationalist ideals of sexual purity and manliness.[39] Yet, there is also evidence to suggest that friends, neighbors, and even gardaí and priests knew of the sexual proclivities of the same-sex-desiring men of Dublin and did not turn them in. Perhaps Dubliners still didn't quite trust the gardaí any more than they had the RIC. It's hard to qualify the reluctance to turn informant as a broad rejection of the state's moral order. After all, hundreds of regular Irish people sent complaints about printed material to the Irish Board of Censors, leading to the banning of various novels, restrictions on what could make it into newspapers, and even censorship of comic books.[40] But, when it came to actually facilitating the arrest and conviction of men who had sex with men, Dubliners interfered so rarely that it is statistically insignificant.[41] Like the juries who flinched at the baiting tactics of the 1930s gardaí, there were limits to the ways civilians were willing to enforce the moral order of the postcolonial state.

Hand's ability to host men in his home also speaks to the resource constraints of the Garda and the Irish state's anti-sex campaign. If the postcolonial moral project was going to be truly successful, the Garda needed the cooperation of the general public. Undoubtedly, Hand's neighbors on either side of his terraced cottage heard the comings and goings of young men. Certainly, Hand's friend Payton knew what kinds of sexual interests Hand had:

> In conversation I asked him why he did not get married. He said "I wouldn't get married, I wouldn't touch a woman, I'd rather have men. . . . I am carrying it on all my life and never touched a woman." While this conversation was going on we were sitting in front of the fire in the kitchen. Hand then leaned across to where I was sitting, put his hand on my private part outside my clothes and said, "Come into the room and we will have trade." I told him not to be mad that I would not go. I remained on until about half ten. He made no further suggestions to me.[42]

Significantly, Hand's sexual overture was not what drove a wedge between him and Payton. It was Hand's rumor spreading that angered his friend, and,

---

39. See the biography of Eoin O'Duffy, and the biography of John Charles McQuaid.

40. NAI, DOJ, Board of Censorship, 2006-148-13.

41. The exception was in the Dublin Union Workhouse. There were cases there in 1926, 1927, 1933, 1935, 1936, 1940, and 1941. In two of those cases, once each in 1927 and 1941, ward attendants caught defendants engaged in sex and turned them over to the Gardaí.

42. NAI, Dublin Circuit Court, State Files, 1C-94-89, 21-Jan-1931, the State v. James Hand, Frank North, Michael Corr.

even then, Payton went to their priest before the Garda. Father Guilds listened to Payton's accusations—that Hand had both spread rumors about him and sexually propositioned him—and invited both men to sit down and talk through it. In their mediation, Hand admitted to Father Guilds that "it was the truth that he had said these things but that he didn't mean them, and that he did keep the house for immoral purposes with men." Father Guilds told Hand that "if police got to hear of it he . . . would get twelve months, and advised him to give it up. Hand said he would give it up. The priest said if you don't I will get you put out of that house and out of the parish altogether."[43] Notably, the priest didn't say he'd go to the police himself—just that he'd use his own sway in the city to have Hand evicted from his home. Neither Payton nor the priest seemed concerned that what Hand was doing was a danger to society. If anything, the priest expressed concern for his parishioner and sought to keep him out of prison. If even the priests, whose ideology of sin and immorality shaped the very laws that threatened Hand's freedom, were unlikely to tip off the police, how could the Garda expect help from the public to enforce the state's moral project?

In some specific cases, the public *did* aid in policing "immoral" sex. We can see this in the way families committed their daughters and sisters to Magdalene institutions for even the hint of rebellion or impropriety, with no actual sexual indiscretion even needed.[44] There was a disturbing ease with which Irish people committed women to institutionalization, as though the rights women were gaining in the Anglo world threatened the Catholicization of postcolonial Ireland. But the average Irish person was only willing to intervene in a man's business when the infraction met very particular conditions, specifically when an adult layman interfered with a minor who was not related to him.[45] Even though the law did not differentiate between sex between adult men and sex between adult men and children/legal minors, the general population did. There were only ten total cases of sex between adult men in private spaces, but there were an additional twenty cases in private spaces that involved boys under twenty-one. The majority of those investigations were launched by an outside party providing information to the gardaí. Since the 1990s, hundreds of men and women have come forward with allegations of their sexual abuse at the hands of their priests and Catholic school teachers when they were children. State investigations have found that the Garda overlooked these issues when they were raised at the time, or simply deferred

---

43. The State v. James Hand, Frank North, Michael Corr.

44. Smith, *Ireland's Magdalen Laundries*, 28.

45. This obviously excluded priest sexual abuse of children and, for the most part, incest as well. See the overwhelming evidence presented in the Ryan Commission on Child Sexual Abuse, available at https://childabusecommission.ie/; Sarah Anne Buckley discusses the prevalence of incest in Ireland prior to 1956 in *The Cruelty Man*, 152–175.

to the Catholic hierarchy for dealing with perpetrators in their employ. Non-interference in those cases, of course, was irreparably damaging to those children.[46] Yet, the Dubliner's preference to err on the side of not turning informant for the Garda likely also benefited men who had sex with other adults outside the official boundaries of social norms.

To be clear, Irish law *allowed* for the policing of same-sex sex in private. The policing of sexuality in Dublin intensified after independence, but policing tactics sought to establish a *public* sphere free of sex. At the same time, this (perhaps inadvertently) created space for same-sex desire to find purchase in private. Just as it was rare for civilians to narc, it was also rare for gardaí to dedicate resources to investigating acts of private consensual same-sex sex. Hand's case thus demonstrates both the norm of policing public sexuality and the limitations the Irish state encountered when trying to police private sexuality.[47]

I cannot, of course, argue that same-sex-desiring men were accepted or escaped ostracism or violence from other Irish people. Regardless of its legality, same-sex desire was regarded as a sin in most Christian-centric societies, and Ireland was no different from the United States or the United Kingdom in that respect. Violence against gay men was more visible in court records after decriminalization in 1993, when queer people were more likely to report such violence. Yet there were few examples of Irish people who took an active part in the state-imposed restrictions on same-sex-desiring men. The reach of the postcolonial moral order was limited by the willingness of the general Irish population to take an active part in helping the state enforce it. The Irish state and religious hierarchy sought to shed the legacy of British rule in Ireland by emphasizing Ireland's Catholicity, rurality, and moral superiority. Though rhetoric from the "top" of Irish society—the politicians and religious officials—emphasized a homogeneous and chaste vision of independent Ireland, the reality was far more complex. Noncompliance and resistance destabilized the tenuous Irish Catholic nationalist moral order.

Most gardaí efforts were focused on picking up men who had sex in public, who disrupted the facade of the Free State's moral purity. This model of policing, with a focus on public over private sex, certainly created a class-based inequality in who was most likely to be arrested. Most men arrested were working class, unemployed, or out-of-towners. But a good number were solidly

---

46. "Commission to Inquire into Child Abuse," available at http://childabusecommission.ie/; the commission was established in 2000 following legislation requiring the state to investigate the multiple allegations of abuse suffered by children in industrial schools and other state-funded institutions in Ireland. The 2009 report, a.k.a. "the Ryan Report," included testimonies from hundreds of abuse survivors.

47. NAI, Dublin Circuit Court, State Files, 1C-94-89, 21-Jan-1931 the State v. James Hand, Frank North, Michael Corr.

middle class: insurance clerks like Frank North, doctors, businessmen, bank officers, solicitors, and an occasional Anglican priest.[48] Perhaps this is simply because their families or wives would have objected to them bringing their lovers home. Perhaps, like James Hand, they had reason to believe their homes were under surveillance. Or, perhaps, they saw the public spaces of Dublin as their spaces and sought anonymous public sex with intentionality. The complexity of Hand's case, then, reveals the complexity, and limitations, of the Free State's efforts to assert its moral authority by exorcising the visibility of sex in Ireland.

As evidenced by Hand's case, not all same-sex-desiring men *had* to rely on the public conveniences of the city, but sometimes they did anyway. For men who had respectable facades to uphold, having a friend like Hand in the city was particularly fortuitous. Frank North, for example, lived in the suburbs, and, when he came to the city, Hand's bachelor pad served as a sanctuary for illicit rendezvous. Since the Garda almost never pursued men who conducted their affairs in private domiciles—which was true in 1930 and continued to be true up until decriminalization—it was a pretty safe bet. If not, of course, for Hand's feud with Payton, North, Hand, and Corr might've gone undetected for their entire lives.

North and Hand met via correspondence. Though neither said where or how they found each other, it is likely that one placed a coded ad in the wanted section of a local paper.[49] They exchanged several letters, and photographs, before meeting in person. In one of those surviving letters, which was seized by the Garda as evidence against both men in their trial, North conveyed his hope that he and Hand would meet soon.

"My dear J," North wrote, "you know I fell for you the first time I saw your photo—also I think I could give you a good time, or try to anyway!!" After proposing a day and time to meet when North would be back in Dublin, emphasizing "the sooner the better," North hinted that he had definite intentions for their first meeting. "I'm trusting to see you in more ways than one!" he exclaimed and implored that Hand "for all sakes be good and don't waste it til Thursday." The sexual overtones of his requests are clear, particularly

---

48. These statistics are hard to quantify, as the occupation was only listed in about 147 of the court records (less than half) from 1924 to 1966.

49. This was a common way for men to meet each other in the nineteenth and twentieth centuries. I haven't to date (despite many hours of browsing through thousands of editions of various Irish dailies) found the paper in Dublin that offered Frank and James this chance to connect; none of the major newspapers (as far as I've been able to find) have personals sections, and, while some men might've slipped a coded ad in among the "in search of" employment ads, I haven't yet spotted one. But we see this kind of connection in Tokyo, New York City, Berlin, and elsewhere. See, e.g., Cocks, *Classified*; Carrington, *Love at Last Sight*; and Jonathan Mackintosh, *Homosexuality and Manliness in Postwar Japan* (Routledge, 2010).

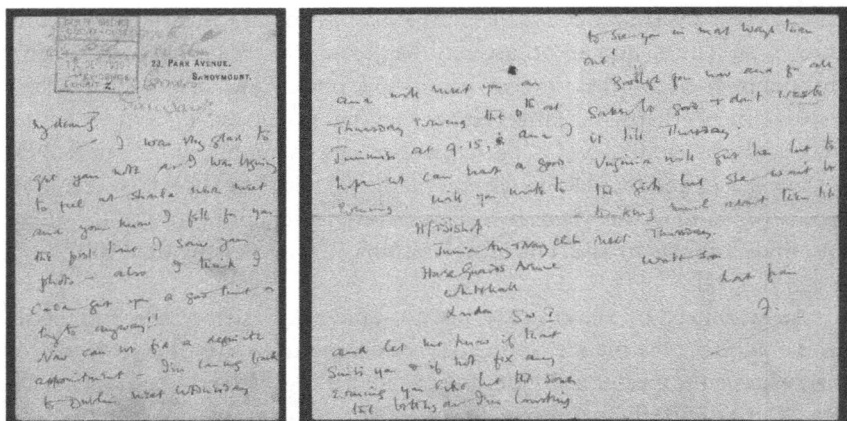

Figure 3.1 A letter from Frank North to James Hand. *(State Files, Dublin Circuit Court, 1C-94-89, 21 January 1931. Reproduced by kind permission of the Director of the National Archives.)*

as he underlined "waste." North was not the only one concerned with when and how frequently a potential lover might have "spent" himself; when Corr and Hand were whispering back and forth between caresses, Hand asked Corr when he last "came off" (a month), and, when prompted, Hand said it had only been a week for him—he clearly had a better handle on the sexual opportunities available to him in Dublin. In his correspondence, North hoped that Hand would save some of his passion for their first meeting.[50] (See Figure 3.1.)

Hand, who was called "Mary" by his queer friends, would likely have been able to decode the next sentence of North's note with ease: "Virginia will give her love to the girls but she won't be thinking much about them til next Thursday." It seems likely that North is giving himself the moniker "Virginia" here. The "girls" might be the rest of their mutual queer acquaintances or may be a sexual euphemism. Regardless, North signs earnestly, "Write soon, Love from, F."[51]

As an adult, North was a respectable middle-class Catholic man, but he grew up in the Liberties, one of Dublin's oldest working-class neighborhoods. His father was a butcher, and four years his mother's junior. By the age of forty-four, his mother had given birth to eight children, six of whom survived to

50. NAI, Dublin Circuit Court, State Files, 1C-94-89, 21-Jan-1931, the State v. James Hand, Frank North, Michael Corr, Letter from Frank North to James Hand.
51. Letter from Frank North to James Hand.

adolescence.[52] In the years before the Easter Rising, the family lived at Fifty-Eight Thomas St., Merchant Quay.[53] They were well off enough to have an entire house and yard to themselves, a testament to Francis Sr.'s relative positionality as a tradesman. None of his family members participated in the Easter Rising, though their home may have been invaded by soldiers on one side or another. Frank North was thirty-two, an insurance clerk living with his family in the middle-class south suburbs of Terenure, when he was accused of having sex with rent boy Michael Hackett.

In 1931, Hackett was the oldest of four children.[54] His parents, typical of their time, married very late.[55] Mary was literate, while her farmer husband was not.[56] Daniel was already forty-one when he married thirty-two-year-old Mary Noone, daughter of a farmer, in 1912. Prior to their marriage, Daniel had been his aging mother's primary caretaker. Maybe he'd been courting Mary for years but couldn't imagine living with her *and* his mother in their tiny two-room cottage in Parkmore, Galway. Maybe his mother simply forbade it. When the two bound their lives together in holy matrimony, they made short work of turning the tiny thatch-roofed cottage into a home for their family. Mary had Michael a year into their marriage, and they adopted a beautiful black sheepdog the year after that. By 1921, the Hacketts had a veritable pack of dogs, with a new puppy every two years or so.[57] On March 1, 1915, Mary had their second son—and the birth killed her. She died twelve days later from septicemia.[58]

At forty-four, a widower, and with two little babies to care for, Daniel remarried almost immediately. In October of that same year, he married Kate. Over the next six years, Daniel and Kate had two more children, adopted

52. Irish Census 1911, Dublin, Merchants Quay, Thomas St; available at https://census.nationalarchives.ie/.

53. Electoral rolls for Div. IV. Merchant's Quay Ward, 1915, p. 105; archived and digitized by the Dublin City Council Libraries and Archive: 1899, 1908, to 1915 Electoral Rolls; available at https://databases.dublincity.ie/burgesses/.

54. The Civil Records on irishgeneaology.ie have birth records for Michael (1913), Patrick (1915), Luke (1917), and Matthew (1920).

55. Irish Geneaology.ie, Church Records, marriage record of Daniel Hackett and Mary Noone, 12 August 1912; available at https://civilrecords.irishgenealogy.ie/.

56. 1911 Census. Entry for the Noone household, house one in Crusheeny (Lackaghbeg, Galway); NAI census, available at http://www.census.nationalarchives.ie/ and Entry for the Hackett household, house four in Parkmore (Galway Rural, Galway), accessed on 16 August 2023, available at http://www.census.nationalarchives.ie/.

57. Ireland Dog License Register, 1914–1921, available at findmypast.ie.

58. Irish Genealogy, death certificate of Mary Hackett, 13 March 1915; digital version of the record accessed on 25 September 2023, available at https://civilrecords.irishgenealogy.ie.

three more dogs, and watched the world get torn apart in World War I.[59] The Hacketts' personal trauma, however, was much closer to home. Heartbreakingly, Kate died at just twenty-seven of heart disease, a year after her second son was born. Even if he were the sort of quiet, brooding recluse you might expect of a man who spent his prime years living alone with his mother on a remote farm on the Wild Atlantic Way, Daniel was surely shaken by these losses. Still, he must have believed it was important for his boys to have a mother—or perhaps he just couldn't live in that house without a womanly presence of some kind—because, in 1923, Hackett once again married. And, again, he made the prudent choice to marry the daughter of a farmer who could be satisfied by the life he could give her.

Mary O'Brien got pregnant shortly after their wedding in February 1923.[60] At thirty-four, she might've given up hope of marriage and children of her own. But giving birth was dangerous in Galway in the Irish Free State. Like most of Ireland outside of Dublin, maternity care was underdeveloped and relied primarily on untrained midwives and handywomen, which led to a high maternal and infant mortality rate.[61] Daniel's first wife had died while giving birth in their home. Though his second wife had died unexpectedly and unrelatedly to childbirth, Daniel was probably nervous about Mary's pregnancy. When his wife began to experience complications, he brought her to Seamount Nursing Home. Despite their best efforts to mitigate the damage pregnancy had done to her body, Mary O'Brien Hackett died in childbirth, a heart attack brought on by eclampsia.[62] Her baby didn't survive.

So Michael Hackett had and lost three mothers in his short lifetime, all before he was twelve. Daniel didn't try to remarry a fourth time. Maybe he relied on his eldest son and extended family to care for the little boys. Maybe he shouldered the parenting on his own, juggling four children and the farm alone. Maybe he turned in on himself, beaten down by a life that took the women he cared for and denied him the pleasures of life. The thrice-widower farmer continued to toil away, caring for the animals on their small farm, planning to pass his house on to one of his sons.[63] Typically, and probably

59. Irish Genealogy, marriage record of Daniel Hackett and Katie Grealish, 23 October 1915; digital version of the record accessed on 25 September 2023, available at https://civilre cords.irishgenealogy.ie.

60. Irish Genealogy, marriage record of Daniel Hackett and Mary O'Brien, 13 February 1923; available at https://civilrecords.irishgenealogy.ie.

61. Breathnach, "Handy Women and Birthing," 34–56.

62. Irish Genealogy, Mary O'Brien death record, 1921, ref. no. 04378170; accessed on 16 August 2023, available at https://civilrecords.irishgenealogy.ie.

63. Daniel was forty-one when he got married for the first time. Before that he'd lived alone with his mother, a widow, in their little house in Castlegar, until her death in 1910. His older brother Pat had married two decades earlier, at the age of twenty-eight, and moved to Terryland, nearer "urban" Galway city. By 1912, Pat already had six children! Meanwhile Daniel

frustratingly for the children in Ireland's large families, the Irish practiced primogeniture to prevent the overparceling of precious farmland. Only one (son) would inherit the Hackett farm in Parkmore, Castlegar. It was a small thatch-roofed two-room cottage built of stone, with its own stable and piggery.[64] Presumably, Daniel thought he'd leave the farm to his oldest son. But, as we know, the farming life did not appeal to Michael Hackett. His brother Patrick would, ultimately, both take over the farm and be the one with their father when he passed in 1938.[65] Apparently uninterested in—or perhaps just unsuited to—the farmer's life that awaited him in the West, Michael made his way to Dublin. There, he sold his body to get by while he mucked about the big city.

According to Michael Hackett's testimony, he first met Frank North in August 1930. When Hackett came to Twelve Thor Place, the door was unlocked. He went inside to find his host, James Hand, by the fire. Hand had invited Hackett up to the house earlier that week for some "paid work." After about a half hour a stranger entered. Hackett learned later that the man was North, an insurance salesman from north of the city. Hand opened three bottles of stout and distributed them. The three conversed in front of the fire for a few more minutes before Hand announced that he had to go out for a bit and would return in an hour.

Once Hand left, North made a move. When Hackett did not reject North's initial advances—over-the-trousers fondling—the two moved to the bedroom at the back of the house. The two sat on the edge of the bed smoking. They took down their trousers, and when Hackett said he was unable to "take it up the back" he rubbed North's penis until North "had an emission" on Hackett's stomach.[66] After they dressed, North gave Hackett five shillings, which would have been over a day's wages for a working-class Dubliner.[67] Hand had returned to the living room with more stout. Hackett finished his before

---

toiled away caring for their aging mother. Pat and his family also lived in a two-room thatch-roofed stone cottage. Pat reported his occupation in 1911 as "farmer," so presumably he and his older sons worked with Daniel at Parkmore.

64. 1911 Census of Ireland, St. Nicholas Parish, Galway; available at http://www.census.nationalarchives.ie/reels/nai002378036/.

65. Irish Death Records, Daniel Hackett death record, 1936, no. 1512288; available at https://civilrecords.irishgenealogy.ie.

66. NAI, Dublin Circuit Court, State Files, 1C-94-89, 21-Jan-1931, the State v. James Hand, Frank North, Michael Corr, Deposition of Michael Hackett.

67. According to the UN Economic Commission for Europe, Research and Planning Division Economic Survey of Europe in 1948 (Geneva: UN Department of Economic Affairs, 1949), 235, the average annual income per person in 1938 Ireland was about $252 American dollars, or £53 British pounds. This means that on average an Irish man might make around £1, or 20 shillings, per week. Five shillings for a few hours of work was a significant sum for an unemployed boy like Hackett.

heading home for the evening. A few months later Hand invited him up for another visit. The same series of events unfolded.[68] This exchange may have gone on indefinitely, were it not for Hand's arrest in Phoenix Park.

The gardaí picked up and questioned eighteen-year-old Hackett and nineteen-year-old John Ormond after they were seen going to and from Hand's cottage at Twelve Thor Place. Whenever Hackett or Ormond visited Hand, they said they ended up in bed with one of Hand's friends. Ormond testified that he had sex with a stout man, maybe an army officer, who paid him after they were finished. When Hand asked if Ormond was satisfied with this arrangement, Ormond said he was, and returned to Thor Place several times for the same reason. Hackett similarly turned up for clandestine meetings with an older man in Hand's house, and, unlike Ormond, he knew the name of the man he had sex with—Frank North, a thirty-one-year-old insurance clerk.[69]

Hand may not have been surprised when he was arrested in Phoenix Park on January 6, 1931, but North was definitely shocked when he was taken in for questioning a couple weeks earlier. The gardaí asked if he knew Hand, if he ever spent time at Hand's house, if he ever encountered other men at Hand's house. He admitted to knowing Hand, having spent many evenings with him, having even met "a kid there last Saturday night—Hackett is his name." But North denied the accusation that he had sex with Hackett or any men.[70]

When the gardaí read Hackett's statement to North, North said it was "disgusting. . . . Nothing like that ever happened. I used to go up there [to Hand's house] for a drink because they object to me drinking at home. I am supposed to be a [teetotaler]. The story you read to me is a composition of lies. The filthy bit is."[71]

Despite his protestations, the gardaí found enough evidence to charge and convict Frank North. In addition to Hackett's statement incriminating North, North's own correspondence with Hand suggested his predilection for the "filthy bits." But his statement does speak to why he might've relied on the privacy of Hand's home for sexual fulfillment. He admitted that he feared the judgment of his family should he drink alcohol at home. For a respectable man like North, then, a gross indecency conviction would have been ruinous.

On February 12, 1931, James Hand was led into the Dublin Circuit Court judge Cahir Davitt's courtroom for sentencing. Unlike his codefendants, Frank North and Michael Corr, Hand had not been released on bail. No one in his life was able to offer up the £100 necessary for his release. Hand came

---

68. Deposition of Michael Hackett.
69. Deposition of Michael Hackett.
70. The State v. James Hand, Frank North, Michael Corr, Statement of Frank North.
71. Statement of Frank North.

from working-class people. His parents had long since passed; Ellen, his oldest sister, was raising seven children, including twins, on her husband's insurance inspector salary. His sister Mary's dressmaking wages probably went to support their disabled sister, Catherine, who was committed to the Grangegorman Mental Hospital for at least the last three years of her life.[72] How Ellen and Mary felt about James's proclivities (or his saucy adoption of his sister's name among his camp friends), we'll never know. While some working-class families showed up for their sons, brothers, nephews, and uncles in these situations, that was not the case for James and his sisters. Certainly Hand's friends might've supported him. North and Hand were close enough that it seems likely that North tipped Hand off about his house being watched and his visitors being questioned by the Garda. Maybe that is why Hand was out with his friends in Phoenix Park and drew his lover into the park shed for a rendezvous instead of going back to his home. But in the end, friendship wasn't sufficient to protect James Hand from state violence.

After the trial, Judge Davitt commended Beggs and his officers for their work on the case. "The public ought to be grateful to these officers for their excellent work in clearing out this ulcer from the city."[73] When he was sentencing Hand, Davitt insisted that he owed it to the community to give the cabbie the maximum sentence. "I hold very strong views about this type of offence," said the judge. "I don't know how many men you corrupted through your agency, I am taking that into account in imposing a sentence on you."[74] Because he was charged in two separate cases—for the attempted sodomy with Corr and the procurement of sexual services from young men for North—Hand was sentenced twice. He was given two years with hard labor, the maximum sentence for a conviction of "gross indecency," and an additional twelve months of imprisonment for running a "male brothel," the sentences to run consecutively.[75]

---

72. Irish Genealogy, marriage license, registration no. 1932118; accessed on 17 August 2023, available at https://civilrecords.irishgenealogy.ie; a search of the Irish civil records turns up the records of all of Ellen Hand and Michael Brohoon's children; they already had three of those children by 1911, according to the 1911 Census of Ireland, available at http://www.census .nationalarchives.ie. Both James Sr. and Elizabeth were living with Ellen and her (enormous) family just off North Circular Road when they passed in 1915 and 1921, respectively. His death is recorded as being caused by a carcinoma of the humorous. Irish civil records, Dublin North, Death Records, group registration ID 5453076, irishgeneaology.ie; accessed on 17 August 2023, available at https://civilrecords.irishgenealogy.ie. Her cause of death as recorded was a broken femur followed by cardiac arrest. She most certainly had a hard life, and her age at death is listed at just fifty-eight. Irish civil records, Dublin North, Death Records, group registration ID 3346062, available at https://civilrecords.irishgenealogy.ie.

73. "Gardai Commended," *Evening Herald*, 23 February 1931, 2.

74. "Gardai Commended," 2.

75. "Wiping Out a Scourge," *Weekly Irish Times*, 28 February 1931, 17.

As Maria Luddy, Morgan Denton, and I have all argued elsewhere, after independence, the arbiters of the Free State endeavored to clear out the embarrassing remnants of British influence.[76] With limited resources and little will to cooperate from the general population, this goal was hard won. As Denton has demonstrated regarding the policing of female prostitution in the Free State, the gardaí only succeeded in driving sex work behind closed doors.[77] For same-sex-desiring men, the Garda never quite succeeded in even doing that. Public spaces were the domain of all men; same-sex-desiring men were not so easy to force underground.

In the crowded housing arrangements for most Dubliners, a private home like Twelve Thor Place was particularly special. Broderick was not the first to imagine Dublin as harboring a sexual subculture. According to biographer Michael O'Sullivan, Brendan Behan described sexual encounters of all kinds in the Catacombs nightclub under Thirteen Fitzwilliam Place, a gathering place for Dublin's artistic crowd.[78] According to Behan, "There would be men having women, men having men, and women having women. A fair field and no favour."[79] Behan's privileged circles felt unaffected by the moral order of the Irish state. It seems likely that the neighboring residents of Thirteen Fitzwilliam Street were at least aware of the people, possibly even the activities, of the Catacombs, and did not interfere. While the sanctuary of Twelve Thor Place wasn't protection enough for James Hand and Frank North, it's important to remember that their story is exceptional. Despite a bevy of people knowing about Hand's "male brothel" and sexual desire, he wasn't arrested until he broke the law in public in Phoenix Park.[80] Even those who *could* enjoy their relationships in relative safety behind closed doors may have chosen to avail themselves of the city's pleasures. As Hand's case suggests, the queer subculture of Dublin was not always content to be hidden. On the night he was arrested, he and his friends were out, strolling together through Phoenix Park, making loud and lewd jokes to one another, laughing, and having a wonderful time—like any group of Irish men could expect to do without excessive garda harassment in their city. When Hand and Corr peeled off from the group for a bit of "trade," they did so knowing—and even discussing—the risks.

---

76. See Luddy, *Prostitution and Irish Society*, intro.; Denton, "Open Secrets," 193; and Earls, "Unnatural Offenses of English Import," 396–424.

77. Denton, "Open Secrets," 190.

78. RTE, "The Catacombs," *Doc on One*, 12 June 2007, available at https://www.rte.ie/radio/docunone/646054-catacombs.

79. O'Sullivan, *Brendan Behan*, 135.

80. The fear of corruption of Ireland's youths and the seriousness with which child sexual abuse (except within industrial schools, families, and churches) was taken is discussed at length in Chapter 5.

They knew they were in danger. Though only a handful were reported in the papers, over sixty Dubliners were tried for gross indecency in the previous seven years. According to the witness statements at their trial, they talked about the threat of gardaí even as they reached for one another. Yet, in the face of that danger, like the queer men before and after them, Hand and Corr claimed public space for themselves. And even though the state succeeded in ruining hundreds of individual men's lives, ultimately, the Garda and courts failed to eradicate same-sex desire from Ireland. Though Hand and Corr's passionate embrace inside a shed was the public evidence the gardaí needed to upend Hand, North, and Corr's lives, their experiences proved exceptional even though the rules would've had it otherwise.

Despite the postcolonial moral project of the Free State, queerness was not stamped out in urban Ireland. This is evidenced both in the mere existence of the subculture we can glimpse in Hand's case and in the persistence of same-sex-desiring men in carving out public spaces for themselves in the homosocial world of twentieth-century Ireland. The Free State *was* successful in making the public sphere a man's world. That was clearly one of the goals of the Free State leaders, particularly during de Valera's reign, but even before, as evidenced by O'Duffy's term as the Garda commissioner. But, in so doing, this forging of a homosocial public Ireland created openings for same-sex-desiring men to blend into the urban landscape.

In the National Archives' folder of evidence that the Garda used to send James Hand to prison, he is silent. There are depositions from two of his friends, five gardaí, and two teen boys, but not a single statement from Hand himself. A newspaper article, from late February 1931, reports that he pleaded guilty to one of the charges levied against him, but the archival record does not show any of Hand's words or writing. This is atypical of the gross indecency records held by the NAI; at the very least, there is usually a statement from the accused included in the Dublin Circuit Court State Files. In the broader scheme of things, of course, stories like Hand's have been omitted from the history of modern Ireland. But his silence is particularly jarring here, when the context of his life—before, during, and after his misfortune—reveals so much about Irish history.

4

The Solicitor

In April 1941, seventeen-year-old British army deserter Leslie Price met Ronald Brown, the forty-one-year-old state solicitor for County Kildare.[1] Price was hungry, drifting from one sketchy place to the next. He had nowhere to go, no money, and no prospects. After their very first meeting, Brown invited Price to stay with him. Brown promised both to help find Price work and to let the boy stay for as long as he needed. Brown took Price to the movies and out to dinner as well as to parties and on hiking holidays. Sometimes, according to Price, they shared a bed "to keep warm."[2] To those who knew him and saw the two together, it appeared that Brown loved the youth.[3] But, in August 1941, Leslie Price was arrested for having sex with another man. A few days later, Ronald Brown was also arrested on charges of "gross indecency."

Brown was like the hundreds of other Irish men who had relationships with men. Those with the means avoided the detection of the Garda with little difficulty, as suggested by the rarity of middle-class and aristocratic-type men represented in the gross indecency court records. It seems likely that these relationships were "open secrets" common in Ireland but infrequently record-

1. A shorter version of this chapter was published as "Solicitor Brown and His Boy: Love, Sex, and Scandal in Twentieth-Century Ireland," *Historical Reflections/Réflexions Historiques*, 46, 1 (2020): 79–94, https://doi.org/10.3167/hrrh.2020.460106.

2. NAI, Attorney General's Office (AGO), 2002-16-466, 29-Aug-1941, the State v. Ronald H. Brown, Deposition of Leslie Price.

3. NAI, AGO, 2002-16-466, 29-Aug-1941, the State v. Ronald H. Brown, Statement of Heinrich Petrie.

ed for posterity, like sex work.[4] For those with the means, or who ran in the right social circles, amorous same-sex relationships might be tactfully ignored or even accepted. The Gate Theatre founders Micheál Mac Liammóir and Hilton Edwards, for example, lived together from the late 1920s until their deaths without resistance and were, according to scholar Éibhear Walshe, Ireland's first openly gay couple.[5] Mary McAuliffe's recent work on revolutionary lesbian couples falls into this camp as well. Kathleen Lynn and Madeleine ffrench-Mullen, heroes of the 1916 Easter Rising, lived together for thirty years; though historians previously viewed their relationship as a "friendship," McAuliffe's work on the women's private writings reveals something much deeper than friendship.[6] Depending on one's social circles and means, it was possible to have a queer relationship in independent Ireland so long as intimacy was limited to hearts, minds, and bedrooms, instead of public parks. Because the Free State founders were more concerned with appearances than bone-deep change, queerness was tolerable as long as it was not visible. Brown had the means and the right social circle; but his story went off the tracks when the visibility of his relationship threatened the already precarious foundation of the Catholic nationalist state. When Solicitor Brown's name was dragged into the proceedings surrounding a gross indecency case, the ideological boundaries of the nascent state were tested.

Gross indecency court cases, though problematic, provide one of the few windows onto this moment in queer Irish history. Such records may appear to be mere documentations of sexual encounters, but if examined closely, they may reveal deep connections, even affection. That such relationships, particularly those that came before the courts, were often transactional or temporary did not mean that they weren't meaningful to both parties. It is difficult to ascertain a man's feelings toward his sexual partner when the only recording of their relationship is a courtroom deposition or interrogation room statement. But a close reading of the case of State Solicitor Brown and his boy suggests that one can find affection, and possibly love, evidenced in some of these vice crime records.

In independent Ireland, generally the testimony of a "boy" like Price would be enough to send a queer man like Brown to prison. Because Brown was a

4. Denton, "Open Secrets."

5. Walshe, "Sexing the Shamrock," 159–167.

6. Patrick Kelleher, "Lesbian Couple Erased from History of Ireland's Easter Rising," *Pink News*, 9 April 2023, available at https://www.thepinknews.com/2023/04/09/ireland-easter-ris ing-lesbian-kathleen-lynn-madeleine-ffrench-mullen/; Ciara McGrattan, "The Hidden Histories of Queer Women of the Easter Rising," *Gay Community News*, 22 March 2016, available at https://gcn.ie/hidden-histories-queer-women-easter-rising/; Mary McAuliffe, recorded lecture, "Dr. Kathleen Lynn: A Life of Service," available at https://www.youtube.com/watch?v= j7NYxqo19P0.

representative of the state, the assigned gardaí conducted an unusually in-depth investigation, and, ultimately, Brown was exonerated. The atypicality of their story is a useful foil for examining the politics of status and sexuality in midcentury Ireland. Most important, the revelation of Solicitor Brown's involvement with Leslie Price was a deep and troubling embarrassment for the Irish government. The nationalists who founded the Free State built their moral authority to rule on the notion that same-sex desire was a particularly English condition.[7] Brown's story reflects the anxiety that still lingered in the young state around sex and nationalism, and his position in the Irish government reveals the precariousness of Irish Catholic nationalist ideology. It was one thing for a state solicitor to have a teen lover; it was quite another for word of that relationship to make it to the papers and for a representative of the state to be implicated in and found guilty of a gross indecency crime. Though errant bombs dropped on Ireland throughout 1941, it was not the war itself that shattered Brown's world. Instead, it was this seventeen-year-old English boy.

Ronald Henry Brown of Naas, County Kildare, was born in 1899 to Stephen and Mary "May" Brown.[8] May Brown, née Ball, was Stephen's second wife, and gave birth to Ronald when she was forty-one.[9] Ronald was May's only surviving child. She was born in Ardbraccan, County Meath, north of Dublin, to a farmer.[10] Even by rural Irish standards, she married quite late, and to a man nearer her age than most women of her time could have expected. After the Great Famine, rural Irish families limited marriage to a "favored Irish son and daughter" to protect assets and consolidate generational wealth.[11] May had at least three siblings; her older brother Richard took over the family farm, and their younger siblings, Maggie and John, lived with Richard on the farm until he died.[12] John married, in 1907, but continued to run the farm in Ardbraccan while also maintaining a wine cellar busi-

7. Earls, "Unnatural Offenses of English Import," 396–424.

8. NAI, 1901 Census, census.ie; Area—DUBLIN (RC), Parish/Church/Congregation—CLONDALKIN, Marriage of STEPHEN J BROWN of NAAS and MARY ANNE BALL of ENFIELD on 18 November 1897, record number DU-RC-MA-1421, available at https://churchrecords.irishgenealogy.ie.

9. Civil Records of Ireland, Marriages, Naas Union, 1899, group registration ID 01785509, available at irishgeneaology.ie.

10. NAI, 1911 Census, Kildare / Naas Urban/ Naas, East/ Residents of a house 1 in Naas, East (Naas Urban, Kildare), available at census.ie.

11. Timothy W. Guinnane, *The Vanishing Irish: Households, Migration, and the Rural Economy in Ireland, 1850–1914* (Princeton, NJ: Princeton University Press, 1997), 134.

12. NAI, 1901 Census, Meath/ Ardbraccan/ Ardbraccan/ Residents of a house 28 in Ardbraccan (Ardbraccan, Meath), available at census.ie.

ness in Trim with his wife, Rose.[13] Her siblings had no children of their own.[14] Without even cousins his own age to play with, one can imagine that young Ronald's childhood was a bit lonely. He probably looked forward to the months away at boarding school. May died in 1918, when Ronald was not yet twenty.[15]

Ronald's father, Stephen, served as the first chairman of the Kildare County Council (1899–1911) and crown solicitor for County Kildare (1915–1921).[16] From local government to farming, Stephen Brown was a bit of a jack of all trades; one obituary notes that he "did not confine himself to law" despite it being his area of expertise.[17] He was initially a supporter of Charles Stewart Parnell, leader of the tenant rights agrarian agitator group, the Land League, until the 1910s, when he "dropped politics to devote himself entirely to professional work"—perhaps in the wake of his second wife's death.[18] In his twilight years, he took up agricultural pursuits. As a boy he'd been particularly fond of dogs; in fact, he always had at least three dogs from the time he was twelve until his death in 1931.[19] Collies, Irish setters, Italian greyhounds, fox terriers, cocker spaniels—he collected and cared for them all. Since all of his dogs were defined breeds, it is possible that he counted himself among the elite Anglo-Irish socialites who invented the modern dog breed(s) and founded the Kennel Club.[20] His wide variety of breeds, however, may point to his affection for the animals, rather than his intention to become a prize-winning dog breeder.

Stephen Brown had four children—Stephen, Mary, John, and Mollie—with his first wife, Catherine Ross, before she died in 1888.[21] As was the custom of prominent rural families, Stephen's eldest son joined the priesthood as a Jesuit and eldest daughter joined a convent, taking the name Rev. Sister Mary Augusta.[22] Both of his other sons, John Barry and Ronald, trained as solicitors and joined the family business. John Barry Brown served in World War

13. NAI, 1911 Census, Meath / Trim Urban / Haggard Street / Residents of a house 38 in Haggard Street (Trim Urban, Meath), available at census.ie.

14. NAI, 1911 Census, Residents of a house 38 in Haggard Street, available at census.ie.

15. Civil Records of Ireland, Deaths, Naas Union, group registration ID 4432921, available at https://civilrecords.irishgenealogy.ie/.

16. "The Demise of Mr. Stephen J. Brown, M.A.," *Kildare Observer*, 7 March 1931.

17. "Death of Mr S. J. Brown, Popular Kildare Lawyer," *Irish Independent*, 25 February 1931.

18. "Notes by Tatler," *Nationalist and Leinster Times*, 14 March 1931, 4.

19. Ireland Dog License Registers, Kildare, 1912 and 1916, available at findmypast.ie.

20. Worboys, Strange, and Pemberton, *Invention of the Modern Dog*.

21. "Notes by Tatler," 4.

22. Catherine Moran, "Stephen James Meredith Brown," *Dictionary of Irish Biography*, available at https://www.dib.ie/biography/brown-stephen-james-meredith-a1017; see also Sara Hillas, "Superior Educational Attainment and Strategies of Land Inheritance in Post-famine Ireland: A Case Study," *History of Education* (Tavistock) 47, no. 1 (2018): 18–35.

I, where he lost an eye and was a German POW for several years.[23] Upon his return, he was appointed to the prestigious position of clerk of the Crown and Peace for County Kildare.[24] Mollie Brown may have married, but she left fewer imprints on the public records.

Collectively, the Brown family was as close to a Catholic aristocracy as existed in Ireland. Their family estate in Naas was Ard Caein, an impressive six-bay, two-story, redbrick house that is now on the historic register.[25] Set back from the road, it was the perfect place for the crown solicitor to retreat to with his dogs, and, later in life, his prize-winning livestock. Perhaps through his brother-in-law John's connections, Stephen started breeding and trading in prize-winning cattle and pigs.[26] The Browns' reputation and social capital in Kildare was captured in Stephen Brown's obituary. In the wake of his death, the *Kildare Observer* remarked that he sprang

> from an ancient and honourable race which through the centuries had given of its best to the welfare of the people, he fulfilled his heritage and from his vantage point of place and family reached new heights of utility and beneficence. Scholarly and enthusiastic, his activities— and they were manifold, were guided by prudence led by vision, and the solid structure of social service that he built will be his most endur- ing monument. His race had given great men in many and diverse positions, and he himself was an outstanding figure in many things that call for deep learning, wide knowledge, and the specialised ap- plication of talent, amounting almost to genius. As was said of an- other great Irishman [Oliver Goldsmith, eighteenth-century poet, novelist, and playwright] everything he touched he ornamented, and his death leaves his fellow man the poorer in knowledge and inspira- tion to deserve material prosperity and the consciousness of work well done.
>
> His loss is irreparable, but his memory will ever remain a thing of worth to his family, his friends and his country, and, indeed, the greatness of the chasm created by his demise was evident in the de- meanour of the thousands who associated themselves with his obse- quies, and his final embarkation on the illimitable sea of Death that has "never known the shadow of a homeward sail."[27]

---

23. "Wounded and a Prisoner," *Leinster Leader*, 29 July 1916, 8.
24. "New Clerk of the Crown and Peace for Co. Kildare," *Leinster Leader*, 8 October 1921, 37.
25. National Inventory of Historic Architecture, available at https://www.buildingsofire land.ie/buildings-search/building/11814103/ard-caien-tipper-road-naas-east-naas-kildare.
26. "Demise of Mr. Stephen J. Brown."
27. "Demise of Mr. Stephen J. Brown."

Apparently beloved by the people of his town and county, Brown was an impressive figure. Undoubtedly, his youngest son found the shoes challenging to fill.

Like his half brothers and his father before him, Ronald attended Clongowes Wood College, a Jesuit boarding school in Kildare just seven miles from his home.[28] He then followed in his father's footsteps and took over the family law practice. How Ronald felt about his father is something we may never know, but, as soon as he was able, he moved to Dublin. In his twilight years, Brown was likely estranged from what remained of his extended family. He left his considerable estate—some £126,000—to friends in Devon, England, and not a member of his large family.[29] Friends, rather than family, issued his death announcement in the newspaper.[30]

Long before his life was turned upside down, Brown earned a place of respect and security in the Free State. Like most lawyers and politicians with family ties to the revolutionaries and nationalists of the nineteenth century, after independence in 1922, he quickly landed a position in the new government as the state solicitor for Kildare County, standing for the state in criminal cases. With his Naas-based firm, Brown and McCann, he handled a range of legal transactions, mostly property and personal law, administering wills and handling estates. In this position, he was required to be at home for much of the early 1920s.[31] But, eventually, his passion and his work for the Office of the Attorney General brought him to Dublin for most of the 1930s.

By all accounts, Brown was a competent lawyer and an avid hiker. In 1931, the year his father died, he helped found An Oige, the Irish Youth Hostel Association. In 1935, An Oige, "that wonderful organisation of the youth of Ireland which aims at discovering Ireland afoot . . . and making a strenuous bid for health and strength outside the beaten paths," numbered fifteen hundred members and was "still growing."[32] It was an organization dedicated to getting young people out and hiking the trails of Ireland, emphasizing fitness, self-discipline, and fun. As John Donald Gustav-Wrathall has shown, youth-oriented fitness organizations like An Oige and the YMCA were common sites for same-sex and intergenerational sexual relationships to flour-

---

28. NAI, 1911 Census, Kildare / Balraheen / Castlebrown (or Clongowes), Residents of a house 8.2 in Castlebrown (or Clongowes) (Balraheen, Kildare), available at census.ie; and "Proud Tradition of Clongowes," *Irish Independent*, 28 November 1928, 11.

29. NAI, Wills and Probate, Ronald Brown, no. 2004-74-45.

30. "Personal—The Late Ronald Brown," *Irish Times*, 22 January 1982, 28.

31. E.g., "Naas Petty Sessions," *Leinster Leader*, 10 September 1921, 16; "Echoe of Curragh Strike," *Leinster Leader*, 8 March 1924, 7; "Appeal Dismissed," *Leinster Leader*, 27 March 1926, 16; and "Mr. J. Conlan's Principal Nomination Paper," *Nationalist and Leinster Times*, 20 June 1931, 12. By November 1931, he was living in Dublin and working with An Oige. "An Oige," *Irish Press*, 11 November 1931, 7.

32. "An Oige Captures a Lighthouse," *Sunday Independent*, 21 July 1935, 9.

PHOTOGRAPH OF COMMITTEE TAKEN AT MEETING LAST NIGHT: Left to right (front row): Ronald Browne, Colm O'Loughlin, Senator Mrs. Wyse-Power, Prof. Felix Hackett, Prof. Art O'Cleirigh. Back row (left to right: C. H. Heron, Miss N. Breslin, Miss M. Lavery, Eoin O'Caoimh, Miss T. Beere, Miss M. Tweedy, T. French, Miss K. Patten.

Figure 4.1 An Oige Committee photo taken in 1931. Ronald Brown is in the bottom row, first on the left. *(Irish Press, November 11, 1931, p. 7. Reproduced with permission of the Irish Newspaper Archive.)*

ish.[33] Most of the An Oige hostels had spaces for both boys and girls, which were segregated by sex. They provided beds and kitchens—and not much else—for very low rates.[34]

Though from a well-off family, and making a decent living as state solicitor, Brown never married. In 1939, An Oige opened a hostel at Thirty-Nine Mountjoy Square, a grand four-story terraced Georgian redbrick house on the south side of the serene Mountjoy Park. Brown moved into a flat in Thirty-Nine Mountjoy, which would be the room he'd share with Price from April through August 1941, and he served as the hostel's warden, overseeing the male An Oige members who wished to stay there. He worked with Mrs. Dorothy Richardson, who fulfilled their female warden position. An Oige served much of the same functions in Ireland as the YMCA in the United States, creating space for homosocial bonds between youths and building connections between

33. Gustav-Wrathall, *Take the Young Stranger by the Hand*.
34. "An Oige Tribute," *Irish Independent*, 31 August 1939, 8.

the adults who supervised individual hostel sites and the young people who frequented them.[35]

Brown encountered dozens, perhaps hundreds of teen boys who passed through the hostel each year. One boy, though, made more of an impact on him and his life than any other. Leslie Price was born in East Acton, London. Leslie's parents were Alfred and Elizabeth Price of Thirty-Five Carlisle Avenue, and he had an older sister, Elsie, who worked as a shorthand typist.[36] His father was a police officer who encouraged (or forced, according to Leslie) his son to join the army in 1939.[37] Leslie deserted St. Lucia barracks in Omagh, Northern Ireland, in 1940. He then worked on a farm for a few months before hitchhiking to Dublin. Almost as soon as he got to Dublin, he was charged with loitering in the Grafton Street area—a common charge for same-sex-desiring men who were cruising—and "failed to give a satisfactory account" for himself.[38] When picked up by gardaí, he gave some fabricated story about working on a ship in Cork that sailed away without him.[39] After he was let off with a warning, he met Tom Levins, a fifty-year-old man who lived at Fourteen Anglesea Street and housed young men in exchange for sex.

Just between 1939 and 1945, while Ireland affected a position of neutrality in World War II, over sixty men were charged with "gross indecency" in Dublin. Among those charged were soldiers, doctors, woodworkers, gardeners, fishermen, boot makers, secretaries, and, of course, at least one lawyer, individuals ranging from well positioned and connected to under and unemployed, men as old as sixty-seven and boys as young as fifteen.[40] Tens of thousands of Irish men joined the British army to fight Germany and thousands more emigrated to the United Kingdom to work in Britain's war factories. Perhaps the sudden population decrease allowed the Garda to focus a bit more investigative effort on things like sex crimes. In 1944 alone, the DMD discovered eleven men using the Howth railway station as a meetup spot, and one man

---

35. Even modern sex education at the YMCA! Unthinkable at *An Oige*. See Gustav-Wrathall, *Take the Young Stranger by the Hand*, 15–16.

36. These data come from the 1939 register, which lists Alfred Price of East Acton as a "retired constable" and his mother as an unpaid domestic worker. Leslie is not listed as residing in the house with his parents, perhaps because his entry into the military was less his choice and more a choice made for him by his parents. Based on the descriptions of his loitering and the kind of company he kept, it seems possible that his parents were at their wits end with him and sent him away accordingly. Available at https://www.findmypast.ie/.

37. NAI, AGO, 2002-16-466, the State v. Ronald H. Brown.

38. NAI, AGO, 2002-16-466, the State v. Ronald H. Brown.

39. "Other Army Promotions," *Irish Independent*, October 19, 1940, 8.

40. See the Dublin State Files, NAI, including 1D-11-119, John McManus (mechanic); 1D-20-108, Michael Doherty (soldier); 1D-24-138, Robinson McClure (secretary); 1D-24-141, James O'Brien (bootmaker); 1D-24-141, Michael Martin (gardener); 1D-27-8, Victor Walter (doctor); 1D-11-118, Leslie Price (woodworker); and 1D-20-105, Ronald Brown (state solicitor).

testified that he'd personally had sex with seven others.[41] He, and six of the men he identified, were found guilty and sentenced to serve prison time with hard labor.[42] Tom Levins, tenement caretaker, was among those offenders; he was arrested on suspicion of gross indecency offenses in July 1941.[43]

Most of the men arrested for same-sex sex crimes in Dublin during World War II were observed engaging in intimate acts in public spaces. Air raid shelters proved as fruitful cruising grounds as lavatories, parks, and alleyways, where gardaí typically caught men having sex with other men. Rarely did the Garda spend resources investigating same-sex sex crimes that took place in private residences, though the gross indecency law did give them that leeway. Based on the records that still survive in the NAI, during the war years, only 17 percent of Dublin's gross indecency cases involved sex in private residences. In the rarer instances when the Garda did investigate allegations of gross indecency crimes in private spaces, as in James Hand's case, chances were high that an older man was suspected of having sex with someone under the age of twenty-one.

But unlike Hand, who ran in very different social circles than the state solicitor of County Kildare, Ronald Brown was never caught having sex with another man in a public space.[44] The rumors of his involvement with Leslie Price came secondhand. While Price and Brown were living together, Price's former benefactor, Tom Levins, had been arrested. Levins was accused of sexually assaulting a thirteen-year-old girl. In addition to Leslie Price, two other young men, seventeen-year-old John Sullivan and nineteen-year-old David Wilson, were also arrested. All three boys provided testimony sufficient to send Levins to prison for many years. Each was also ultimately convicted of having sex with Levins and sentenced to six months in the juvenile detention wing of Mountjoy Prison.[45] Apparently Leslie Price was still in communication with Levins, Sullivan, and Wilson while he was living with Ronald Brown, because while interrogating those three, the gardaí were given reason to believe that Leslie Price was engaged in a sexual relationship with the state solicitor of County Kildare.

When Price was picked up in connection with the Levins case, he was brought in for questioning at the end of August 1941. During his interrogation, Price revealed the nature of his relationship with his forty-one-year-old

---

41. Fintan Moore was witness against seven of the ten other men arrested, and the other three were implicated in his testimony. NAI, Dublin Circuit Court, State Files, 1D-24-141, dockets 103, 105, 108, 110, 111, 112, 113, 114, and 167, 1-Jun-44.

42. "Seven Men Sentenced," *Irish Press*, 1 August 1944, 3.

43. NAI, AGO, 2002-16-466, the State v. Ronald H. Brown.

44. See Chapter 3.

45. NAI, Dublin Circuit Court, State Files, 1D-11-118, docket 47, 10-Oct-41, the State v. Thomas Levins. See also dockets 52, 53, and 54 in that box.

roommate, Ronald Brown. The version of the Brown-Price saga that Leslie Price first described to the gardaí when they arrested and interrogated him was quite chaste. He described a good man who took in a wayward teen, offering him shelter, employment opportunities, even holidays together. But Price's account of his life with Brown was apparently unsatisfactory to the gardaí, because they kept at him, demanding that he describe the true nature of his relationship with the state solicitor.

Whatever the gardaí said to Leslie Price in that interrogation room went unrecorded. Perhaps they threatened him, perhaps they talked over his head or lulled him into a sense of security: *Just between us, we know what goes on between a boy and a man in a dark bedroom, tell us the truth, there's no use hiding what is obvious, don't you want to get this secret off your chest?* Speculation aside, in the end, Price gave in. Sometime after he gave his first statement, which was signed, stamped, dated, and already filed away, the garda recording the interrogation started a new statement sheet. This time, Price had a slightly different story to tell:

> I now want to tell you that everything I told you [in the previous statement] is the truth, except that of my relations and associations with Mr. Brown. Mr. Brown came home to Mountjoy Square about the month of June 1941 one night, and we both slept in Mr. Brown's Bed. Both of us was half drunk at the time as we had been drinking together all that day, and we carried on with each other that night. Mr. Brown was very good to me. . . . I now want [to] . . . tell you the truth about everything that happened between Mr. Brown and me.[46]

Price's revised narrative of his life at Thirty-Nine Mountjoy Square was sufficiently compelling for the Garda to take the information to the attorney general, who, in turn, instructed the responsible gardaí to launch a full-scale investigation. Detectives Bernard McShane and Redmond Shea followed Price's story across the country, seeking confirmation of their travels and their relationship. It was a story they'd press Price to rehash coherently again at Bridewell Station on September 6, 1941, and over several days on the stand in the courtroom. To the Garda, it mattered little that Mr. Brown was good to Leslie Price. All that mattered was that Price claimed they'd "carried on" with each other.

In Price's second version of the story, many of the original details were the same. The day after they first met, Ronald Brown invited Leslie Price to come live at Thirty-Nine Mountjoy. Brown had the house manager set up a

---

46. NAI, AGO, 2002-16-466, 29-Aug-1941, the State v. Ronald H. Brown, Deposition of Leslie Price.

bed for Price in Brown's bedroom. But, Price finally confessed, he rarely slept in that separate bed. After that first encounter for "warmth" in April, they slept together regularly. In May, air raid sirens and the constant threat of bombings jangled Brown's nerves. He headed out of the city for a night in a Wicklow hotel. Price didn't say if he was invited, but he joined Brown just a few days before Dublin was hit by four German bombs. They shared a double bed that evening, though the housekeeper, whom the gardaí interviewed, didn't notice anything "unusual" on the bedsheets when she made up the room.[47] According to Price, in the evenings they'd regularly "pull" each other's penises until each ejaculated. A few times Brown attempted anal sex with Price, but gently—unlike previous partners Price had had—not inserting his penis more than an inch or two.[48] Brown bought Price a new suit, helped him get a job working for Brown's friend, Heinrich Petrie, and gave him an allowance each week. Brown and Price lived together at Thirty-Nine Mountjoy throughout the summer of 1941 and went on an extended hiking holiday in West Ireland in August. They shared a bed and "carried on" with each other at Thirty-Nine Mountjoy and while on holiday. Such was the account Price gave after hours in an interrogation room on August 29; he rehashed something similar a week later when questioned again on September 6, and again when on the stand in Brown's trial. This was the evidence that the gardaí brought to Attorney General Kevin O'Hanrahan Haugh, who issued the warrant for Brown's arrest. Under normal circumstances, this testimony would likely have been sufficient to send Brown to prison for at least two years. Midcentury Irish ideas about youths and sexuality would typically have cast Brown as the bad influence and Price as a misguided youth in need of rehabilitation but still savable.[49] That things played out differently here is significant.

Before the gardaí arrested Price and collected his first two statements on August 29, the Garda had a fair idea of what was going on at Thirty-Nine Mountjoy. The investigating officers brought those suspicions to the attorney general, who insisted that the gardaí not rush things, that they needed more evidence. In a memo to the investigating officers, O'Hanrahan Haugh said, "If there are developments following their return to Dublin that would justify a prosecution of Brown, I would like to be informed at once."[50] The gardaí followed the proscription, tracking down witnesses from Brown and Price's holiday in the West, interviewing Brown's friends, and interrogating Leslie Price mercilessly. Price struggled to find a "truth" to tell, revealing his "gross inde-

---

47. NAI, AGO, 2002-16-466, 6-Sep-1941, the State v. Ronald H. Brown, Deposition of Margaret Kelly.
48. NAI, AGO, 2002-16-466, the State v. Ronald H. Brown, Depositions of Leslie Price, 29 August 1941 and 6 September 1941.
49. See Chapter 5.
50. NAI, AGO, Folder no. 5-2002-16-466, Indecent Assault Case File.

cencies" with Brown only after hours of being questioned by the gardaí. Held in an interrogation room at Bridewell Station, asked again and again about the nature of his relationship to Ronald Brown, the man with whom he was living, he finally broke and made his second statement. That Price's testimony was insufficient to convict Brown may be more reflective of who Brown was and what the Irish state had to lose if he was convicted.

Much of Ireland's official position of neutrality during World War II was posturing under the leadership of de Valera. From his ascension to power in 1932 through 1948, de Valera firmly guided the nascent Irish state. In 1937, he oversaw the writing of a new Irish constitution, one that entrenched Ireland in a rigid Catholic-nationalist ideology, with all the associated sex hangups one might expect. Like the nineteenth-century Home Rulers who blew open the Dublin Castle scandal in 1884, Irish nationalists in the independent state acted morally superior to their former colonial rulers.[51] In a sermon in 1929, Catholic priest P. J. Gannon said that "Europe is forgetting" the morality of Christianity, while "we Irishmen" would never forget.[52] The assertion of Ireland's moral superiority was repeated throughout the twentieth century, particularly with regard to Ireland's role as a producer of missionaries, priests, and religious sisters.[53] The evidence to the contrary at home—unwed mothers, excessive drunkenness, child neglect, prostitution, gambling, and same-sex sex—was forcefully suppressed or willfully ignored by the politicians and plebeians alike.

Most certainly to distance themselves from their "immoral" English predecessors, the Irish politicians were careful in the first two decades of independence. It would have been deeply embarrassing for one of their own to be embroiled in something so shocking as a same-sex sex scandal. Indeed, it's surprising that Attorney General Kevin O'Hanrahan Haugh even decided to go ahead with the charges, though he wrote that "the association of Brown and Price is a distressing affair (in view of Brown's position and relation to this office) but I fear the Gardaí are more than justified in their suspicions. . . . I would not like to rush into a prosecution."[54] O'Hanrahan Haugh's hesitation was well warranted in the political climate, as Ireland's neutrality in the war was at least in part to flex their autonomous muscles at Britain. But, undoubtedly, O'Hanrahan considered the options carefully, as Brown's name would

51. Earls, "Unnatural Offenses of English Import," 396–424; see also De Nie, *Eternal Paddy.*

52. "How Ireland Has Clung to the Faith," *Irish Independent,* 8 July 1929, 7.

53. I.e., "Responsibility of Catholic Irishmen," *Donegal News,* 26 October 1940, 5; "Ireland's Vocation," *Irish Independent,* 9 October 1933, 10; "Striking Sermon in Dublin," *Strabane Chronicle,* 26 October 1940, 3.

54. NAI, AGO, 2002-16-466, the State v. Ronald H. Brown, Letter from K. O'H.H., Attorney General, dated 25 August 1941.

come up in the Tom Levins case. Instead, they put together a case so thoroughly exonerating, they eliminated the scandal before it could break.

According to those who observed them, Brown and Price's relationship didn't seem particularly suspicious. In addition to the three statements from Price, the gardaí traveled to Wicklow and Sligo to interview the staff at every hotel Brown and Price visited, and they interviewed the Richardsons, who worked with Brown at Thirty-Nine Mountjoy, and Brown's friend Petrie. Petrie said that "Mr. Brown referred to Price as his adopted son."[55] In August 1941, Brown brought Price on a hiking holiday in the beautiful West Ireland. A hotel manager, Mrs. K. Holmes, said she "took them to be two pals going about on holidays."[56] Through interviews with hotel staff, the detectives confirmed that Brown secured one room at each hotel on their tour, usually with only one double bed, for the two of them to share. Only one hotel employee of the handful interviewed made any suggestion of possible funny business. Evelyn McCarrick, hotel proprietress of Central Hotel in County Leitrim, noted, "They did not ask for separate rooms although there were a number of them—four in all—vacant in the hotel at the time, and which would cost the same."[57] But, of course, those who witnessed their relationship wouldn't have assumed it was sexual. That was not the norm.

Only Price's statements supported the claim that his relationship with Brown was sexual. Though the hotel staff didn't take the two to be lovers, there was no doubt that Brown and Price did, indeed, share beds everywhere they went. Quite salaciously, by media standards of the time, the *Irish Times* reported that Mrs. Dorothy Richardson, the other warden at Thirty-Nine Mountjoy, came upon Price in Brown's bed when she brought breakfast to Mr. Brown's room. According to the *Times*, Mrs. Richardson noted that "on the occasion when Price was in Mr. Brown's bed, Mr. Brown told her that the boy had been cold in the camp bed, and had had insufficient blankets."[58] Though this evidence corroborated Price's claim that the two slept in the same bed, Brown's attorney attempted to spin it, asking Mrs. Richardson if she could blame the boy for sleeping in Brown's bed instead of his own. She responded that she "would not say that the camp bed was very comfortable or warm."[59]

---

55. NAI, AGO, 2002-16-466, the State v. Ronald H. Brown, Statement of Heinrich Petrie, 8 September 1941.

56. NAI, AGO, 2002-16-466, the State v. Ronald H. Brown, Statement of Mrs. K. Holmes, 4 September 1941.

57. NAI, AGO, 2002-16-466, the State v. Ronald H. Brown, Statement of Evelyn McCarrick, 4 September 1941.

58. NAI, AGO, 2002-16-466, the State v. Ronald H. Brown, Statement of Dorothy Richardson, 4 September 1941.

59. "Charges against State Solicitor," *Irish Times*, 26 September 1941.

Was Brown exonerated because of who he was, or because of how the court saw Price? Price's Englishness seemed of little consequence, going without comment in the course of the trial, though perhaps it added doubt to his statements. That circuit court judge Cahir Davitt seemed convinced at the outset of Price's untrustworthiness is surprising only in that it exonerated Brown but not Tom Levins. Davitt, who frequently presided over gross indecency cases and was known for his press statements about the danger and disgustingness of gross indecency offenders, seemed quite confident in Brown's innocence.[60] He commented that "never had so heavy and distasteful a task fallen to his lot. . . . [Brown] was a solicitor of some twenty years standing, a servant of the High Court, a person who had served his country, participating in the national struggle . . . [Price] had a bad record. He had contradicted himself in the box time and again, and had failed to give a consistent account of any one incident."[61]

Even if the account of their sexual relationship was a fabrication, as Solicitor Brown's attorney, ultimately, convinced the jury, theirs was certainly an unconventional relationship. Though some informal fostering system might have been possible among Catholics like Brown, particularly among family members, it was limited to children rather than late adolescents like Price. Catholics relied mostly on Catholic industrial schools and orphanages.[62] The first Irish statute to provide for state-based childcare, the Health Act, was passed in 1953. So, for Ronald Brown to suddenly take in this older boy after one conversation, even to treat him like "an adopted son," was unusual by Irish Catholic societal standards.

But the jury chose not to interpret the evidence as damning of Brown. The gardaí interviewed over a dozen witnesses, subjected Price to three separate interrogations, and assembled a thick folder of evidence to support their case. It was rare for the Garda to dedicate considerable resources to investigating same-sex sex crimes, though not unprecedented. Sometimes they went to quite extensive lengths to actively root out same-sex sex offenders. As I discussed in Chapter 2, in the 1920s and 1930s, they sent plainclothes officers out to entrap men cruising the public lavatories and parks. In Chapter 6, I discuss the period after World War II, when they staked out lavs all around Dublin, perching on the roof of the Jameson Distillery, hanging off of a railway bridge, and piling into cramped observation booths of public lavatories. But

---

60. "Vice Prevalent in Dublin," *Irish Times*, 13 February 1931, 13; "Sentence of Seven Years Penal Servitude," *Irish Times*, 14 February 1931, 15; "Strong Comment by Dublin Judge," *Irish Times*, 1 August 1931, 9; and "Not Uncommon in This City," *Irish Times*, 7 February 1931, 6.

61. "State Solicitor Acquitted," *Irish Press*, 17 January 1942, 3.

62. Commission Report, Commission to Inquire into Child Abuse, accessed on 29 May 2019, available at http://www.childabusecommission.ie/rpt/pdfs/. See also Smith, *Ireland's Magdalen Laundries*, 23–86.

no other case file in the Dublin Circuit Court records has the depth of witness statements and evidence collected. Certainly, there are no records so well padded that then resulted in the decisive exoneration of the defendant. It seems most likely that the paper trail and extensive investigation was actually built up to clear Brown's name before he and the office of the attorney general were sullied by association with the Levins case.

On August 25, 1941, O'Hanrahan Haugh warned the gardaí that they needed more evidence before he'd seek a warrant for Brown's arrest. When Price and Brown returned from their August holiday, Price was promptly arrested and interrogated between August 28 and August 29. Following up on the details of Price's statement, the two investigating officers went to every hotel and hostel Price and Brown visited and collected statements from the staff; for three days, September 4–6, they crisscrossed the country, building up a file and list of witnesses. On September 8, one of Brown's coworkers, having heard of Brown's impending charges, let Brown know what was coming—it seems safe to assume that Brown also knew at that point, since Price was in custody—and the coworker told him that Brown was not allowed to stand for the state in any cases, pending his own trial. Brown's trial and associated depositions dragged on for months, from as early as September 13, 1941, until its ultimate five-day conclusion, between January 12 and January 16, 1942.[63]

When Brown's case finally returned to trial in 1942, it was covered gently by nationalist-leaning Irish newspapers. This was not the Dublin Castle scandal, an opportunity to challenge the rule of a foreign oppressor in Ireland. Were Brown a more important figure in the government, it's possible that de Valera might've censored its coverage entirely. Certainly the taoiseach, or Irish prime minister, was not above censorship and manipulating the presses for the good of the state; throughout World War II, de Valera used the Irish press to create a "moat of silence" around Ireland, supporting Irish neutrality throughout the war by downplaying the conflict on the continent.[64] But, in the Brown case, the state did not step in to censor the press.

The *Irish Times*—an Anglo-Irish newspaper that generally aligned itself with the United Kingdom rather than the nationalist movement in Ireland—broke the story when Brown first appeared in court on September 8, 1941. Even the *Times* was vague about the charges levied against Brown, perhaps fearing censorship or in acknowledgment of the sensitivity of the matter. With the war raging on, and the newspapers dedicating most of their energy to delicately report on global news without overstepping Dublin Castle's censor-

---

63. NAI, AGO, 2002-16-466, the State v. Ronald H. Brown.
64. Robert Cole, *Propaganda, Censorship, and Irish Neutrality in the Second World War* (Edinburgh: Edinburgh University Press, 2006), 2.

ship boundaries regarding the war, Solicitor Brown never made front-page news. A headline announced, "State Solicitor on Serious Charge" on page three of the Monday *Times* and gave bare-bones details from the trial itself.

> The State Solicitor . . . was remanded in custody until today . . . having . . . committed a serious offence. Detective Officer Bernard Mc-Shaen who arrested Brown in O'Connell street, Dublin, on Friday night, said that after reading the warrant he said: "I will say nothing for the moment." At the Bridgewell Brown remarked "That charge is ridiculous," and, after being charged, "The charge is completely false." . . . Two bails of £500 each were offered.[65]

The same report was published again in the Saturday edition of the paper, on page twelve. The *Times* published a much longer report on the trial on September 17, again buried on page six, but focused on the testimony and examination of Leslie Price.

> Leslie Price's deposition, part of which had been made the previous day, was to the effect that he had been in Dublin for about a year and had got in touch with Mr. Brown who promised him a job. He was to help clean offices at Mountjoy square and to be paid £1 per week and to be provided with lodging. He was to lodge in Mr. Brown's flat. He alleged that the offence with which Mr. Brown was charged had taken place in Mr. Brown's flat and in other places where he had been with Mr. Brown on holidays.
>
> Mr. Burne [Brown's attorney] asked the Justice to allow him to reserve his cross-examination of the witness in that Court, as the deposition was very long and he could not do justice either to Price or to Mr. Brown without analysing it.
>
> The Justice agreed to give any time necessary to study the deposition, but said that if he did give time, he would not take another witness in the meanwhile.
>
> Price was then cross-examined by Mr. Burne and stated that when he was arrested it was on a charge of an attempted offence with a man who was not Mr. Brown. Already he had pleaded guilty to a charge of larceny on another occasion. He had deserted from the British Army, although he made no attestation or taken an oath when joining it. The man with whom he was alleged to have attempted to commit an of-

---

65. "State Solicitor on Serious Charge," *Irish Times*, 8 September 1941, 3.

fence was a man whom he had met a considerable time before he had seen Mr. Brown.[66]

Burne's cross examination didn't continue until September 27. In a very short report, on page fifteen of the *Irish Times*, the words "gross indecency" were first published in connection with Ronald Brown's case.[67] The papers made no mention of Brown or his gross indecency case again until October 28, and then only to say that he was remanded on bail again. When finally the state solicitor's trial resumed in January, the *Times* had apparently lost interest, publishing one-sentence updates three times throughout the trial with a final update on January 17 that simply read, "Ronald H. Brown, State Solicitor, Co. Kildare, was found not guilty on counts of gross indecency, and discharged by Judge Davitt and a jury in the Dublin Circuit Criminal Court yesterday."[68]

Conversely, the nationalist-leaning newspapers like the *Irish Press* gave little space to the early months of the trial and its complicated implications for the Catholic-nationalist state. It was only in January, when the milquetoast evidence was laid out in full, and Brown was clearly on track to exoneration, that the *Press* engaged with the scandal. The *Irish Press* was a nationalist-leaning newspaper founded in 1931 to support de Valera's party, Fianna Fáil. Though Brown's case was never given the attention of front-page news, the *Irish Press* published updates every day of the January proceedings. For the first few days, the reporting was limited, with no more than two sentences a day, stating that "evidence was continued before Judge Davitt in . . . the case in which Ronald H. Brown, State Solicitor for Co. Kildare . . . is charged with having committed acts of gross indecency."[69] The end of the trial, in which the not guilty verdict was returned, however, was significantly more robust in its detail:

Ronald H. Brown, State Solicitor for Co. Kildare (42), single, whose address was given as at Mountjoy Square, Dublin, was found not guilty on all counts, by a unanimous verdict of the jury at the Circuit Criminal Court, Green Street, Dublin, yesterday, where he was charged with gross indecency. The trial had lasted five days, and when the jury, after an absence of two hours, brought in their verdict, Judge Davitt ordered his release. Judge Davitt, in summon-up, said that never had so heavy and distasteful a task fallen to his lot. The defendant was a solicitor

---

66. "Charge against State Solicitor further Hearing Adjourned," *Irish Times*, 17 September 1941, 6.
67. "State Solicitor Charged," *Irish Times*, 27 September 1941, 15.
68. "State Solicitor Acquitted," 7.
69. "State Solicitor's Trial," *Irish Press*, 14 January 1942, 3.

of some 20 years standing, a servant of the High Court, a person who had served his country, participating in the national struggle.

Referring to remarks made by counsel for the defense, Judge Davitt said he realised that the position of the Press in cases of the kind was one of considerable difficulty. The facts were of a kind that the public did not wish to read, and accordingly, the Press had always treated those cases with extreme reticence.[70]

Judge Davitt commended the *Press* for taking such a light touch when covering the Brown trial. Certainly, fifty years earlier, when it was British administrators in Ireland embroiled in queer scandal, the nationalist presses pulled no punches. As soon as an Irish representative was in the spotlight, however, the press's qualms abounded. The *Irish Times* reticence is perhaps more surprising, but it was still World War II, and the *Times* was one of a handful of newspapers that got into trouble with the censors.[71] Perhaps the early reporting reflects a bit of that subtle jabbing at de Valera's government, and the milder January reporting was the result of censorial intervention, or, like the *Press*, the *Times* court reporters saw the writing on the wall and realized that this was a case of a scandal averted.

And, indeed, the scandal was averted: through unusually thorough police investigation, bland press coverage, and a decisive not guilty verdict, returned after just two hours of jury deliberation. The state's representative was cleared of his association with Tom Levins, whom the judge described as being "the most disgusting blackguard who had ever appeared before him" just before sentencing him to nine years of penal servitude.[72] Ronald Brown was absolved officially and for all the public to see. But, as was true of all of the gross indecency charges in twentieth-century Ireland, the damage was done. Certainly, Brown's resignation from the state solicitor position in February 1942 and his retreat to spiritual solitude speak to the immense loneliness inflicted by the Catholic nationalist state and its homophobic postcolonial state building.

While the circumstances that exonerated Brown and left Price to the mercy of the judge in the Levins case make this story stand apart, it is still representative of the same-sex relationships that were common in independent Ireland. Even as his Englishness and transience ought to have condemned him, Price was still treated by the Irish judicial system as another savable boy—a categorical distinction that I discuss at length in the next chapter. Even though he was acquitted, Brown was presumed throughout the investigations to be the responsible party in the relationship, rather than the victim of a

---

70. "State Solicitor Acquitted," 3.

71. Horgan, *Irish Media*, 38–45.

72. "Circuit Court Sentences," *Irish Times*, 10 December 1941, 2.

predatory boy. Their relationship was taboo, but not because of the considerable age gap between the two. By today's standards we might judge this as inappropriate because Price was seventeen and Brown forty-one. But in 1941 Ireland, the same age gap between a man and a teen girl would have raised little concern; significant age differences were actually quite common in heterosexual marriages. What made Price and Brown's relationship taboo was, of course, the sex of the participants.

Today it is hard to see past the obvious power dynamics that shaped their relationship: a well-to-do solicitor and a homeless boy, with nearly fifteen years dividing them. But in some ways, Price held even more power over Brown. The illegality of Brown's interest in Price put him at huge risk. As a representative of the state legal system, Brown would have been all too aware of that risk. That Price endeavored to protect Brown when interrogated speaks volumes. Whatever the power dynamics, it is possible to see genuine affection, perhaps even love, in their story. It is possible to read beyond the antagonisms created by a court case to reveal the heart of their relationship.

Petrie told investigators that Brown "referred to Price as his adopted son."[73] As Nicholas Syrett and Rachel Hope Cleves both evidence in their recent books, use of familial titles was common in twentieth-century intergenerational same-sex relationships.[74] It was language that made close, intimate same-sex bonds comprehensible to outsiders. That Brown referred to Price thus in the company of one of his closest friends is significant. When Petrie met up with Brown for lunch in the days after Price's arrest, Petrie remarked that Brown "appeared to be very depressed and was not in his usual form."[75] Though Petrie never liked Price, and had told Brown so on several occasions, he saw how deeply the loss of Price affected Brown. Though he didn't yet know of Price's betrayal, Brown was clearly heartbroken. "It is the first time I thought I'd done a real good deed," Brown confided in his friend, "but fate seems to be against me." Whether his sadness was triggered by the thought that the boy he'd tried to help had disappeared into a life of crime, or if he was mourning the loss of a lover, we cannot know.

Leslie Price described their first night together as a moment of one warming the other's bed. "One night, when I was in the room with Mr. Brown, we were talking and complaining that it was cold in bed. We decided that we would sleep together in the one bed. I got up and went into Mr. Brown's bed."[76] He describes his own agency in that first instance, though at other times he

---

73. NAI, AGO, 2002-16-466, the State v. Ronald H. Brown, Statement of Heinrich Petrie, September 8, 1941.

74. Syrett, *An Open Secret*; Cleves, *Unspeakable*.

75. Statement of Heinrich Petrie.

76. NAI, AGO, 2002-16-466, the State v. Ronald H. Brown, Statement of Leslie Price, 29 August 1941.

also mentions that he and Brown were intoxicated on that night. He never suggested that Brown made his stay at Thirty-Nine Mountjoy Square contingent on their sleeping together, and the second bed remained in Brown's room throughout their tenure together.

Probably the most heartbreaking statement Leslie Price made was just as he was about to break under questioning by the gardaí on August 29. Even as he prepared to tell a different story, he underscored what was most true about his recollection of the previous three months: "Mr. Brown was very good to me."[77]

In the end, the jury acquitted Ronald Brown; they also convicted Leslie Price for having sex with Tom Levins. Despite his exoneration, Brown resigned from his post as state solicitor. Perhaps it was his choice, or one forced by the attorney general. Even cleared of charges, the taint of a same-sex sex scandal was impossible to shake off. He continued to serve as legal counsel for An Oige until 1945. At some point, he picked up and moved to Essex, England. According to his estate papers, he passed away at the age of eighty-two while living in the Kham Tibetan House, which was, before becoming a Buddhist retreat in 1976, a home for "stray and wayward boys."[78] Leslie Price disappears from the Irish records after his six months in Mountjoy Prison's juvenile wing.

The necessity of vice crime records for exploring the histories of same-sex love and desire, particularly intergenerational relationships, remains problematic but also rife with potential. In the harrowing circumstances of an interrogation room, a boy might try to protect his older lover from scrutiny, only to break under pressure. Under the watchful gaze of a uniformed police officer, a witness might be compelled to tell a truth that revealed the depth of feeling two men had for each other. In the tense and traumatic conditions of the courtroom, alleged perpetrators might be pressed to admit to intimacies that they'd never confess to friends or family in the restrictive sex regime of twentieth-century Ireland. If Ronald Brown did invite the youth into his bed, and if Leslie Price did, as he told the gardaí, slide willingly under the covers, maybe they found each other again when it was all over. Maybe there is a love story buried in these court records.

While Solicitor Brown could never have hoped to attain the acceptance that Micheál Mac Liammóir and Hilton Edwards enjoyed, he was able to take his lover to parties with friends, to hotels and hostels, and around town. For three months, they lived together without any trouble. But when Solicitor Brown's name was connected to Tom Levins, who'd corrupted numerous boys and assaulted a teen girl, Brown's private life—and home—were put under

---

77. Statement of Leslie Price.

78. Marpa House History, accessed on 9 December 2019, available at http://www.marpa house.org.uk/marpa-house/history/.

police scrutiny. The level of investigation was extraordinary, with very few examples reaching that level of resource dedication. But, it seems clear, that this was not the same sort of scrutiny that James Hand experienced a decade earlier. If anything, the deep investigation of Brown's private life and residence was intended to secure sufficient evidence to exonerate him. So, Brown's case was unusual, involving a relatively extraordinary amount of investigative police work, and all to find the man innocent while the boy was implicated in a different case.

While his relationship with Leslie Price was certainly unconventional, unusual, and probably off-putting to the jury, no one except the flustered and harassed Leslie Price ever asserted that the two had sex. The attorney general's office presented a case so undamning of the defendant that the jury could do nothing but acquit him. In Hand's case, the prosecution sought to prove that he was conducting a male brothel, that he'd himself been guilty of having sex with men in a public park, and that he was the sort that had to be locked away for the protection of Ireland's vulnerable boys. When it came to presenting the case of Solicitor Brown and his boy, the prosecution presented a case laden with doubt as to the nature of Brown's relationship with Price. It was in the attorney general's interest to dissuade the jury from believing Leslie Price's testimony, because Ronald Brown was one of them. In the still young Irish state, the stakes were too high for a representative of a government office to be outed as a man who had sex with other men, let alone a transient seventeen-year-old British army deserter. Such a scandal would . . . what? Evidence the depth of same-sex love as something more than the seedy public sex of Dublin's streets that the Garda was tasked with driving underground? Suggest that a true campaign to eliminate queerness from Ireland would have to turn an eye to the private lives of even the most powerful? Reveal the cracks in the foundation of the Catholic nationalist Irish state? Whatever Attorney General Kevin O'Hanrahan Haugh and his colleagues believed was at stake in this case—and perhaps it was only the reputation and freedom of their friend and coworker—they ensured that Brown would be found not guilty by a jury of his peers.

Brown was a representative of the state. He came from a family that fought for Home Rule. He served the Dáil Éireann from its revolutionary formation and served the state for over a decade. Was Leslie Price his first? Maybe. His recorded reactions to the entire ordeal might indicate that this was the first time he'd gone out on a limb to love another man (or boy, in this case). The resulting scandal led to his resignation, leaving the country to join a Buddhist monastery, and, ultimately, being buried by his German friend instead of his own family. Though exonerated at trial, his life was shattered. The loss of his position in the state and his rejection by his family suggest that the state could not continue to employ a man who had been discovered defying the rigid

Catholic nationalist sexual habitus and ethos. Does his ultimate retreat from the world point to a brokenhearted man who lost his first love and never recovered? Or did he internalize the disgrace he brought to his family and country? Perhaps it's a little of both. Unlike Hand, Brown didn't go to prison. But he lost his livelihood and his lover all the same.

5

The Boys

On a fair day in January 1931, fifteen-year-old Matthew Nyhan's father sent him into the city to look for a day's work.[1] Matthew's father was David Nyhan, and his mother was Margaret Nyhan, née Hayes. Before Matthew was born, the Nyhans had rooms at Thirty-Four Marrowbone Lane, a tenement building in the Liberties, a firmly working-class and poor area of Dublin.[2] But Matthew grew up in a small single-story, single-family cottage on Maxwell Street in the Saint Catherine's neighborhood of South Dublin. The shift from the Liberties to Saint Catherine's would have been a significant improvement in the family's quality of life. They were a moderately sized family by Irish standards. Matthew had five siblings total: David Jr., the eldest, born September 12, 1907; Norah, born February 1, 1909; James, born February 4, 1911; Mary, born April 3, 1913; and John, the youngest, born February 8, 1918.[3] Matthew was born July 5, 1915, which meant poor Margaret had a new baby every two years, on average.[4] When Matthew was arrested in 1931, his brother David was already married and a father himself;

---

1. "The Weather Today," *Irish Examiner*, 2 January 1931, 6.
2. "Residents of a house 34.1 in Marrowbone Lane (Usher's Quay, Dublin)," NAI, Irish Census 1911, available at http://census.nationalarchives.ie.
3. All of David Nyhan and Margaret Hayes' children's births are listed on the Civic Records of irishgeneaology.ie.
4. Birth Registry for South Dublin, ref. no. 01564279, 1915, available at https://civilrecords .irishgenealogy.ie/churchrecords.

Nora too had married and moved out of their parents' home.[5] His father, David Sr., was a laborer. He worked for about nineteen years in a brewery, but, by the time Nora married, he'd moved to working as a weaver. He was probably a hard worker, if he'd made enough as an unskilled laborer first in brewing and then in weaving to move his family out of the Liberties. But he probably also managed the family with a firm hand. With the children marrying and moving out in their early twenties, one can imagine that the Nyhan household was one where the children were expected to grow up early and contribute to the household income.[6]

So when David Nyhan told his second youngest son to get out of the house and find some work, the boy partially complied. Matthew went to Hawkins Street but did not bother to ask for a job. Instead he perched on Butt Bridge, watching the men working the docks below. (See Figure 5.1.)

As he stood idly by, a forty-three-year-old man named Robert Byrne came up to him and offered him a cigarette. Nyhan declined. When Byrne asked Nyhan to go for a walk, Nyhan agreed; the two walked up to O'Connell Bridge to catch a tram to Phoenix Park. On the way to the tram stop, Byrne gave Nyhan sixpence "to go to the pictures" that night.[7] Nyhan recounted their stroll through Phoenix Park: "After we passed the Barracks [Byrne] . . . said come on down and we'll have a 'pump.' We went to the lavatory near the Zoo and went in, he went into one part and I went into another."[8] Nyhan testified that he waited for Byrne to come out of the public toilet. When Byrne emerged, his pants were still open, and he held his penis in his hand. Nyhan said Byrne asked, "Did you ever see one as big as that?" and asked Nyhan to "come on in for a while."[9] Nyhan was faced with a choice: walk away (with sixpence already in his pocket) or fulfill the implied (or explicit) terms of their deal. Nyhan

5. Marriage Registry for Dublin, ref. no. 05274566, 1930, available at https://civilrecords .irishgenealogy.ie/churchrecords/; and Marriage Registry for Dublin, ref. no. 0527961, 1929, available at https://civilrecords.irishgenealogy.ie/churchrecords.

6. According to David Dickson, marriage patterns in the city followed rural patterns, though first births occurred sooner after marriage in the city than in most rural areas. Dickson's analysis, however, is based on a single report from a Stanley Lyons survey of birth rates in 1941 and 1942. Most marriage pattern studies focus on the rural (i.e., K. H. Connell, *ThePopulation of Ireland, 1750–1845* (Westport, CT: Greenwood Press, 1975); T. W. Guinnane, *The Vanishing Irish: Households, Migration, and the Rural Economy in Ireland, 1850–1914* (Princeton: Princeton University, Press, 1998); Maria Luddy and Mary Daly also draw on broader national statistics rather than the narrower Dublin-based statistics, in their various discussions of marriage and family patterns.) Dickson, *Dublin*, 494–495.

7. NAI, Dublin Circuit Court, State Files, 1C-94-88, 6-Jun-1931, the State v. Matthew Nyhan and Robert Byrne, Deposition of Matthew Nyhan.

8. Deposition of Matthew Nyhan.

9. Deposition of Matthew Nyhan.

Figure 5.1 Irish Tourist Association postcard of the River Liffey taken from Butt Bridge, Dublin with boats moored in the river and alongside the quays, Joe Williams Postcard Collection. *(Reproduced with permission of the South Dublin Libraries.)*

didn't leave or shout for help; in his testimony, he didn't even describe any hesitation. He simply said, "I went in."[10]

In twentieth-century Ireland, middle and late adolescence was a fuzzy period between the state's direct control over youths in compulsory schooling and their ascension to full Irish citizenship. Those years in between when boys left school and, at twenty-one, were deemed full adults by the Irish state were dangerous and formative. From the point of view of Ireland's lawmakers, under the wrong influence, a boy could be led astray, into a life of corruption and sin. The Irish state thus employed a system of punitive and redemptory education for "juvenile" (under seventeen) and "juvenile-adult" (seventeen to twenty-one) offenders. Juvenile offenders could be sent to industrial schools, which were effectively state-run detention centers for both orphans and misdemeanor offenders, and juvenile-adults could be sent to the borstal institutions that were reformatory schools specifically for "boys" aged seventeen to twenty-one. Borstals employed military-like regimes of discipline, job training, and religious instruction in an effort to reform these wayward "boys." When judges, newspaper editors, and gardaí referred to juvenile and juvenile-adult offenders, they generally referred to them as "youths" or "boys," not as "men,"

---

10. Deposition of Matthew Nyhan.

rarely even as "young men."[11] Their culpability in crimes, most specifically sex crimes, was subjectively decided by the gardaí and judges who *were* the twentieth-century justice system. And the men with whom they had sex were as likely to bear the brunt of the sexual encounter, regardless of ideas about "consent" and willing participation.

In the previous two chapters, I introduced a couple of other "boys." In Chapter 3, Michael Hackett was eighteen years old when the gardaí picked him up for questioning. He quickly spilled the story of how James Hand introduced him to Frank North, and how he (Michael) had sex with North for money. In Chapter 4, the gardaí squeezed a confession out of seventeen-year-old Leslie Price about his intimate relationship with Ronald Brown. Hackett was never charged in the Hand case, though he readily admitted his part in sex with North. Price, conversely, tried to deny the accusations that he'd had sex with older men for money, but he was charged, found guilty, and spent six months in juvenile detention as a result of his relationship with Tom Levins (not, as you'll recall, because of his relationship with Ronald Brown, who was exonerated). Nyhan, at fifteen, pleaded guilty to sodomy and gross indecency in 1931, and Byrne got nine years.[12] In all of their cases, the "men" (over twenty-one, and, in both cases, ten or more years older) with whom the "boys" were charged and found guilty received much harsher punishments. The contrasting experiences of Hackett, Price, and Nyhan, and of "boys" and "men" in the court records, highlight the inconsistencies and oppressive nature of Ireland's moral crusade.

As I discussed in the introduction, I decided to include cases involving boys aged fifteen and up because fifteen was the age of the youngest person, Matthew Nyhan, charged with gross indecency in Ireland between 1922 and 1972. Nyhan's charge and conviction, and the conviction of "boys" aged fifteen to twenty-one, did not mean that the Irish state always held boys responsible for their participation in sex crimes, but sometimes it did. The Irish state inconsistently produced fictive boundaries for defining appropriate male sexuality, boyhood innocence, and masculinity, intentionally and unintentionally, through the policing of same-sex sex.

It's important to situate boys like Hackett, Price, and Nyhan in the history of Dublin's homosocial and queer cityscape and Ireland's postcolonial moral machinations. As historians Rachel Hope Cleves, Nicholas Syrett, and John Gustav-Wrathall point out, intergenerational relationships were deeply en-

---

11. Irish childhood is a developing field, but Irish children's sexuality is particularly understudied. For a recent treatment, see Luddy and Smith, *Children, Childhood and Irish Society*.
12. The State v. Matthew Nyhan and Robert Byrne.

trenched in early twentieth-century same-sex subcultures.[13] For long-term relationships, age gaps between lovers often made life easier on a couple. Like the Allertons of the Chicago area, an intergenerational couple could refer to one another by familial terms—uncle-nephew, father-son, mother-daughter, aunt-niece—and use formal legal systems like adoption to ensure that a lover was able to inherit property or travel together without attracting attention.[14] Ronald Brown and Leslie Price, discussed in Chapter 4, used familial language to describe their short but intense relationship. In more transactional relationships, too, so-called rent boys could ply their trade without the fear of repercussions, because their youthfulness was a kind of shield from familial and societal expectations. Whether they sold their bodies for pleasure, material gain, or both, these boys were an undeniable part of Dublin's sexual subculture.

There wasn't really a norm in the state's procedure for dealing with under twenty-one-year-olds involved in gross indecency cases. Some, like Price and Nyhan, were charged and convicted. Some, like Hackett, at eighteen and with no prospects, straightforwardly confessed to having sex with a man and walked away without any formal repercussions, not even a slap on the wrist.[15] Between 1922 and 1972, 11 percent of the individuals arrested for same-sex sex crimes were aged fifteen to twenty-one; 80 percent had sexual relation-

---

13. Cleves, *Unspeakable*; Syrett, *An Open Secret*; Gustav-Wrathall, *Take the Young Stranger by the Hand*.

14. Syrett, *An Open Secret*, 83–104.

15. Hackett was a Galway boy who probably moved to Dublin in search of work, freedom, or both, who slipped into obscurity after his involvement in the Hand case. I say this with a deep sigh of disappointment, because there was another Michael Hackett who was arrested at Beresford Place in 1950 for committing an act of gross indecency, and I briefly thought they might be the same man, which would be a useful anecdote for understanding if/when boys who entered the sexual subculture as rent boys became continued to pursue same-sex sex as adults. But the 1950 Michael Hackett was born in 1919. Even if the 1931 Michael Hackett had lied about his age, it seems unlikely that the gardaí—or James Hand—would have believed he was eighteen if he was, in fact, twelve. The Michael Hackett of 1931 was almost certainly the Michael Hackett born on 11 August 1913, to Daniel and Mary Hackett of Galway, per the Irish civil records available on irishgenealogy.ie (the digital record is available at https://civilrecords.irishgenealogy.ie/churchrecords/images/birth_returns/births_1913/01437/1588871.pdf.) As far as I can tell, Michael Hackett, born in 1913, emigrated to Massachusetts in 1950. By then he'd found work as a porter. Notably another Michael Hackett—probably his cousin from Galway—went to Massachusetts as a tourist in 1953. Emigration record: "New York, New York Passenger and Crew Lists, 1909, 1925–1957," National Archives and Records Administration (NARA) Microfilm T715, 7882-vol. 17148-17150, 2 September 1950, (Washington DC); and Tourist record: "New York, New York Passenger and Crew Lists, 1909, 1925–1957," NARA microfilm publication T715, 8443, vol. 18454-18455, 19 April 1954, (Washington DC). It turns out, actually, that Michael Hackett was a very common name in early twentieth-century Ireland. There was as yet another Michael Hackett born in the 1910s who grew up to be a member of An Garda Síochána!

ships, either economically or romantically motivated, with older men, usually ten to thirty years older.[16] Some took money, gifts, or lodging in exchange for sex. When pressed by gardaí, some insisted they'd taken nothing. Denying material gain might've been a strategy to waylay the consequences for selling sex, or to assert their victimhood, or even to express genuine feeling for their sexual partners. Court records are opaque at best in assessing the feelings of those accused of crimes. Whatever their motivations for participating in the sexual economy of Dublin or for having sex with Dublin's men, 32 percent of the boys aged fifteen to twenty-one named in gross indecency cases were not themselves charged.[17] Men over twenty-one who were implicated in a gross indecency crime were always charged unless they were gardaí or, in a few cases, victims of assaults. "Assault" charges were usually reserved for cases in which adult men sexually assaulted children under fifteen, but, in a few cases, a victim of an assault went to the police and was not themselves charged.[18] And, while the court records give us some insights into the world of rent boys, the arrested and implicated represent only a fraction of those who participated in Dublin's sexual economy and queer subculture. There were likely hundreds of boys aged fifteen to twenty-one who had sex with the residents of and visitors to Ireland's capital.[19]

Intergenerational sexual relationships are, broadly speaking, hard to quantify in the court records. The ages of defendants and (if not also defendants) their sexual partners are only identified in about half of the digitally available Irish newspapers and/or the state files and books held by the NAI. Yet, when the age difference was significant, it was discussed or demarcated in the records. When a defendant or witness (like Michael Hackett) was much younger than his sexual partner, the gardaí and/or solicitors made a point of asking their age when collecting depositions. Within the dataset where age *is* known, the results of those cases are telling.

---

16. Calculated from my personal database of gross indecency court records, based on those available in the NAI.

17. Of thirty-eight named fifteen- to twenty-one-year-olds, twelve were not charged at all.

18. There are seventeen cases in which one man was charged with indecent assault, but the victim was over fifteen; in four of those cases, the victim was aged sixteen to twenty-one. All men accused of assaulting a boy were found guilty. Of the remaining thirteen, five were found not guilty or their case was thrown out because of a hung jury. For example, Charles Lambe was accused by Richard O'Flaherty of an attempted sexual assault, but the jury resulted in a *nolle prosequi*. NAI, Dublin Circuit Court, State Files, V15-14-38, docket 25, 21-Jun-1954, the State v. Charles Lambe.

19. There are thirty-eight boys fifteen to twenty-one who were named in court records; since the court records are incomplete and only represent a fraction of the actual goings-on of Dublin in the twentieth century, it's pretty safe to assume there were at least hundreds and possibly thousands.

Though Nyhan and Price were charged, and both found guilty, their positionality as youths afforded them a leniency that their "adult" counterparts did not experience. Nyhan, Price, and Hackett all enjoyed the Irish judicial system's forgiving approach to the follies of youth. The treatment of the boys involved in intergenerational sex reflects a broader Irish sentiment in this period: boys under twenty-one were in a formative period of their lives, and they could be saved or reformed, even when mixed up in something as "heinous" as same-sex sex.[20] This is notably different from what historian Alessio Ponzio reveals about Italy at the same time, where teen sex workers were considered tempters and predators.[21] Like many nascent and postcolonial states, Ireland funneled a great deal of charity into its young men, even as it imprisoned its young women for various undesirable behaviors.[22] The anxieties of the "pure" independent Irish state played out on the bodies of women, and its hopes were pinned on young men.

When Nyhan followed Robert Byrne's exposed penis back into the lavatory, he tacitly agreed to the sexual exchange. Byrne kissed Nyhan and asked the boy to take down his trousers. Nyhan did. Byrne produced a little tin of Vaseline, bright yellow and small enough to fit in the palm of his hand, and used it to lubricate Nyhan's "backside." (See Figure 5.2.) When Nyhan expressed his discomfort with the attempted anal sex, Byrne stopped, pulled him back into a front-to-front embrace, and proceeded with lubricated intercrural sex until he "came off." In his statement at Bridewell Garda Station, Nyhan said that he'd told Byrne he "didn't like it" and would have preferred to continue on their walk.[23]

Nyhan was comfortable telling Byrne when he didn't want to do something, and his willingness to follow an exposed penis into a public lavatory for the promise of sixpence suggests that he'd done something like this before. At the same time, his description of the encounter—"he pulled his hand along his thing and knocked off a lot of yellow stuff," and "when he was at the front he wet my legs"—could be real or feigned naivety.[24] Certainly, with the

---

20. See Reidy, *Ireland's "Moral Hospital."*

21. Ponzio, "What They Had," 62–78.

22. On boy culture, as it was cultivated in the revolutionary era, see Marnie Hay, *Na Fianna Eireann and the Irish Revolution 1909–23: Scouting for Rebels* (Manchester: Manchester University Press, 2019); Gail Baylis, "Boy Culture and Ireland 1916," *Early Popular Visual Culture* 13, no. 3 (2015): 192–208. For an overview of the Borstal institutions, which were created for the rehabilitation of boys under twenty-one, see Reidy, *Ireland's "Moral Hospital."* On the systems put in place to control women and particularly their sexuality and bodies, see Smith, *Ireland's Magdalen Laundries*; Luddy, *Prostitution and Irish Society*; and Cara Delay, *Irish Women and the Creation of Modern Catholicism, 1850–1950* (Manchester: Manchester University Press, 2019).

23. Deposition of Matthew Nyhan. Spectacularly, the tin of lube is still in evidence—pinned to the court file at the National Archives. See Figure 5.2.

24. Deposition of Matthew Nyhan.

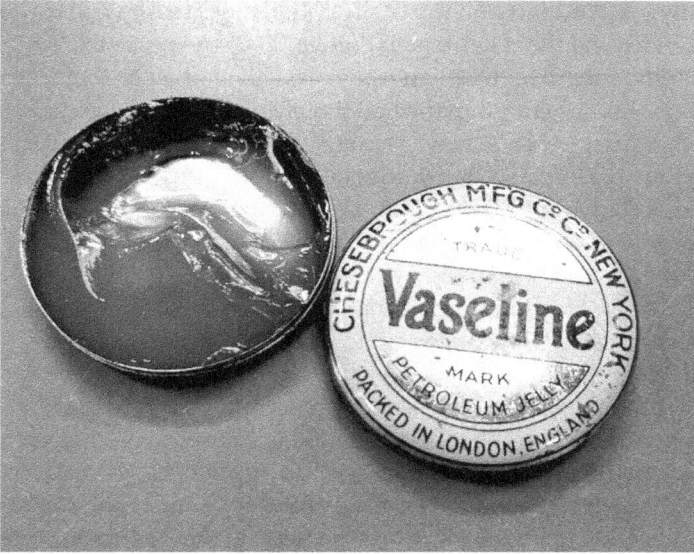

Figure 5.2 The tin of lube described in Nyhan's statement, collected as evidence by the Gardaí and preserved in the National Archives to this very day, at least as of August 14, 2023. *(NAI, State Files, County and City of Dublin, 1C-94-88. Reproduced by kind permission of the Director of the National Archives.)*

state of the Irish sex education system in 1931, Nyhan might not have had the words or a true understanding of things like ejaculation. Yet he had all manner of slang for genitals, referring to Byrne's penis as "prick," "private part," and "thing," interchangeably.[25]

It is clear that Nyhan wasn't interested in following his father's directions to find work on Hawkins Street. Maybe he was actively cruising on Butt Bridge, looking for a mark. Maybe the encounter with Byrne was just a lark he decided to indulge on a whim. Whatever his motivations, once the coast was clear in the lav, Nyhan followed Byrne's exposed penis back into a stall for sex. In the recorded statement, his description of events, and his participation, is presented with a deliberateness and matter-of-factness. At the time of their arrest, the garda who caught Byrne and Nyhan did not entertain the idea that Nyhan was somehow innocent. He was arrested and charged right alongside Byrne.

The courtroom results, however, evidence the stark contrast between the "innocent" rent boy and his corrupter. Nyhan admitted to going off with a stranger, following the exposed and erect penis into the lavatory stall, and

---

25. Deposition of Matthew Nyhan.

kissing Byrne. And then, on top of that, Nyhan pleaded guilty. He got away with a £25 fee and the requirement that he "keep the peace for two years."[26] Significantly, even though Nyhan really messed up when he went with Byrne to the park, his father put up the bail money of £200 and then paid the £25 fine so that his son could avoid prison.[27] It would have been a devastating sum for the working-class family to shoulder in 1931. By the 1950s, working-class wages could range from £3 10s to £7 10s per week.[28] In 1931, then, £25 was an exorbitant amount for a family like the Nyhans, even with David Nyhan doing skilled weaver work. Still, with a relative slap on the wrist, Nyhan was sent on his way. He didn't get off completely scot-free the way Hackett had a few months earlier, but things could have been worse, as in Price's case a decade later.

Robert Byrne, conversely, was found guilty and sentenced to a total of nine years imprisonment.[29] The maximum sentence for one count of gross indecency was two years imprisonment with hard labor. Likely because of Nyhan's relative age, and perhaps because of Byrne's connection to the British army, the judge threw the book at him, giving him the maximum sentence on all charges. Byrne wrote the presiding judge a letter, explaining his situation. "I have served in the British Army since 1905 to 1913 . . . 6 years in India . . . and from 1914 to 1915 in France. . . . I have been wounded both in the leg and head. I have already gone under twenty operations. . . . In the event of me being found guilty I would like to ask that you make allowings out of my pension to my mother as I am her only Dependent." Judge George Shannon read the letter aloud to the jury, but it earned the former soldier no sympathy.[30] Remarking on the case, Shannon said "he had not sufficient words to condemn the accused's conduct, and he was punishing him in order to warn others, so that society might be protected, so far as possible, from the evil action of men like him."[31] While the boy walked away intact, Byrne was castigated for his alleged corruption of an Irish boy.

The Irish state and society believed that "boys" could be redeemed through education, even when they were associated with sex crimes. Education was central to the early vision of the Irish state, more generally, particularly under the influence of Cumann na nGaedheal, the pro-Treaty party in power in independent Ireland's early years. Cumann na nGaedheal passed the 1926 School

26. The State v. Robert Byrne and Matthew Nyhan.
27. The State v. Robert Byrne and Matthew Nyhan.
28. Brady, *Dublin, 1930–1950*, 246.
29. The State v. Robert Byrne and Matthew Nyhan.
30. Notation in the case file. The State v. Robert Byrne and Matthew Nyhan.
31. "Another Case: Sentence of Seven Years," *Irish Independent*, 30 January 1931, 2.

Attendance Act, which made schooling compulsory until the age of fourteen.[32] Though, in 1942, the Dáil debated raising the compulsory age to sixteen, it did not pass because, under the auspices of the 1937 Constitution, it was the right of the family to oversee the education of its children.[33] Though the structure of the Irish school system did not change under William Cosgrave's government, which sought to maintain its relationship with the Catholic Church much in the way that de Valera would in his tenure as leader of Ireland, the curriculum the state established emphasized the building of good Irish citizens.[34] This included the formalization of the traditions of the Gaelic League, with the revival of the Irish language and emphasis on Irish music and a nationalist interpretation of Irish history.[35]

Addressing a group of teachers, Reverend John Flanagan, who represented Archbishop William Walsh on a committee seeking to cut education costs, lauded the part that the National Schools played in "building up the nation," but he also noted that teachers' responsibility ended when the school years close, and it was the duty of parents and employers to ensure that the teachers' "good work" not be wasted.[36] An ideal independent Ireland was to be achieved through Catholic instruction and Gaelic revivalist initiatives, particularly the emphasis of the Irish language in schools. The Catholic Church had from the late nineteenth century gained almost exclusive control of both primary and secondary schooling and continued to run the schools in the twenty-six counties with subsidiaries from the government.[37] The local parish priest oversaw the schools, and appointed teachers, presumably individuals who exhibited a commitment to the salvation of Irish souls.[38]

Boys were expected by their parents to start earning income after leaving school, and sometimes before. Since compulsory schooling didn't extend to secondary school, that meant that someone like the fifteen-year-old working-class Matthew Nyhan was most likely finished with school when he was arrested in 1931. Very few Irish students went on to secondary school before the 1960s. Certainly, we know that his father expected him to be working that day in May, which would otherwise have been a school day. Some boys, like Nyhan, lived at home, working as newspaper sellers or telegram boys by day and rent boys when there was an opportunity for extra spending money. Others, like Hackett and Price, were forced to or chose to leave home. (Though

---

32. Irish Statute Book, Number 17 of 1926, "1926 School Attendance Act," available at https://www.irishstatutebook.ie/eli/1926/act/17/enacted/en/html.

33. Helleiner, "For the Protection of the Children," 51–62.

34. Ó Buachalla, *Education Policy*, 60–61.

35. Ó Buachalla, 59.

36. "National Thrift: The Part Schools Can Play," *Irish Independent*, 13 April 1928, 9.

37. "Bishop Stresses Dual Purpose of Education," *Irish Independent*, 9 September 1953, 7.

38. J. Duffy, *The Lay Teacher* (Dublin: Fallons, 1967), 27.

Price was English, not Irish, he would have been required to go to school until he was fourteen, per the Fisher Act of 1918. Urban working-class men, like Price's and Nyhan's fathers, expected and needed their sons to be gainfully employed.) Sex for money or lodging was, in some cases, the price of independence or the alternative to sleeping on the streets.

Yet, the judicial system used additional "schooling" as punitive sanctions for those who were fifteen to twenty-one years old to remove the boys from their criminal environments and make them wards of the state for redemptive instruction.[39] The British government established reformatory and industrial schools in the late nineteenth and early twentieth centuries with the mission to provide for the "industrial training of juvenile offenders / children, in which juvenile offenders / children are lodged, clothed and fed, as well as taught."[40] In Ireland, both Catholic and Protestant religious orders established reformatory and industrial schools, though, by the 1920s, only Catholic institutions were still open. The use of education to reform juvenile and also adult offenders was a development of the nineteenth century.

Starting in the late Victorian period, British penal reformers saw the need to separate youthful offenders from adult criminals. Previously men, women, and children were detained in the same institutions. The negative influence of "hardened" adult criminals on youths, and particularly boys—who represented at least two-thirds of the youth criminal population at any given time—was addressed with the establishment of penal institutions and separate juvenile wards.[41] The British, American, and Irish continued to use education as a redemptive tool in dealing with youthful offenders throughout the twentieth century.[42] Job training programs were implemented in prisons for adults, and that approach was expanded on and coupled with the creation of separate facilities and institutions for juvenile offenders. In addition, the state introduced a new category of offender, the "juvenile-adult," identified as needing special treatment.[43] In a gross indecency case in 1935, for example, the jury made a statement about eighteen-year-old Patrick Delaney, recommending "mercy on account of his youth, his previous good character, and being under the influence of the other man."[44] Judges and juries had a great

39. Investment in Education—Report of the Survey Team (Dublin: Stationery Office, 1966), 51.

40. Justice Sean Ryan, *Commission to Inquire into Child Abuse*, vol. 1, chap. 2: "History of Industrial Schools and Reformatories" (May 2004), 37, available at http://www.childabuscom mission.ie/rpt/pdfs/CICA-VOL1-02.PDF.

41. Reidy, *Ireland's "Moral Hospital,"* 17.

42. Justice Sean Ryan, *Commission to Inquire into Child Abuse*, 36.

43. Reidy, *Ireland's "Moral Hospital,"* 6.

44. NAI, Dublin Circuit Court, State Books, 1D-55-76, docket 52, 30-Apr-1935, the State v. Patrick Delaney and Percy Frazer.

deal more sympathy for "boys" seemingly led into the life of crime, even a crime as "disgusting" as gross indecency.

The juvenile-adult offender was not a child, nor was he a man.[45] According to historian Conor Reidy, the Irish juvenile-adult was one of two kinds in the Irish imagination. He was either one of the "street-wise" Dickensian youths "who possess all the cunning and wit of a man twice his age . . . often 'run' by a Fagin-like, older, criminal mentor," or he was an accidental criminal. The boy "fell into criminality . . . may have committed his first offence and was unlucky enough to be caught, or too inexperienced to escape detection."[46] The Departmental Committee on Prisons, commonly referred to as the Gladstone Committee, was set up in 1895 as a response to the problems in dealing with youthful offenders as well as the "poor moral condition of convicts leaving English prisons." The committee found that criminal habits were formed between the ages of sixteen and twenty-one, and thus it was decided that a different sort of institution was needed to deal with those "juvenile-adult" offenders.[47]

In the late nineteenth century, a reformatory institution for juvenile-adult offenders was piloted in Elmira, New York. Impressed by the success there, the prison commissioner and former civil servant Evelyn John Ruggles Brise proposed and established a similar system first in Kent, England, in 1901, and then in Clonmel, Ireland, in 1906. The principle of the "borstal" was to use education—reading, writing, and numeracy—and job skills training, coupled with a system of privileges and sanctions, to guide inmates (not "prisoners") to self-reformation. Also key to that system was a program that helped boys obtain job placements and housing once released from the program, efforts managed by a group called the Borstal Association of Ireland. The borstal institutions were intended for offenders with at least a two-year sentence, and generally not first-time offenders; according to its designers, the self-reforming process required a minimum commitment to the program to be effective.[48]

The borstal reformatory system and the judicial system in twentieth-century Ireland were not always in sync. Courts tended to hand out sentences to juvenile-adult offenders that prison reformers deemed too short for effective borstal treatment. This was most often true for the boys found guilty of gross indecency. The courts tended to give minimal sentences of under twelve months to boys aged fourteen to twenty-one. In 1910, a modified borstal system was established in a ward of Mountjoy Prison in Dublin for juvenile-adult

---

45. Legally, juvenile-adults were seventeen to twenty-one, and juveniles were fourteen to sixteen.

46. Reidy, *Ireland's "Moral Hospital,"* 7.

47. Reidy, 29–30.

48. Reidy, 58–87, 139–166.

offenders, which offered education, job training, and a similar system of privileges and sanctions to the borstal but without the two-year sentence requirement. Mountjoy was thus the primary destination for Dublin's juvenile-adult gross indecency offenders who had shorter sentences.[49]

The borstal in Clonmel, the adapted program at Mountjoy, and other juvenile prison wings emphasized rudimentary education, stability, and job training in their reformation of the juvenile-adult offenders. Boys were put on a regimented daily schedule to establish discipline and stability. Privileges, from eating with other boys to having visitors, were based on merits and demerits and intended to encourage self-reflection and moral transformation. Inmates received lessons in reading, writing, and rudimentary mathematics.[50] Theoretically they had to achieve a minimum level of literacy before beginning job training, though that standard was not always adhered to. When they entered training programs, the boys spent between six and nine hours of the day working. Carpentry, tailoring, gardening, laundry, painting, whitewashing, and shoemaking were among the trades and skills that boys were trained on throughout the United Kingdom and Ireland. After independence, Irish borstal and juvenile detention facilities focused on tailoring, gardening, carpentry, shoemaking, and agriculture.[51] Irish nationalism, which was grounded in a particular reverence for the rural, emphasized the hale and heartiness of rural masculinity. Thus rural vocations were carried into the reformatory efforts exerted over juvenile-adult offenders in the Irish institutions. According to William Casey of the Borstal Association of Ireland, a "healthy outdoor occupation . . . would improve and strengthen them physically and morally, removing them from their original vicious surroundings (the city)."[52] Job training, education, and disciplined routines were intended to give the boys the tools to reform themselves and thus building moral Irish men for the nation.

Of course, the theoretical principles and tactics of the borstal system did not always reflect its reality. When E. J. Flanagan, an Irish-born priest who founded the orphanage and educational complex known as Boys Town in Omaha, Nebraska in 1917, visited the Irish penal institutions for boys and juvenile-adult offenders in 1946, he found the use of physical punishment

---

49. Reidy, 29–51. Out of 397 males charged with gross indecency, the age is identified for 177 defendants; thirty-four are between fourteen and twenty-one, and of those thirty-four, only one got the maximum sentence of two years imprisonment with hard labor. Five were found not guilty or the case was thrown out, two were given three months, nine were given six months, six were given nine months, two were given ten months, four were given twelve months, and two were given fines. The rest were found guilty, but their sentences were not listed.

50. Reidy, *Ireland's "Moral Hospital,"* 146, 152.

51. Reidy, 152.

52. Quoted in Reidy, 155.

deplorable.[53] Flanagan believed that penal servitude should be "a place of rescue rather than dehumanising punishment."[54] The conditions he found and heard about in Irish juvenile reform institutions prompted Flanagan to urge "the good people of Ireland" to do "what Christian charity demands," and step in to put a stop to the abuse of boys in the penal system.[55] Boys were just as likely to receive physical punishment as job training in the borstal institutions. Yet the system was still endorsed by the people doing the sentencing. When considering how to sentence an offender in 1950, one judge noted that the boy's companions had received training in one of the institutions and had not been in trouble since. For that judge, the reform of those boys was enough to convince him that the youth on trial ought to be sent to the borstal, where he could receive the instruction to turn his life around and become a good Irishman.[56]

As Jonathan Coleman, Matt Houlbrook, and Charles Upchurch have shown, the teens and young men who engaged in sex work were essential to the fabric of same-sex sexual subcultures in the United Kingdom.[57] In Britain, "rent boys" were often portrayed as working-class men for hire by elite queer British men, with the decadence of the upper class exerting immoral influence over the working classes.[58] These anxieties spilled over into Ireland under British rule, particularly surrounding the case of the Dublin Castle scandal of 1884, in which British administrators in Ireland had sex with Irish men.[59] Absent the British, who was to blame for Ireland's ongoing problem with that most "unnatural offence"? Class *was* a clear factor in who was most likely to be policed in Ireland, both before and after independence; more working-class and unemployed men were arrested than middle-class men, and virtually none of Ireland's elite were troubled by the laws. But when it came to the

---

53. Edward John Flanagan of Boys Town is not to be confused with the John Flanagan mentioned previously in this chapter. E. J. Flanagan was born and ordained as a priest in Ireland, but emigrated to the United States in 1904 with his sister Nellie, then founded Boys Town, and died in the United States in 1948. J. Flanagan served the Fairview parish of Dublin from 1926 until his death in 1935.

54. "Father Flanagan's Statement about Physical Punishment in Ireland," *Tuam Herald*, 19 October 1946, 4.

55. "Father Flanagan's Statement," 4.

56. "Youth Sent to Borstal," *Meath Chronicle*, 1 July 1950, 3.

57. Jonathan Coleman, "Rent: Same-Sex Prostitution in Modern Britain, 1885–1957," Dissertation, University of Kentucky (2014), 3–5; Matt Houlbrook, "Soldier Heroes and Rent Boys: Homosex, Masculinities, and Britishness in the Brigade of Gardaí, circa 1900–1960," *Journal of British Studies* 42, no. 3 (July 2003): 351–388; and Charles Upchurch, "Forgetting the Unthinkable: Cross-Dressers and British Society in the Case of the Queen v. Boulton and Others," *Gender and History* 12, no. 1 (April 2000): 125–157.

58. Coleman, "Rent," 1–4.

59. See Earls, "Unnatural Offenses of English Import," 396–424; Coleman, "Rent"; and Aleardo Zanghellini, *The Sexual Constitution of Political Authority* (Routledge, 2015), 127–161.

ways that judges and newspapers talked about the corruptive nature of same-sex sex, class wasn't at the foreground of Irish anxieties the way it was in the United Kingdom. Instead, youth was the marker of innocence, and susceptibility to moral corruption from older, inherently sinful, adults.

Same-sex desire was not just unmanly or criminal; it was un-Irish. Consistently, juries recommended "mercy on account of youth" for juvenile-adult sex offenders, and, conversely, judges meted out the harshest possible punishment for adult offenders who involved themselves with those under twenty-one. Judges commented that same-sex sex offenders posed a danger to "children," even in cases absent any children or even juvenile-adults.[60] While the Irish conflation of same-sex-desiring men with pedophiles echoes similar moral panics in the mid-twentieth century across the Atlantic, it is also a marker of the struggle that faced the postcolonial state in identifying enemies to blame for Ireland's social ills.[61] How the Irish understood and talked about the "vice prevalent in Dublin" isn't quite as simple as antipedophilia, or even homophobia. There wasn't a strong tradition of sexological discourse in Ireland (in part because all sexology texts were officially banned in independent Ireland), and same-sex sex was still characterized as a "vice" or sin, making it a moral issue rather than a sexuality or identity issue. When an Irish judge conflated sex between men with a danger to Ireland's youths, they were expressing a fear of corruption more than a fear of sexual predation.

For some boys who entered the market, sexual exchanges were necessary for establishing a social network and longer-term relationships. In his work on 1870s Paris, the historian William Peniston argues that the "networks of relationships developed by these men fulfilled several important functions. . . . They formed a community based on emotional ties, financial support, common experiences, and shared identities."[62] There is evidence of such relationships in Dublin. In the 1940s, the Garda uncovered two networks of men and boys involved in same-sex sexual-economic exchanges, one in Howth, a seaside village north of the city in Dublin County, and one in the city. In both groupings, the boys implicated reported economic gains. Many also implied a sense that their relationships with the older men were predicated on mutual affection. Those boys generally lived for spans of time with their adult benefactors, and the adults provided them with employment opportunities, clothes, food, and spending money. Furthermore, testimonies in those cas-

60. "Vice Prevalent in Dublin," *Irish Times*, 13 February 1931, 13.
61. See Jenkins, *Moral Panic*.
62. William Peniston, "Pederasts, Prostitutes, and Pickpockets in Paris of the 1870s," *Journal of Homosexuality* 41, no. 3–4 (2001), 183.

es revealed that the arrested men and boys all knew one another, which suggests that there was an established network of same-sex-desiring individuals.[63]

In all of the cases of intergenerational sex preserved in the NAI, the older man provided something material to their younger lovers. An older, sometimes much older, sexual partner might provide protection, food, affection, drugs/alcohol, shelter, or money. This was generally true if the relationship was enduring or transactional. Alcohol was common as a bribe and social lubricant in the gross indecency files. Hand and North gave Hackett bottles of stout, perhaps to ease the awkwardness of the situation. It could also be a marker of a "good time" or a mask for suffering. In addition to a home and affection, Ronald Brown gave Leslie Price money, took him on dates and holidays, and took him out on the town and to parties, where both overimbibed in drink. Price told the gardaí that both he and Brown were under the influence of drink the first night they had sex. Additionally, Price, Brown's friend Petrie, and hotel staff all commented on the two men being in various states of intoxication when together. Petrie told the detectives that he'd cautioned Brown that "Price was too young to be drinking, and was not a suitable member of our party." He "requested Mr. Brown not to bring Price to any future parties," or "to my house, as he had been in my house on one previous occasion with Mr. Brown, and my wife strongly objected to his presence there."[64] Though Petrie also acknowledged the clear and genuine affection Brown felt for Price, he disapproved of the way the man treated the boy as an equal (or partner), rather than as a ward.

In extreme but also common cases, intergenerational sex was a tool for survival. This was particularly true among homeless and underemployed teens like Hackett and Price, and was not, of course, not limited to Ireland.[65] The trauma of homelessness, and the particularly harrowing experiences of same-

---

63. The Howth case relied primarily on the finger-pointing of one Fintan Moore, who so implicated eleven other men. The Dublin case revealed five men involved, including Ronald Brown, who was the state solicitor for Kildare at that time. See NAI, Dublin Circuit Court, State Files, 1D-20-104, dockets 2, 47, 52, 53, 54, 10-Oct-1941, and 1D-24-141, dockets 103, 105, 108, 109, 110, 111, 112, 113, 114, and 167, 1-Jun-1944.

64. NAI, AGO, 2002-16-466, the State v. Ronald H. Brown, Statement of Heinrich Petrie given on 8 September 1941.

65. Chauncey, *Gay New York*, 75–91; Evans, "Bahnhof Boys," 605–636; Stephen L. Eyre, Emily Arnold, Eric Peterson, and Thomas Strong, "Romantic Relationships and Their Social Context among Gay/Bisexual Male Youth in the Castro District of San Francisco," *Journal of Homosexuality* 53, no. 4 (2007): 1–29; Martha W. Moon, William Mcfarland, Timothy Kellogg, Michael Baxter, Mitchell H. Katz, Duncan Mackellar, and Linda A. Valleroy, "HIV Risk Behavior of Runaway Youth in San Francisco: Age of Onset and Relation to Sexual Orientation," *Youth and Society* 32, no. 2 (2000): 184–201; Jen Reck, "Homeless Gay and Transgender Youth of Color in San Francisco: 'No One Likes Street Kids'—Even in the Castro," *Journal of LGBT Youth* 6, nos. 2–3 (2009): 223–242.

sex-desiring youths who experience homelessness or run away from home, is well studied and documented by current social workers, psychologists, sociologists, and historians.[66] Hackett and Price clearly *needed* to participate in Dublin's sexual economy. Neither had other jobs nor the security of a family member with which to stay. Nyhan's immediate family were all well within reach, and he slipped into the sexual economy not in search of stability or a meal but because he wanted to go to the cinema.[67] Motivation was not factored into the judicial decisions. When judges like George Shannon and Cahir Davitt offered comments for the newspapers, they didn't even acknowledge the boys involved in these cases. They were more likely to lament the threat that same-sex-desiring men posed to abstract boys rather than the actual boys who passed through their courtrooms.

O'Duffy, the Garda commissioner from its founding through the early 1930s, identified "street trade," or selling sex, as a major problem in his report to the 1930 Carrigan Committee. O'Duffy told the committee that child sex abuse and street trade were disturbingly common; sex abuse was more common in rural areas, and trade in urban areas, with girls at the greatest risk in his estimation, but boys as well.[68] From the founding of the Free State, Ireland had to deal with high levels of visible middle and late adolescents on city streets. The state established a Commission on Youth Unemployment in 1943, and then the Juvenile Liaison Officer Scheme in 1962.[69] For the large number of visibly vagrant street youths, there were few ways to make money. Combined with running messages and hocking papers for pennies, selling sex was a necessary part of survival. From the 1884 Dublin Castle scandal right up until the decriminalization of same-sex sex in 1993, those youths relied on the illicit and illegal sexual marketplace to counter homelessness and unem-

66. See, e.g., Douglas Bruce, Ron Stall, Aimee Fata, and Richard T. Campbell, "Modeling Minority Stress Effects on Homelessness and Health Disparities among Young Men Who Have Sex with Men," *Journal of Urban Health*, 91, no. 3 (2014) 568–580; Kerwin Kaye, "Male Prostitution in the Twentieth Century," *Journal of Homosexuality* 46 nos. 1–2 (2004) 1–77; Angela Stewart, Mandy Stiman, Ana Mari Cauce, Bryan Cochran, Les B. Whitbeck, and Dan Hoyt, "Victimization and Posttraumatic Stress Disorder among Homeless Adolescents," *Journal of American Academy Child Adolescent Psychiatry* 43, no. 3 (March 2004): 325–331; Kimberley Tyler and Katherine Johnson, "Trading Sex: Voluntary or Coerced? The Experiences of Homeless Youth," *Journal of Sex Research* 43, no. 3 (2006): 208–216.
67. In this way, rent boys and transient queer youths in Dublin operated much in the same way young women and girls did at the same time in New York City, London, etc., where "treating" culture was acceptable. See, e.g., Kathy Peiss's *Cheap Amusements* or her short article "Charity Girls and City Pleasures."
68. Maguire, *Precarious Childhood in Post-independence Ireland*, 121–123.
69. Buckley and O'Riordan, "Childhood since 1740," 335–340.

ployment, and older men relied on those youths to fulfill their sexual desire for male-to-male intimacy.[70]

Intergenerational relationships could be enduring or purely transactional. By Price's own estimation of their relationship, Brown gave him a home, a job, and a sense of security. Both Price and Brown expressed open affection and care for the other, remarkable considering the circumstances under which their words were recorded. As state solicitor, Brown was certainly aware of the consequences of the accusation. While Price probably didn't have the same legal wherewithal, he knew that sex between men was illegal, and he did everything in his power to deny the charges. Conversely, when eighteen-year-old Hackett met thirty-two-year-old North, and fifteen-year-old Nyhan met forty-two-year-old Byrne, the exchanges were purely transactional. In Hackett's case, the encounter took place in Hand's house, North paid the boy directly after they had sex, and then the two parted ways.[71] Nyhan and Byrne both described a chance meeting on Butt Bridge; they might've been lying and could have arranged the meeting earlier, but neither made any effort to protect the other from the gardaí. If Nyhan felt true affection for Byrne the way Price did for Brown, I'd expect a recording of at least some kind of deflection or lying rather than open admission of a sexual encounter. In many of these cases, the police wielded the boys as weapons. Some boys may have flipped for promised immunity; others may have been intimidated or worn down into compliance. Some may have held no allegiances to the men with whom they had sex and turned on them easily. It's hard to tell from the court records. Neither Hackett nor Nyhan seemed to feel that kind of beholden to the men with whom they had sex. And, of course, the depth of feeling between man and boy didn't matter to the judge and jury. Price and Nyhan were charged, while Hackett wasn't. Price's charge for involvement with Brown was technically thrown out, because Brown was found not guilty, but Price spent six months in prison anyway. Nyhan was convicted but only had to pay a fine.[72]

For judges and juries in Ireland, the default position was to give second chances, to recommend "mercy on account of youth" to juvenile-adults. When one nineteen-year-old was convicted of gross indecency in 1934, the presiding judge gave him a light sentence of just three months imprisonment. "That was a very proper and humane thing to do," reflected a different judge in 1935, "to give a young prisoner a chance of making good."[73] If convicted of gross indecency, most boys got three to nine months. Price and Nyhan were no more

70. See Coleman, "Rent"; and Earls, "Unnatural Offenses of English Import."

71. NAI, Dublin Circuit Court, State Files, 1C-94-89, 21-Jan-1931, Attorney General v. James Hand, Frank North, Michael Corr, Letter from Frank North to James Hand.

72. The State v. Robert Byrne and Matthew Nyhan.

73. "Penal Servitude for Young Man," *Irish Examiner*, 11 October 1935.

or less "rough," transient, or unemployed youths than most of the boys charged in gross indecency cases in the first four decades of independence. As you'll recall from Chapter 4, Judge Davitt saw Leslie Price as one of those streetwise Dickensian youths, and one with a history of criminal misdeeds, whose word couldn't be trusted.[74] And yet, he was still just a boy. Davitt sentenced Price to six months in the juvenile detention wing of Mountjoy Prison in Dublin. A punishment for a boy, not a man.[75]

For men involved with boys, the courts rarely granted mercy. Judges described such men as "bad characters," asserting that they "corrupt the life of the city" and "bring permanent shame on their families."[76] When an older man was convicted of having sex with a juvenile-adult, even if the youth testified that he was a willing participant in that relationship, the older man bore the brunt of the punishment. The gross indecency law of 1885 allowed a maximum sentence of up to two years imprisonment with hard labor. The 1861 sodomy law allowed a maximum of up to life imprisonment. Between 1922 and 1972, the chief state solicitor's office tended to aim for higher sentences when older men had sex with juvenile-adults. An over-twenty-one defendant could expect between two and five years imprisonment for having sex with a juvenile or juvenile-adult.[77]

Boys who sold sex were, as O'Duffy reported to the Carrigan Committee in 1931, a significant problem in the Free State—and continued to be a problem in Ireland for the rest of the century.[78] Recent work by journalist Evanna Kearins reveals that Dublin's illegal sexual economy for men seeking other men and teen boys persisted well into the 1990s.[79] British administrators revealed Dublin's male sex work scene on a national scale to the public in 1884 when the Dublin Castle scandal exposed the extensive network of male sex

---

74. "State Solicitor Acquitted," *Irish Press*, 17 January 1942, 3.

75. NAI, Dublin Circuit Court, State Files, 1D-20-105, 10-Oct-1941, State v. Leslie Price, Thomas Levins, David Wilson and John O'Sullivan.

76. "Judge Postpones Sentence," *Irish Independent*, 12 February 1931; *Evening Herald*, 13 February 1931; "Strong Comments by Judge—Two Men Sentenced—Outside the Pale of Civilisation," *Irish Independent*, 30 January 1931, 2.

77. In cases involving children under fourteen, the courts really hit offenders with the book, stacking multiple charges like attempt to commit sodomy, sodomy, indecent assault, attempt to commit an indecent assault, gross indecency, and procuration of an act of gross indecency; a combination of charges, if the jury found the defendant guilty, could culminate in decades of imprisonment. This most certainly demonstrates the state/justice systems greater concern for the health and safety of Ireland's children—even though these only represent one-quarter of the gross indecency cases preserved in the NAI.

78. NAI, Department of Justice, H247.41A, Evidence from Eoin O'Duffy to the Carrigan Committee.

79. Kearins, *Rent*. See also "Male Order Where Sex Is for Sale," *Irish Examiner*, 20 March 2000, 14; "TD Faces Rent Boy Quiz," *Belfast Newsletter*, 7 March 1994, 3; "Vice Blitz on Phoenix Park," *Evening Herald*, 16 February 1994, 76.

workers engaged.[80] The British government's leak of Roger Casement's "Black Diaries" in 1916 again illustrated the availability of sex for hire through meticulous records of all of his expenditures, including what he paid for sex in Dublin, Belfast, and around the world.[81] In the 1930s, Hand's "male brothel" was covered by major national Irish newspapers, despite the salacious topic in an age of censorship.[82] As recently as 1994, police harassed a prominent politician, Emmet Staggs, when he invited a rent boy into his car just outside of Phoenix Park.[83] These boys were a feature of Dublin's sexual economy for at least a century, probably more. In other European countries, including Italy, Germany, Turkey, and elsewhere, boys like Hackett, Nyhan, and Price were considered responsible for the same-sex sex crimes they instigated.[84] In Ireland, it was always the older man at fault.

Socioeconomic and home life circumstances left a lot of Ireland's transient youth population in flux and often in trouble with the law in the mid-twentieth century. Those boys were both suspicious to the gardaí—because many had histories of loitering, larceny, making a public nuisance, and other petty crimes—and afforded mercy when on trial, because there was hope yet for their futures. Short of exonerating self-confessed gross indecency offenders, the sentences meted out were minimal. Gardaí and judges seemed to believe that the boys were transient interlopers or unwilling victims of this same-sex-desiring world. State officials' beliefs were shaped, in part, by the statements that the boys gave in the courtroom. Hackett noted that he "did not like" the game, and Nyhan alleged that he cried out and said he did not like it.[85] These claims counterbalanced their seeming willingness to participate in those transactions. They might've been coached by other rent boys about how to give testimony that highlighted their transience in the sexual economy, or they may have simply been unenthusiastic participants speaking their truth. Whatever conditions shaped their testimonies, the end results were the same. Boys were held to a different standard than their adult corrupters. Rent boys' manipulation or navigation of the court system was similar to that of women sex workers. Denton notes that many women presented "themselves as 'un-

---

80. See Earls, "Unnatural Offenses of English Import."

81. Conrad, "Queer Treasons," 124–137; see also Roger Casement and Jeffrey Dudgeon, *Roger Casement: The Black Diaries—With a Study of His Background, Sexuality, and Irish Political Life* (Belfast Press, 2002).

82. The court proceedings and decisions were reported in the *Irish Times*, 21 and 28 February 1931, and the *Irish Independent*, 1 March 1931.

83. Alan Murdoch, "Irish Official Set to Survive Scandal," *Irish Independent*, 9 March 1994, available at http://www.independent.co.uk/news/uk/politics/irish-minister-set-to-survive-scandal-1427878.html.

84. Ponzio, "What They Had"; Kayaal, "Twisted Desires"; Marhoefer, *Sex and the Weimar Republic*; and Marhoefer, Research Presentation.

85. The State v. Robert Byrne and Matthew Nyhan.

fortunates,' . . . playing to the potential sympathies of a justice."[86] Much like the boys who sold sex in Dublin, the women who sold sex claimed that they were victims of circumstance to avoid harsher punishments. True to form, though, the Irish courts were almost universally more lenient with boys suspected of selling sex than women. These boys were more often than not released back into the world. Though policing same-sex sex was common in most of Europe and North America in the twentieth century, the way those under twenty-one were coddled in the Free State was unique.[87] The Irish state treated boys as victims of corrupters, going so far as to overlook admissions of willing participation in sexual activity and meting out reformation rather than punishment.

Curiously, there are very few cases in the court records of those over twenty-one receiving monetary compensation for same-sex sex. There are a number of possible explanations for this. It may be that there was a low demand for adult male prostitutes and thus an equally low supply. It may be that some of the cases examined in the earlier chapters of this book, particularly those involving men in public lavatories, were *going* to involve the exchange of money, but the gardaí interrupted the transaction. Perhaps rent boys aged out of the economy; some may have assimilated to what they believed to be appropriate masculine and sexual behavior in Ireland, or, for those who enjoyed having sex with men, they may have shifted from service provider to clientele. Or professional adult male prostitutes may have just been more adept at avoiding detection and policing. The sources in the NAI and NLI don't point one way or another. There is, in fact, only one surviving record of a man over twenty-one admitting to taking money in exchange for sex. The results of that case are, in some ways, completely baffling but also revealing of the fictions that the Irish state wove into the association of sex-for-pay, boyhood, and temporality in Dublin's sexual economy.

In April 1934, thirty-five-year-old Patrick Forde stopped into a public lavatory at Parliament Row.[88] At the time he was living in the East Wall neighborhood of Dublin, in a narrow two-story terraced house on a cul-de-sac off of East Road. He'd been unemployed for some time; his last good employment was in 1932, when he worked three years for an off-license wine and liquor store. Prior to that, in 1929, he'd worked for a grocer, also for three years. Though both employers sent him away with positive letters of recommendation, describing him as "sober, honest, and obliging," he was still (or, perhaps,

86. Denton, "Open Secret," 217.

87. See Maynard, "Through a Hole in the Lavatory Wall," 207–242, for a study of Toronto's gross indecency laws; and Houlbrook, *Queer London*, for a study of the policing of London same-sex desire leading up to the Wolfenden Commission, which recommended the removal of the gross indecency laws.

88. NAI, Dublin Circuit Courts, State Files, 1D-44-28, 10-Apr-1934, the State v. Patrick Forde.

again) between jobs in 1934.[89] Parliament Row is in the Temple Bar area of Dublin, and would have been about 3 km from Forde's residence. He didn't tell the gardaí what brought him to Temple Bar on a Thursday evening in April. Maybe he'd headed to the area for a drink after a day of inquiring for positions in the city center; maybe he was cruising. The docks of Dublin along the River Liffey weren't a bustling industrial hub like the docks in London or even Belfast, but the pubs and lavatories were plentiful and traversed by locals and visitors alike.[90] Whether he was looking to get paid or laid on Parliament Row, he was in the right place.

In the lavatory, Forde saw that sixty-seven-year-old George Gaw was loitering. According to Forde, when he opened his trousers and took out his "person to have a pumpship [urinate]," Gaw caught hold of Forde's penis, said it was "lovely."[91] Gaw proceeded to get down on his knees and put Forde's penis into his mouth, sucking enthusiastically until Forde "overflowed, and he then let it out of his mouth."[92] Apparently nonplussed by this sudden turn of events, Forde went with Gaw to a nearby pub, the O'Mara Public House at Aston Quay. Gaw bought the younger man a bottle of stout and a packet of Players cigarettes and gave him £1.[93] After they'd finished their drinks, Gaw asked if they could meet again the next night, in the same lavatory, at 7:00 P.M. Forde agreed. They met as arranged, fellatio again took place—with Gaw (according to Forde) doing all the work—and they again went to O'Mara's for a drink, and Gaw gave Forde another £1. After they finished their drinks Friday, though, they didn't part ways. Instead, they went back to the lav. There, Forde said that "Gaw put his hand into my trousers, took my person and said it is a lovely big prick, and put it into his mouth. I went to force away from him but he would not let go my person out of his mouth, so then I put my hand into his trousers pocket and took his purse and ran away and was caught by two men at Bedford Row off Fleet St."[94] The men who caught the fleeing Forde (were his trousers still open as he ran?) dragged him back to Gaw, who demanded Forde return his purse. When Forde refused, the two men helped haul Forde to the

---

89. The State v. Patrick Forde, Statement of Patrick Forde, taken 14 April 1934.

90. By the early 1800s, the River Liffey was too shallow and narrow to keep up with the ships of industry. Without that kind of traffic, Dublin Corporation built pedestrian bridges linking North and South Dublin all along the Liffey. The port continued to serve passenger ships, however, and, throughout the twentieth century, Dublin was one of the main hubs for departing emigrants, along with Belfast and Derry.

91. Statement of Patrick Forde.

92. Statement of Patrick Forde.

93. The transcript reads "a packet of Players." Players cigarettes were a common brand in Ireland in the 1930s that came with collectible playing cards, typically sexy headshots of film stars. Players were made in Dublin.

94. Statement of Patrick Forde.

College Street Garda Station. After collecting statements from both men, the gardaí arrested Forde *and* Gaw (probably to Gaw's surprise).[95]

Bizarrely, Gaw's statement was identical to Forde's in the details of when and how they met, the drinks that Gaw bought Forde, and the money he gave him. The only details missing were the fellatio and talk of how big Forde's penis was. I'm sure the gardaí listened to these two stories and wondered the same things that I wondered. Why would Gaw arrange to meet Forde the second time at the lavatory instead of the pub? Why did he give Forde money in the first place? What kind of man buys a drink for another man he met in a public convenience? The gardaí came to the same conclusion that I did: probably a man who had sex with that other man.

Forde's assertion that he rejected the older man's advances on the third trip to the lavatory likely rang false to the jury. At the trial, the *Irish Times* reported that "[Forde's] plea was that it was at the instigation of Gaw he committed the offence of indecency."[96] He tried to frame his case as one of naivety or innocence corrupted by an older man. But Forde was thirty-five years old. There was no mistaking him for even the twenty-one-year-olds who'd filtered through that same courtroom over the past decade. His obvious willingness to continue a sexual arrangement with Gaw combined with his admission to taking clear sexual pleasure from Gaw's actions were confoundingly problematic.

Likely to obtain sympathy from the jury, both men concluded their versions of the story with cries of their victimhood. Forde asserted that on the third sexual encounter he tried to stop Gaw from performing fellatio but was unable because Gaw would not let him go. Gaw claimed that just as he had his penis in his hand, ready to urinate, he was attacked by Forde. Gaw's version of events was a marker of vulnerability as well; he was unable to stop Forde from taking the purse because he was caught literally with his pants down. In admitting to arranging to meet at a lavatory, Gaw effectively admitted to seeking sex with this other man. In describing two counts of fellatio, Forde admitted to committing an act of gross indecency. The difference was that Gaw didn't actually confess to sex acts. Forde, on the other hand, laid it all out there. The consequences were dire.

If the jury felt sympathy for Forde, there was no overcoming the fact that he pleaded guilty to the charges. While Gaw, who pleaded not guilty, was discharged, Forde was found guilty on all charges, one charge of taking £2 off of Gaw and two counts of gross indecency. He was sentenced in total to thirty-six months with hard labor—and only six months was for the theft.[97] I don't

---

95. Statement of Patrick Forde.

96. "Dublin Circuit (Criminal) Court Prison for Robbery," *Irish Times*, 8 May 1934, 10.

97. The State v. Patrick Forde.

know how the jury and the circuit court judge Shannon justified this strange finding. Though Forde's confession was enough to convict him, it was not enough (in the eyes of the jury) to convict Gaw. What did Forde think to achieve by making the statement that he did? For youths, claiming that an older man instigated forays into sexual indiscretions usually worked out. From the case results it would seem that his susceptibility to influence from the older man actually worked against him in the eyes of the jury.

In cases where the rent boy was used as a witness, like Hackett and his cowitnesses in the Hand/North case, the importance of distancing the seemingly innocent boy from knowledge of or desire for sex was clear in their testimonies and self-presentation. Hackett said that North asked him if he could "put it up his back passage." They tried and failed, because "it wouldn't go up," and instead went back to mutual fondling.[98] Nyhan similarly claimed that when Byrne tried to penetrate him anally, he asked the man to stop. When North asked Hackett how long he had been selling sex, and if he liked it, Hackett replied that he did not like it but he did it for the money.[99] When Byrne asked Nyhan if he was enjoying their sexual contact, Nyhan replied that he didn't like it, and he wished they would continue their walk instead.[100] Though Nyhan and Hackett didn't claim that they felt coerced or abused, it is evident that they were uncomfortable with the sexual economy even as they relied on it for money. To the listening juries, their statements undoubtedly established their naivety and need for protection.

Yet the rent boys of independent Ireland didn't actually have to worry about being too knowledgeable about same-sex sex. Unlike Hackett and Nyhan, the majority of the boys named in gross indecency cases didn't vocalize dislike for sexual contact with men. Of the boys implicated in a gross indecency case after 1922, one-third testified that they objected in some way to the sex act, while 20 percent testified that they explicitly consented to the sex act. Half testified that they had an erection at some point in the encounter, and, of those, most testified that their own "nature flowed" as a result of the sexual contact. And, despite these admissions, all of the boys still skated by when it came to charging or sentencing.

Like the rent boys, Forde was economically disadvantaged when he turned to begging and then selling sexual favors. Unlike the rent boys, Forde was an adult man who engaged in acts of gross indecency and was, by his own account, willing. Not once but three times he went with Gaw into the lavatory. He tried to assert his passivity in the encounter, telling the gardaí that he "had

98. NAI, Dublin Circuit Court, State Files, 1C-94-89, 21-Jan-1931, the State v. James Hand, Frank North, Michael Corr, Deposition of Michael Hackett.
99. Deposition of Michael Hackett. "5/-" denotes five shillings.
100. The State v. Robert Byrne and Matthew Nyhan.

nothing to do with Gaw, and [Gaw] had done it all with me." But, while boys like Nyhan and Hackett were careful to assert their dislike of the sexual transaction, Forde never claimed that he didn't like having sex with another man.[101] Finally, while the authorities in Ireland were willing to show leniency to boys who sold sex, a thirty-five-year-old was no boy. The penalty that the judge exacted for Forde's follies suggests that he was in even more trouble than most consenting adults who were caught by the gardaí in public lavs and parks. It may have been shocking to the jury and judge to hear a man describe oral sex so clearly. It may have been even more shocking to see an Irishman debase himself by taking money for sex. Three years imprisonment, a sentence typically reserved for men who assaulted children under fourteen, was a loud warning to men like Forde.

It is possible that the rent boys like Hackett, Price, and Nyhan quit the "game" as full-fledged adults. It's also possible that they saw the sexual economy not just as a form of work but as an entrance into a world where they could express their own sexual desires and receive pleasure.[102] However these boys saw themselves in the same-sex-desiring world of Dublin, the state saw them as Ireland's future. Children were meant to be educated in "good" Christian endeavors and mannerisms, emphasized in the corporal punishment and nationalist curriculum of the National Schools, stressed again at home in the education of the family, and repeated yet again in the weekly Mass.[103] With such a strong theoretical foundation, it was likely baffling that boys should act outside the norms of the Christian society, and a corrupting external influence was easier to blame. When a man was found guilty not only of submitting to same-sex desire himself but of corrupting the future of the Irish state, the punishment was consistent with the crime. And when a boy didn't grow out of his youthful transgressions, he paid the price.

---

101. Statement of Patrick Forde.

102. George Chauncey suggests that Irish immigrant men seeking sex with other men existed in New York City in the early twentieth century, but they were primarily the active partners of "fairies." Chauncey points to Charles Tomlinson Griffes, a self-identified "fairy" who flirted with the Irish cops, got to know them as they walked their beats, and asked them to meet up at the theater for an evening on the town. Chauncey, *Gay New York*, 72, 107–108.

103. "Christian Education of Youth," *Fermanagh Herald*, 19 April 1930, 6.

6

The Predators

I n October 1950, seven Dublin gardaí took turns on the stand for a series of
cases being heard before judge George Shannon in the Green Street Circuit
Court.[1] The seven gardaí—Thomas Morris, James Cullen, Fred Ryan, William
Fennessey, Anthony Diamond, Patrick Cusack, and Michael Byrne—delivered testimonies about their summer stakeouts of the public conveniences

---

1. These case files are contained in the NAI, Dublin Circuit Courts, State Files, 1D-28-124 /
docket 17, the State v. Patrick O'Mahony; 1D-28-124/18, the State v. Robert Brenna; 1D-50-
0031/29, the State v. Maurice Cahill and Daniel Duggan; 1D-28-125/31, the State v. William
Kerrigan and Maurice Cahill; 1D-28-127/32, the State v. Edward Lewis and William Jones; 1D-
28-125/33, the State v. Domick Delaney; 1D-28-125/36, the State v. Thomas Bevine; 1D-28-125/36,
the State v. Michael Hackett; 1D-28-123/38, 1D-28-125/36, the State v. Samuel Jones and Christopher O'Connor; 1D-28-126/45, the State v. Patrick McShea; 1D-28-126/45, the State v. Henry
O'Kelly; 1D-28-126/49, the State v. Joseph Farrell and James Gordon Thomas; 1D-28-126/50,
the State v. John Kane and John Hughes; 1D-28-126/51, the State v. William Robert Stewart;
1D-28-126/52, the State v. Charles Gifford; 1D-28-127/62, the State v. John Clarke; 1D-28-127/63,
the State v. Charles Kellett; 1D-28-127/67, the State v. Hengry Doherty and John Brady; 1D-28-
127/68, the State v. James Fagan and Patrick McCabe; 1D-28-127/69, the State v. John O'Reilly
and William Harris; 1D-28-127/70, the State v. Liam Walsh and Thomas Kelly; 1D-28-128/71,
the State v. Vincent Treacy and Michael Carley; 1D-28-128/74, the State v. William Harold Bachelor and John Moran; 1D-28-128/75, the State v. Denis Hyland and Sydney Taylor; 1D-28-128/78,
the State v. Phelim Sheridan; 1D-28-128/83, the State v. Patrick McKeon and James Seally; 1D-
28-123/41 and 42, the State v. Phillip O'Connor and Patrick Seery; 1D-28-126/45A, the State
v. John Bowe; 1D-28-123/40, the State v. Michael O'Connor and Richard Kelly; 1D-28-127/64,
the State v. George Thompson; 1D-28-125/35, the State v. Gordon McWilliams; 1D-28-128, the
State v. William Murray; 1D-50-32/19, the State v. William Mullen and Jeremiah Ryan.

at Beresford Place and St. Stephen's Green. From June to September, several nights each week, the gardaí watched the comings and goings of these lavatories. The testimonies they delivered made the goal of their stakeout quite clear: they were watching for men having sex with other men.

While there was a sense of anxiety about the vices of Dublin, the use of the gross indecency and sodomy laws was never consistent or pervasive. What the gross indecency and sodomy records indicate is, as I've emphasized throughout this book, the stark contrast in policing of sex between men in the colonial period in comparison to the postcolonial period. Even more significantly, extensive use of the gross indecency and sodomy laws was episodic. O'Duffy led the first charge against vice, in a campaign targeting both the sex between men and the women who sold sex, between 1922 and 1932. The next concentrated policing episode was during World War II.[2] And finally, with the arrest of fifty-one men at the Beresford Place and St. Stephen's Green lavatories, the last major deployment of Section 11 of the Criminal Law Amendment took place over the course of just four months in 1950. There were years between 1922 and 1972 when only one or no men at all were charged with gross indecency in Dublin. Police harassment of men seeking sexual partners in public, using vagrancy and loitering charges, was likely more regular in those years, as evidenced by the collective trauma recorded in oral histories and memoirs in the 1970s.[3] But the relative absence of those more severe charges, the ones that would have sent a more public message about the state's stance on same-sex desire, is indicative of the realities and limitations of the postcolonial moral order in Ireland.

Compared to the gardaí who worked under O'Duffy in the late 1920s and early 1930s, the seven gardaí of 1950 comported themselves quite differently on the job.[4] None used their own bodies to bait unsuspecting men. None went on gross indecency watches alone. They demonstrated, efficiently and effectively, how to arrest and provide adequate evidence to secure convictions. Though four cases don't have clear results recorded in the NAI, the other forty-seven were found guilty. Judge George Shannon—who'd been a pretty firm proponent of clearing the streets of vice back in the 1930s—allowed one-quarter of the men convicted to be released after they paid a fine, rang-

---

2. See Chapter 4.

3. See, e.g., Rose, *Diverse Communities*; A. Madden, *Fear and Loathing in Dublin*; and Boyd et al., *Out for Ourselves*, 54. As I discussed in the Introduction, the actual number of how many men were impacted by these lesser charges and police harassment is hard to quantify, as there aren't many detailed court records for loitering charges. There were dozens of men serving brief sentences in prisons like Mountjoy at any given time for "Loitering," but it's impossible to determine if that loitering was some form of "public indecency" (being in the company of a prostitute or exposing genitals—entirely possible in the course of a tryst with another man).

4. See Chapter 2.

ing from £10 to £100, with instructions to keep the peace for two years. The rest, presumably, served sentences of between two and six months imprisonment with hard labor.[5]

For the gardaí, the 1950 summer arrests and October convictions were an unmitigated success. Through their work, they demonstrated that (1) there were a *lot* more men having sex with men in Dublin than prior arrest numbers suggested, and (2) with dedicated resources, the Garda could be quite effective in policing the "vice" of same-sex sex. The work and success of this "vice squad"—my phrase, not theirs—further shows that, when motivated, the state was capable of exercising considerable policing power over same-sex-desiring men. The policing between 1922 and 1931 was at the behest of O'Duffy. What, then, moved the team of gardaí in the summer of 1950 to spend their evenings cramped in lavatory attendant booths or surrounding the Beresford Place lavatory? Was it a similar order from the commissioner's office? Was it a desperate move to demonstrate the value and necessity of the Garda to protect the Irish public? Was it the effort of a group of true believers striking out on their own initiative to take on vice? A close reading of the court records, investigation into the vice squad members themselves, and the historical context substantiates each of these possible explanations, though, in truth, until an explicit directive from the Garda commissioner is discovered, we may never know for certain.

Significantly, though the vice squad was immensely successful at the October circuit court sessions, their initiative was not without risk. The care with which these seven gardaí approached the task of apprehending same-sex-desiring men is telling of the moral climate of the period. Observing sex acts was a step above engaging in sex acts, but it was still uncomfortable, disconcerting work. More so in these gross indecency and sodomy trials, because the gardaí had to recount their observations before a jury and all present in the courtroom. Again, this wasn't as troubling as the gardaí who, in the 1920s and 1930s, themselves engaged in sex with men; but it certainly toed the line of appropriate and inappropriate sexual behavior for Irish men. Not all gardaí were as processual as the 1950 vice squad. And even the detached formula of the vice squad's testimonies was revelatory.

All of the men on the vice squad were established members of the DMD by 1940, having served in the Dublin Garda for at least ten years.[6] Three joined

---

5. It's possible more were given this opportunity, and that information wasn't recorded. As you may recall, John Bodkin was given this reprieve back in 1927, and that information was not recorded in the original court documents. The presiding judge, in fact, was quite livid that Bodkin was roaming the streets rather than serving his sentence in prison. NAI, Department of Justice, ref. no. 2019-85-299, "John Bodkin's Deportation."

6. Service records for Patrick Cusack, Michael Byrne, and James Cullen were accessed through the DMD and Garda registers through UCD's digitization project. The others are

at the creation of An Garda Síochána, between 1922 and 1924, the four others joined between 1933—during de Valera's tactical hiring surge to counterbalance officers loyal to O'Duffy—and 1940, during World War II, when Michael Kissane came on as commissioner. The highest-ranking member of the vice squad was Detective Garda James J. Cullen, though three years after their campaign, Michael Byrne would make sergeant and go on to serve as station sergeant in 1959.[7] All the officers of the vice squad also, significantly, served over thirty years. Patrick Cusack served thirty-nine years.[8] Considering the flux the Garda was in at the time the vice squad was staking out Beresford Place lav, with two-thirds of the force preparing for retirement, this is actually quite remarkable.

As demonstrated by scholars of the Garda, like Vicky Conway, Liam McNiffe, Anastasia Dukova, and Gregory Allen, men joined the force for any number of reasons, ideological or practical.[9] We can't know for sure what prompted Cullen, Cusack, and Byrne to join just as the Garda was being formed. Certainly, the Garda promised a steady if modest paycheck, lodging, and job security in a state very much in flux. Based on their positive and long service records, they probably weren't among the "bad characters" hired and fired in the 1920s, men who wanted the authority to wield brutal power over others.[10] They might've been motivated by nationalist fervor and true belief in the mission of a Catholic-grounded "police force for the people." All were born before independence and raised up in a turbulent and independence-seeking colonial state.

James Cullen was a laborer like his father when he enlisted in the force in 1923. The military life must've felt familiar as he'd served in the British Army during World War I. He was born and raised in Dublin, by John and Ellen Cullen, and then served his entire thirty-two-year career in the DMD.[11] While

---

held by the Garda Museum Archives. I was initially granted access to those records, but after the Press Office of the archives learned the nature of my project, I was informed that those records were shared in error. I have requested permission to use the records but, at the time of this final manuscript proofing, my request continues to be denied. I have, however, been able to locate most of them through other genealogical tools.

7. UCD, DMP general register, Michael Byrne, registration no. 12490, p. 250, available at https://digital.ucd.ie/view-media/ucdlib:53467/canvas/ucdlib:53728.

8. UCD, DMP general register, Patrick Cusack, registration no. 12492, p. 250, available at https://digital.ucd.ie/view-media/ucdlib:53467/canvas/ucdlib:53728.

9. McNiffe, *History of the Garda Síochána*, 150–165; Conway, *Policing Twentieth Century Ireland*, 70–80.

10. "Committee on Finance, Vote 33—Gárda Síochána," House of the Oireachtas, Dáil debates online, 19 June 1936. Accessed on 12 November 2015, available at http://debates.oireachtas.ie/dail/1936/06/19/00007.asp; and the acting minister for justice asked Mr. Dillon to "please, moderate your language."

11. NAI, 1911 Census, Dublin / Arran Quay / Prussia Street / Residents of a house 64.2 in Prussia Street (Arran Quay, Dublin), census.ie; UCD, DMP general register, Warrant #11918, 231.

the Garda preferred to station men far from home, they must've felt Dublin was big enough that he wouldn't be too familiar with the civilians in his area. He served steadily, generally unobtrusively, on the force in that time, but, in 1950—just five years before his retirement—he headed up the vice squad.

Besides Cullen, the two oldest members of the vice squad, Michael Byrne and Patrick Cusack, were also two of the longest serving. Both served in the National Army for two years after the establishment of the Free State, and both served their entire Garda careers in DMD postings. Byrne was born in Mountmellick (in Ireland's midlands, a town just north of Portlaoise, where one of the major state prisons is located) on July 13, 1899.[12] Byrne worked as a laborer for a time, like his father, and then as a chauffeur. He was already married when he joined first the National Army, in 1923, and then the Garda, in 1924.[13] He died while still in service, after thirty-five years as a Garda. Cusack, three years younger than Byrne, was also from the midlands, just 40 km west of Mountmellick.[14] He married a bookkeeper in 1928.[15] Though Byrne had more aspirations than Cusack for his time in the service, the two must've worked well together to take up the work of the vice squad that summer.[16]

Detective Sergeant Michael P. Wall was not part of the team that staked out lavatories that summer, but he was, ultimately, important to the procedure of 1950s arrests and convictions. Wall belonged to the technical division of the DMD and was the primary photographer for Dublin. He provided the 1950 cases with illustrative crime scene photos to orient the jury. Understanding how public the Beresford Place urinal was likely motivated the jury's decision to convict in all forty-seven cases. He also served as an expert witness in most of the 1950 cases, describing the scene and his documentation of the street, urinal, and placement of officers. His contributions to the vice squad were important in the process of force modernization.

An Garda Síochána was supposed to be the police force for the people. For leaders like O'Duffy, this meant that they were supposed to be Catholic,

---

12. Born to Michael and Margaret Byrne, née Kane; birth reported by Mary Meagher, probably a midwife. Church Records, IrishGeneaology.ie, registration ID 9906882, available at https://civilrecords.irishgenealogy.ie/churchrecords.

13. Irish Civic Records, irishgeneaology.ie, available at https://civilrecords.irishgenealogy.ie/churchrecords.

14. Son of a milesman for the Greater Southern and Western Railway, registration ID 7177417, available at https://civilrecords.irishgenealogy.ie/churchrecords.

15. She was the daughter of a schoolmaster, available at https://civilrecords.irishgenealogy.ie/churchrecords.

16. The Garda Museum and Archives holds the service records for the other four officers, and I am unable to divulge the details provided by those records per instructions from the Garda Press Office.

exude athletic manliness, and uphold a chaste view of Irish morality.[17] For de Valera, that meant they were supposed to reorient Ireland along Fianna Fáil's political axis, where the Catholic Church had a "special place" and sex continued to be problematically visible. For gavels of the justice system like Cahir Davitt and George Shannon, this meant protecting Ireland's boys from sexual predators and clearing the vice from the streets of Dublin. In practice, the police force for the people was saddled with collecting census data, serving as social workers, dealing with stolen bicycles, and, though persistently underpaid and understaffed, also do the daily patrolling and investigative police work of a modern force. By the 1950s, a typical garda worked one hundred hours a week, at least eight of those on patrol, and 40 percent of their time was dedicated to nonpolicing work, like recording agricultural statistics, keeping track of children's school attendance, verifying weights and measures, and distributing pension books.[18] It isn't really that surprising then that there aren't *more* formal cases of things like gross indecency and sodomy cases that were heard in courts. There simply weren't the resources available, and probably a lot of gardaí felt the same way juries and justices did: that it was distasteful work, and no one wanted to do it.

It is significant that the 1950 vice squad members were all hired in the formative decades of postcolonial state building. They're like a bizarre buddy system of O'Duffy-, Dev-, and Kinnane-recruited gardaí. Though evenly distributed across those hiring initiatives, all were raised on nationalist politics, and some even served in the fight for Irish independence. We can't know, of course, their motivations for serving in either the army or the Garda. Undoubtedly, like young men around the world wanted, these institutions offered employment, job security, and power in a time and place where all of those things were hard to come by. Most of the vice squad members earned both monetary awards during their years of service for "Good Police Duty" and an "Exemplary Service" notation on their records. They were all committed members of the force with full service records. Maybe they were just cogs in the public service machine, doing their time, or maybe they were true believers in the Garda mission and system.[19]

By limiting their surveillance and policing to just two spots in the city, the vice squad demonstrated how commonly men were using the public conveniences of the city to meet sexual partners. Of course, Ireland's politicians

---

17. See Chapter 2, and also Conway, *Policing Twentieth Century Ireland*, 29; and McNiffe, *History of the Garda Síochána*, 20–45.

18. Denton, "Open Secrets," 148.

19. UCD, DMP general register, available at https://digital.ucd.ie/view-media/ucdlib:53467/canvas/ucdlib:53728.

and agents of the justice system had been concerned about that very thing for decades. Most queer men used the lavs *only* to meet. After the almost ritualistic exchange of signals and conversation that opened the door for sex, the most careful men left the lavs and went to find more private spaces for their dalliance. Others were less careful. Garda Fred Ryan described one such episode.

> [Henry Percival Pollard] stood at a cubicle + took out his penis + proceeded to pull it up + down with his hand for about 3 minutes or so. He then left the urinal + in approximately 20 minutes I again saw him enter + did the same thing as before for about 3 minutes. He again left the urinal. He went + stood in the second cubicle from Butt Bridge. He took out his penis + was pulling it up + down with his hand for about 3 minutes.

Shortly after Henry Pollard's third return to the urinal, another man, Thomas Hughes entered and stood in the fourth cubicle. The second man also took out his penis, and, rather than urinate, "was pulling it up + down with his hand for 2 or 3 minutes." The two men then spoke to each other. Following their conversation the second man turned to the first and displayed his erect penis. The first man responded immediately, stepping into the urinal stall with the second man, and "grasped [the second man's] penis in his hand. He pulled it up + down for a minute or so. He then bent down on one knee + I observed him put his mouth to [the second man's] penis for about a minute."[20]

Fred Ryan observed all of this alongside his watch partner for the evening, William Fennessey. They were perched, quite literally, on the Loopline Bridge overlooking Beresford Place. The Loopline is not a pedestrian or even automobile bridge. Rather, it's a bridge suspended some forty feet above the ground and serves a rail line that crosses the River Liffey over Butt Bridge and joins services at Connolly Station. It's not the sort of bridge where you might comfortably lean over the edge and watch the passersby below. As you can see from Figure 6.1, the railway bridge was girded by crosshatched steel barricades. The gardaí who took a position on the Loopline Bridge were lying across the tracks and hanging their heads over the edge to peer into the top of the Beresford Place lavatory below.

Ryan and Fennessey had clamored up onto the bridge just after dark on that August evening, probably around 9:00 P.M. or so, with the goal of monitoring the men who stopped at the urinal on their way home from the pubs.

---

20. NAI, Dublin Circuit Court, State Files, V14-30-27, docket 4, 10-Oct-1950, Deposition of Garda Frederick Ryan. Notably these two were arrested in the summer of 1950, but their trial got pushed back twice, and they weren't actually tried until January 1951.

Figure 6.1 View in 1917 of the Loopline Railway Bridge from Beresford Place. *(Keogh Brothers, call number 177. Reproduced courtesy of the National Library of Ireland.)*

Though months of stakeouts at this very spot might've desensitized Ryan and Fennessey to the sight of men touching each other, no other gardaí had witnessed fellatio that summer. I wonder what Ryan and Fennessey were thinking and feeling in that moment. Did they look at each other, wide-eyed, in surprise? Did they have to suppress laughter or scoffs of disgust? Did they carefully *not* look at each other? Did the sight thrill them, turn their stomachs, or a little of both? Or were they so disciplined that even the unusual sight of one man taking another's erection in his mouth didn't phase them in the least? On the stand, giving testimony against Pollard and Hughes, neither Ryan nor Fennessey gave any indication of their interiority. Each stuck to the detached formula of their testimonies throughout the October and January circuit court sessions.

It was 11:30 P.M. in the evening. Despite the bold turn of their encounter in the lav, Pollard and Hughes weren't planning to finish there in the exposed stall where any drunk (or garda) might turn up. Clearly interested in pursuing their sexual chemistry to its logical conclusion, they spoke quietly to each other, making plans as they buttoned up their trousers and made to leave. Ryan was again "unable to hear the conversation" in the stall below, but he "signaled by means of a flash lamp to [the four gardaí in the street below]." Pollard and Hughes left the urinal together, heading in the direction of Butt Bridge. Four gardaí, a short distance down the street, intercepted them. Both men were arrested, taken to a Garda station, and charged. Because of testimony provided by the six gardaí, both were found guilty and sentenced to six months imprisonment with hard labor.[21]

The policing of public same-sex sex in Dublin reached its crescendo in the summer of 1950 under the efforts of these seven gardaí. After its establishment in 1922, the concern with gross indecency by the Dublin metropolitan Garda was limited to brief, sporadic campaigns of concentrated policing, as shown in Table 1.1. Significantly, though, of nearly 300 arrests made for sex between men and a partner aged fifteen plus, 271 were before 1951. From 1952 to 1972, only twenty-four men were prosecuted for gross indecency crimes, and of those twenty-four, ten were found not guilty or cases thrown out, and four of those found guilty were allowed to pay a fine and keep the peace.[22] Efforts to police same-sex sex in Dublin were inconsistent, but there were brief surges in policing activity.

Under O'Duffy, the gardaí experimented with various active policing tactics to determine the best and safest (morally) methods for policing sex between men. By 1950, surveillance had long been identified as the best option of a lot of bad options. Over the course of the 1940s, the Garda was also modernized and developed into a force that looked quite different even from the original "police force for the people" founded back in 1922. Cars and motorcycles, a photography unit, and the use of expert witnesses, like doctors, were standardized by 1950. When it came to policing sex, procedure was also a tool that—when used appropriately, when gardaí didn't go off script—was particularly effective, as in the summer cases from 1950.

Still, there was a fine line between garda and offender, even with the physical distance of a suspended bridge or a lav attendant booth separating the two. While using their own bodies as bait was absolutely out of bounds by then, there were times when even observing and reporting were called into question. With a good solicitor, a man charged with gross indecency based on a police observation could potentially challenge the validity of a garda's testimony, calling into question their motivations and methods. While the vice squad of 1950 developed a procedure for the streets and courtroom that proved effective, not all gardaí in the DMD were as savvy.

---

21. NAI, Dublin Circuit Court, State Files, V14-30-27, docket 4, 10-Oct-1950, Deposition of Garda Frederick Ryan.

22. Men were still at risk of arrest for consensual sex between two adults until 1993. According to Chrystel Hug, between 1962 and 1972 (for all of Ireland), there were 455 convictions of men for crimes of gross indecency with males, and 342 of those convicted were over the age of twenty-one. See Hug, *The Politics of Sexual Morality in Ireland*, 207–211.

In cities, police have been part of the urban sexual landscape since their invention in the nineteenth century.[23] Studies of cities like London and Toronto provide models for how to look at and contextualize the DMD's policing of sex between men. Dublin is difficult to compare to London simply because there were not as many police (one thousand[24] vs. twenty thousand), not as many people (six hundred thousand vs. eight million), and a much smaller area (about 44 sq. mi. vs. over 600 sq. mi.), respectively.[25] Similarly, Toronto is considerably larger than Dublin; its 1950 population was over one million, the area of the city was over 200 sq. mi., and the police force had sufficient resources to devote to a dedicated "Morality Department" that targeted same-sex-desiring men, prostitutes, and others perceived as morally dangerous.[26] With larger populations and police forces, there are many more resources for the examination of the policing of same-sex sex in London and Toronto. However, proportionally, the numbers are quite comparable. For example, historian Matt Houlbrook identifies the year in which the most arrests occurred in London (1947: 637 cases). In comparison, the year in which the most arrests occurred in Dublin (1950: 54 cases) shows that this equals eight arrests in London and nine in Dublin per one hundred thousand residents.[27] Houlbrook shows that in London police developed knowledge of the where and when of same-sex sexual activity—from the ever popular urinal to the Turkish bathhouses, basement lounges, pubs, cafés, and more—in order to surveil those spaces.[28] They dressed in plainclothes (and sometimes women's clothes and makeup) to infiltrate drag balls and gatherings of same-sex-desiring men. Some used their bodies to bait same-sex-desiring men into offenses deemed grossly indecent.[29] Similarly, using court records from 1890 to 1930, Steven Maynard examines the ways that gross indecency offenders and the men who arrested them in Toronto identified the queer spaces of the city and "furnished information on the social characteristics of the men who participated in the

---

23. Maynard, "Through a Hole in the Lavatory Wall," 207–242; and Houlbrook, *Queer London.*

24. This is an estimate. There were only seventy-five hundred gardaí for all of Ireland in 1950 (Conway, *Policing Twentieth Century Ireland,* 104), and McNiffe notes that there were one thousand men in the DMP force in 1890 and that the gardaí actually operated with fewer officers in 1925 than the DMP and RIC had before the War of Independence.

25. London police statistics: Clive Emsley, *The English Police* (New York: St. Martin's Press, 1991), 186. These numbers are for 1950. Also, for a discussion of Dublin as a queer urban space, see Chapter 2 of this book.

26. Maynard, "Through a Hole in the Lavatory Wall."

27. Ferriter, O'Malley, and Hug do not consider the policemen specifically as part of the same-sex-desiring world, although they all employ court records in their discussions of same-sex desire prior to 1965.

28. Houlbrook, *Queer London,* 23–25.

29. Houlbrook, 27–29.

homosexual subculture."[30] In both London and Toronto, the expansion of vice policing coincided with the modernization of their respective police forces. While Ireland's Garda was generally and slightly behind the modernization curve, the DMD pursued parallel tactics, courtroom spectacles, and trends as those in larger cities.

Gardaí recruitment was a topic in the Dáil that was "among the traditional inspirers of lively interest—and possible frayed tempers."[31] In particular, there were long discussions about the recruitment process, who was being recruited, if and when a new recruitment cycle would begin, and problems with the requirements for new recruits. From 1935 to 1948, recruitment for the Garda was suspended. In 1938, 1942, and 1943 there were rumors of recruitment starting, but those were just rumors, leaving "hopes of young men all over Ireland dashed."[32] There was a recruitment cycle in 1947, which added two hundred candidates to the list to fill open positions as they became available.[33] Recruitment reopened again briefly in February 1948 but was stopped in March, which prompted some anxiety in places like Dublin. Dublin experienced a "crime wave" in 1948, and the gardaí felt that the work they were doing—which included administrative tasks from the compilation of agricultural statistics to the delivery of old-age pension books in addition to their regular policing duties—far exceeded their force strength, and, in some cases, capabilities.[34] The annual recruits were generally expected to replenish the two hundred or so who retired every year, but, due to budgetary constraints, the government decided to halt new recruitment, which became particularly problematic in the early 1950s.[35]

The need predicted by the *Irish Press* in 1948 came about in 1952, when hundreds of gardaí, who had joined the force at its inception, reached their full thirty-year service commitment and began retiring in droves. A 1952 recruitment ad was criticized because it did not communicate what work was done by "Eire's clerical police force," and the members of the Dáil and the public challenged the stagnated recruitment tactics:

> It was announced some days ago that 250 recruits are to be sought for the Garda Síochána. It would appear from the announcement that no improvement is being made into the method of selection or in the standard of education required. . . . It is significant while the official advertisement gives precise details of the height and chest measure-

30. Maynard, "Through a Hole in the Lavatory Wall," 209.
31. "Garda Sichoana," *Connacht Sentinel*, 13 May 1952, 2.
32. "Eire's Clerical Police Force," *Connacht Tribune*, 16 April 1938, 18.
33. "Government Notices," *Irish Press*, 16 December 1943, 2.
34. "Anxiety about Ban on Gardai Recruiting," *Irish Press*, 15 March 1948.
35. "Recruiting for Garda Is Stopped," *Irish Press*, 13 March 1948, 1.

ments demanded of aspirants it contains no indication as to what subjects figure in the qualifying examination of the "selected candidates." . . . In every other walk of life the tendency has been to require higher standard of education. Those who control the Irish police force seem to be satisfied that inches count for more than intellect. This is grossly unfair to men who under modern conditions have much more complex and delicate duties than controlling crowds after a football match.[36]

The recruitment ad itself had changed little in thirty years. The major requirements continued to demand that applicants be "unmarried and of good character," between nineteen and twenty-three years of age, meet the chest and height measurement requirements, and be in "good health, of sound constitution, and fitted physically and mentally to perform the duties of a member of the force."[37]

When the 1952 and 1953 calls failed to drum up the desired number of recruits—in 1953 alone, the Garda expected to take five hundred new recruits—the age cap was changed to twenty-five.[38] For the first substantial recruitment effort since, really, the early 1930s, when Fianna Fáil sought to pack the force with loyal policemen, the recruitment ad was woefully inadequate for the modern police force. The emphasis was still on "character" (subtext: Christian, preferably Catholic, and loyal to the party in power), physical ability, youth, and bachelordom/unattachedness. Critics wondered why there was not a demand for applicants with Leaving Certificates from secondary school or even college educations. The duties of gardaí in 1950 differed greatly from those of gardaí in the 1920s or even 1930s. Political violence was no longer a part of everyday life in the Republic, and the gardaí of 1950 were more civil servants than keepers of the peace. Critics found the continued use of an ad not much changed since 1922 unacceptable.[39]

Conversely, while there were criticisms of how men were recruited, for the most part, the opinion of the gardaí themselves was positive in Ireland. Most gardaí walked the beat, which gave them an intimate and detailed knowledge of the areas they patrolled.[40] Their closeness with the community also augmented the positive public opinion of the gardaí, as revealed in letters to the editor between 1923 and 1955.[41]

36. "Recruiting Gardai," *Irish Independent*, 1 February 1952, 4.
37. "Government Notices," 4.
38. "Recruiting for Garda Síochána," *Irish Independent*, 17 September 1953, 4.
39. Conway, *Policing Twentieth Century Ireland*, 79–90.
40. Conway, 38, 58.
41. These statistics are calculated from 125 op-ed articles in which "Garda" and "Sir" were mentioned between 1922 and 1955. "Sir" is how letters to the editor begin in Irish newspapers.

Letter writers frequently praised the force. A 1937 letter criticized the government for not issuing a practical response to the gardaí pay claims, calling the Garda a "fine body of policemen."[42] In 1949, a laborer of the Dublin Corporation agreed that the Garda was a "body of splendid men."[43] In particular, in the early 1950s, there were a series of letters criticizing the government for denying officers who served before 1950 the new pension benefits passed in 1952.[44] In letters to the editor mentioning "Garda" from 1926 to 1953, only 8 percent were criticisms of the Garda, and 20 percent were not commentaries on the Garda at all but rather mentioned them tangentially. The remaining 72 percent were positive reflections or commentaries on the work the Garda was doing, or appeals to the Garda to do even more, such as requests that gardaí begin doing traffic patrols in the 1950s. Letters to the editor reflected a general public approval of the Garda. While the RIC had been resented by the Catholic population for its perceived (and actual) role as an arm of British control of Ireland, the Garda was Ireland's police force. This was an identity that the leaders of the Garda worked to forge; as O'Duffy wrote in 1922, "You [Ireland] now have a police force of your own, who are not out to force law and order down your throat with a gun like their predecessors, but to cooperate with you in the protection of life and property."[45] That positive relationship was further entrenched during World War II (the Emergency).

Though Ireland was officially neutral during the war, a position that reflected the continued tension between Britain and Ireland and de Valera's leadership, the war still impacted Irish lives. Rogue bombs, German POWs, and the significant contingent of Irish soldiers who volunteered to serve in the British military were reminders of the violence tearing Europe apart. Though the Irish government suppressed the magnitude of the war in the press through censorship laws, the 1940s were certainly not peacetime in neutral Ireland.[46] Bomb and air raid shelters were integrated into Dubliner life—several of the men charged with gross indecency utilized the raid shelters for sexual liaisons—and the Garda was essential in organizing volunteers and overseeing the protection of their communities. This too brought the gardaí into close contact with their citizenry and created a positive opinion of the organization.[47]

---

42. "Garda Pay Claims," *Irish Independent*, 17 December 1937, 12.

43. "Questions of Pay," *Sunday Independent*, 16 January 1949, 6.

44. "Our National Police Force," *Irish Examiner*, 10 December 1952, 6.

45. "General O'Duffy's Speech," *Irish Independent*, 20 November 1922, 5.

46. For a discussion of the success of wartime censorship in Ireland, see Donal Ó Disceoil, *Censorship in Ireland 1939–1945: Neutrality, Politics, and Society* (Cork: Cork University Press, 1996).

47. Conway, *Policing Twentieth Century Ireland*, 59.

These positive opinions of the Garda worked to their advantage, particularly as there was the potential for negative reception of any police force after the experience of colonialism. The rebranding of policing and the insistence that the gardaí embody masculine ideals were central to the development of the force and its reception by the public. As Conway argues:

> Members of an Garda Síochána were pioneers, sportsmen, devout Catholics, Irish speakers and educated. These were values that had been suppressed under British rule but which would be celebrated and promoted in independent Ireland. These efforts are evident in the earliest days of the force and in time they contributed to engendering an intense national pride and confidence in the police.[48]

The pride in the Garda is evidenced in op-eds from the 1920s through the mid-1940s, after which the caliber of articles changed. It is much easier to find criticisms of the Garda after 1949.

In the 1920s and 1930s, tactics were unorganized, seemingly random, and produced varying results in the courtroom. Despite this, it was in the 1920s that the Irish gardaí first testified that their pursuit of an individual suspected of grossly indecent behavior was encouraged or initiated because of "special instructions" or "special duty," presumably passed down from their superior officers. Particularly between 1924 and 1936, the tasks of that "special duty" included stakeouts of public conveniences, following men deemed suspicious because they spent too much time in and around public lavatories and dressing in plainclothes and attempting to entice men into illegal sexual liaisons. By the summer of 1950, gardaí testimonies reflect an emphasis on a clear physical distance between the offender and the officer. Enticement tactics appear to have been abandoned, and gardaí did not dedicate much effort to following suspects around the city—there are no testimonies outlining those particular tactics after 1944.

Instead, the lessons of the 1920s and 1930s were adapted into a procedural approach to finding and catching same-sex-desiring men in action. The seven gardaí discussed at the start of this chapter relied exclusively on the stakeout of public conveniences, which were well suited to concealing the watching gardaí. This was the best tactic for maintaining distance between the officer and offender, for observing the damning sexual activity, and for conveying that distance was maintained even while the gardaí gathered evidence for the judge and jury. None of these tactics were unique to Ireland. Between 1890 and 1930, the Toronto "Morality Department" included police and park rangers sworn in as "special constables" who patrolled public spaces under the auspices of that

---

48. Conway, 210.

institution.[49] Maynard discusses the "technology of surveillance," which developed in that period to enable the special constables to police same-sex-desiring men, including platforms constructed outside lavatory buildings for peering into holes, the introduction of hand lamps to the police force for revealing illicit sexual activity, and photography for documenting crime scenes and offenders.[50]

Policing same-sex desire in any sort of tactical way came much later to Dublin than to Toronto or London and coincided with what Conway calls the "move towards modernization" of the Garda.[51] In particular, the use of the technologies of surveillance, tools such as hand lamps, a Photography Division, and patrol cars, became more common between 1930 and 1950 and were essential to the observation and prosecution of same-sex sex offenses. Hand lamps were used to reveal illicit behavior in dark alleys and parks, but, in the case of the surveillance of the Beresford Place lavatory, they were more important as signaling tools. Even in the 1950s, the Dublin gardaí did not have walkie-talkies or other means of wireless communication, which limited the ease with which several gardaí could spread over an area. Thus, when Detectives Ryan and Fennessey sat atop the Loopline Bridge peering down into the already well-lit urinal of Beresford Place and observed individuals they identified as gross indecency offenders, they could not radio their colleagues who were scattered about the street below, leaning on lampposts or sitting in doorways. Nor did they want to shout to those colleagues and give away their position, which proved so fruitful in their crackdown on gross indecency that summer. Instead they used their hand lamps to signal to their colleagues on the ground that the men exiting the lavatory were offenders.

Most gardaí walked their patrols, largely because there simply were not many vehicles to go around, and there were stations in walking distance of just about anywhere in Dublin. Though Dublin had more patrol cars than any other city in Ireland, they were still few and not regularly in use in the 1930s and 1940s. In 1945, the Dublin force had a total of thirty-eight vehicles (motorcycles and cars).[52] When a vehicle was involved in a case of gross indecency, the offenders were usually stumbled upon at random in a dark alleyway or when a garda decided to stop and check a public lavatory on a regular patrol route. Gardaí developed a familiarity with the city streets while walking the beat, which was invaluable to their knowledge of popular sex spots like the

---

49. Maynard, "Through a Hole in the Lavatory Wall," 222–223.

50. Similarly in West Germany at this time police started installing two-way mirrors in public bathrooms to observe and catch men engaging in "indecent" sexual behavior in the stalls. W. Jake Newsome, *Pink Triangle Legacies: Coming Out in the Shadow of the Holocaust* (Cornell: Cornell University Press, 2022).

51. Conway, *Policing Twentieth Century Ireland*, 62–63.

52. Conway, 62.

Figure 6.2 Beresford Place lavatory, view from the street. *(National Archives of Ireland, State Files, Dublin Circuit Courts, 1D-28-123, photograph taken by D/Sergeant M. Wall, Photographic Division, Garda Headquarters, Kilmainham. Reproduced by kind permission of the Director of the National Archives.)*

Beresford Place lav, the various nooks and crannies of Phoenix Park or St. Stephen's Green, and the neighborhoods like Monto that were associated with prostitution.[53]

The introduction of a Photography Division changed the way gardaí could paint a picture for a listening jury. It provided the imagery of crime scenes, like Figures 6.2, 6.3, and 6.4. The gardaí testimonies referenced these images. They were used to prove that the area was well lit and that the interior of the lavatory was fully visible to the gardaí perched on the bridge overlooking it (Figure 6.3).

The images of views from the street (Figures 6.2 and 6.4) both situated the scene of the crime in the minds of the judge and jury and suggested how indecently these men were behaving, engaging in sex acts in spaces where they could easily be seen by other good, respectable Irish people coming and going from the public convenience. These were never photographs of the defendants themselves but, rather, the landscape in which the alleged crime took place. With an image of the lighting of the interior of the lav, a garda could assure the jury that, indeed, he could clearly see the people in the cubicles below. It was a nonhuman corroboration of a human testimony.

---

53. Denton, "Open Secrets."

Figure 6.3 Beresford Place public convenience, photograph of the fluorescent light that illuminates the interior of the urinal. *(National Archives of Ireland, State Files, Dublin Circuit Courts, 1D-28-123, photograph taken by D/Sergeant M. Wall, Photographic Division, Garda Headquarters, Kilmainham. Reproduced by kind permission of the Director of the National Archives.)*

Figure 6.4 View of the Loopline Bridge and Beresford Place public convenience from across the street. *(National Archives of Ireland, State Files, Dublin Circuit Courts, 1D-28-123, photograph taken by D/Sergeant M. Wall, Photographic Division, Garda Headquarters, Kilmainham. Reproduced by kind permission of the Director of the National Archives.)*

A different but also significant aspect of the modernization of the force was the addition of specialists, including doctors and pathologists, who were paid by the state to support the efforts of the police and evidence collection. Doctors were not utilized as witnesses with any sort of regularity in the pursuance of gross indecency cases, but they were used far more in the 1940s and 1950s—again, when Conway identifies the "modernization" of the force—than in the 1920s or 1930s. As early as 1947, there were several doctors on retainer for police investigations, including Dr. John Ryan, Dr. Francis Burke, and Dr. Sean Lavan. Generally, a doctor's evidence carried considerable weight. However, in 1953, the Irish Supreme Court found that for a doctor's evidence to be admissible in court the defendant needed to agree to an examination, a condition that was not met in a case of a drunk driver in that year.[54]

By the 1940s, men arrested for gross indecency offenses or sodomy were given the option to be examined by a doctor. In cases where legal minors were involved, the doctor was also often called in to examine the victim of sexual assaults.[55] Presumably, a man like Henry Keown, who submitted to that medical exam, thought that there would be no physical signs of their same-sex desire or activity. When Lavan examined Keown and eighteen-year-old Peter Harte, he searched their bodies for physical "signs" of sexual activity. Lavan found no "irritation around the anus" and testified, "It seemed to have been . . . normal in my opinion in the sphincter," with "no evidence of any lubricant." But when Lavan examined the penis, he found that it was moist, there appeared to be "abrasions in the corona on the dorsum"—redness on the tip of the penis—although there was no blood left on the swab he used. Lavan thought it important to note that, in the course of the examination, Keown's penis became erect because of the "manipulation" of the examination ("phinosis or swelling appeared at the end of my manipulation which was not present when I examined him at first.") Lavan concluded that there appeared to have been a "recent emission of semen from the penis . . . within a few hours." Lavan also examined Harte, with many of the same findings, and collected Harte's clothing, which had, by his estimation, seminal stains on them, and sent them to the pathologist. According to Lavan, Harte's anus "was normal," and, in fact, "there was nothing abnormal about that boy at all. The stains on his clothes were an abnormality but I couldn't say that they were a recent abnormality."[56]

54. "Garda Officer's Appeal Struck Out," *Irish Independent*, 28 November 1953, 12.

55. NAI, Dublin Circuit Court, State Files, 1C-90-35, docket 46, 10-Oct-1950, the State v. Constantin Kyriacco, Deposition of Dr. John M. Ryan.

56. NAI, Dublin Circuit Court, State Files, 1D-28-76, docket 18, 3-Jun-1947, the State v. Henry Keown and Peter Harte.

In all of the court records and newspaper articles about gross indecency cases I consulted for this book, this is the first instance of anyone referring to an individual in a sex crime as "normal" or "abnormal." Judges, police men, and witnesses in cases talk about same-sex sex in the terms of vice, sin, or abominations. Same-sex desire was, in other words, still a biblical issue, and policing it was an extension of the independent state's obsession with presenting as Catholic. The lack of a major psychiatry movement in Ireland stagnated the spread of the language of normality and abnormality. The doctor's classification of Harte reflects a shift, at least in the medical profession, in conceptualizations of sexuality in 1940s Ireland.

The use of the medical language to describe the anatomical condition of these male bodies created a professional barrier between Lavan himself and these two men accused of gross indecency. Further, Lavan's testimony provided evidence that, on the one hand, anal sex had not occurred, but, on the other hand, there were signs to suggest that the two men were involved in activity that created seminal stains on Harte's clothing and produced (seminal) moisture on Keown's penis. Further, Keown's apparent arousal at being handled by the doctor was important enough for Lavan to take note. In an attempt to turn Dr. Lavan's testimony against him, Keown's attorney pursued a line of cross-examination. The solicitor asked if Lavan had inserted his fingers into Keown in a rectal exam; the doctor had not. Still, the defense attempted to suggest that Keown's bowels or Lavan's examination of Keown's anus had produced the moisture that Lavan found on Keown's penis. Ultimately, the doctor admitted that the moisture could have been the result of a strained prostate, and the pathologist's findings seemed to suggest that the sample collected had no spermatozoa. The doubts that Keown's lawyer cast on Lavan's testimony were sufficient to undermine the case against him, leaving the jury undecided. But the "evidence" he found on Harte's body was enough to convict the boy of acts of gross indecency.[57]

A pathologist was also employed by the state and was at the disposal of the Garda as early as 1935.[58] Dr. John McGrath, who served in the Garda as the state pathologist, was expected to use his microscope to assist in criminal investigations. Upon his retirement in 1953, the *Sligo Champion* described McGrath as,

a man who gave evidence in virtually every Irish murder trial in the past twenty years. . . . A very unassuming man is Dr. McGrath, but he is a man whose meticulous attention to detail, his forensic skill and

57. The State v. Henry Keown and Peter Harte.
58. "Louth Poison Tragedy," *Irish Press*, 11 January 1935, 1.

his innate sense of justice made him one of the best-known figures in legal history.[59]

Though McGrath's talents were more frequently used in murder trials, there were two examples of his use in gross indecency cases. In both cases, he was asked to identify whether the stains on some clothing were seminal. In the Keown and Harte case, McGrath was also asked to examine under a microscope the swabs that Lavan took of the moisture on Keown and Harte's penises. In this case, McGrath found that Harte's clothing was covered in dry seminal stains, which he concluded were probably obtained in the hours before they were sent to his lab, but that the penis swabs were devoid of semen.[60]

The use of these "experts" was generally favorable. In the Keown/Harte case, only Harte was found guilty, likely because, per the doctor and the pathologist's testimony, there was no evidence of sexual emission anywhere on Keown, while there was on Harte. There were twenty-four gross indecency cases, about 10 percent of all cases between 1922 and 1972, in which a doctor or pathologist was employed in a criminal investigation. Of those consultations, 75 percent were between 1940 and 1972. Significantly, one-third of the cases involved victims under the age of fourteen. This suggests that when the gardaí wanted to pursue cases in which the primary witness was a child, the doctor was solicited to add a credible and "professional" witness to the case. In 86 percent of all the gross indecency cases in which a doctor or pathologist was consulted and testified as an expert witness, the doctor's findings matched the outcome of the case. This was true of 100 percent of the cases in which the other witness was a child; the doctor's expert opinion of whether a child had been "interfered with" was taken at face value, including in cases where the accused was found not guilty.[61] Though by no means regularly or consistently, these "experts" were used to lend credibility to or discredit witnesses and were part of the shaping of the legal definition of and procedures for policing gross indecency, as human and scientific manifestations of the technologies of surveillance.

The tactics of policing same-sex sex ranged from following suspicious characters, following up on tips (though these were rare, unless the sex crime involved a legal minor), staking out places suspected of sexual activity, or baiting men into making sexual propositions. The most common of these tactics was the stakeout, largely because a stakeout allowed the observing gardaí to

---

59. "Murder Trial Expert Retires," *Sligo Champion*, 20 June 1953, 4.

60. The State v. Henry Keown and Peter Harte.

61. NAI, Dublin Circuit Court, State Files, 1C-90-32, docket 56, 27-Apr-1926, the State v. John Nugent; and 1D-11-1117, docket 25, 10-Oct-1941, the State v. Michael White.

become the witnesses needed to secure a conviction. Although men were arrested (and convicted) for visiting public lavatories too frequently, for the most part convictions for gross indecency crimes between adult men were obtained through stakeouts.

Further, no matter how factual and impersonal the gardaí were when they served as "witnesses" to the alleged crime, the fact remained that they recounted graphic sexual testimonies in these cases; the formula of testimony that the gardaí gave still involved graphic descriptions of men engaged in intimate sexual acts. Juries found the testimonies of cops who baited highly problematic. Some were equally as uncomfortable with the descriptions of testimonies that inserted a garda, however distantly, into those intimate moments. Even if it were their job to do just that, the act of seeking out places where men had sex with other men was a moral gray zone. Numerous men—especially after 1951—were exonerated because of a garda's ill-planned or timed arrest. A single garda's testimony that he actively saw a man having sex with another man was not a formula for a conviction.

In the confessional of the courtroom, the Irish policemen were required to recount their viewing of gross indecency crimes to a listening judge and jury. By engaging directly and indirectly with the same-sex-desiring men who sought out sex in public spaces, gardaí danced a fine line between officer and offender. Their entanglement in that world required carefully negotiating their relationship to the loosely defined laws of gross indecency and to their roles as respectable Irish Catholic men. From the voyeurism of the stakeout to the eroticization and knowledge production of the courtroom testimony, the gardaí were immersed in the world they were instructed to stamp out. Though a procedural approach to the lav stakeout did not come until the summer of 1950, the Garda were aware of and attempting to police the illicit sex going on in public spaces in the early years of the force. The public lavatory became an easy and favored target. In 1931, 40 percent of all gross indecency arrests that year were around public lavatories. By 1950, 91 percent of the gross indecency arrests were men caught by gardaí concealed in and around public lavatories.

The stakeout procedure that the 1950 vice squad employed was clearly intended to create a distance, literal and figurative, between the officer and the offender. Unlike enticement or even the tailing of suspected offenders, the stakeout put barriers—the wall of an attendant's booth, or fifteen feet from the overhang of a bridge to the heads of men in the lav below—between the gardaí and the men they watched. The seven gardaí of 1950 built yet another buffer into their effort by rotating who took up that position each night they staked out Beresford Place. Watching was treacherous; how long was it before observation became voyeurism? One might imagine that the positions atop the Loopline Bridge or piled into a lav attendant's booth were fraught with anxiety, watching men stroke their penises to erection repeatedly throughout a night.

A few blocks west of O'Connell Street, the main thoroughfare in Dublin, Beresford Place intersects with Customs Quay on the River Liffey in two places. In 1950 on Beresford Place, across from the northwest corner of the Customs House, was an open-topped four-stall urinal.[62] The gardaí positioned themselves over that urinal with a clear view of the men who came and went. The urinal was "brightly lighted by one fluorescent light," and there was "a second fluorescent light which also shows light in the interior of the lavatory." Leaning over the edge of the railway bridge, the gardaí monitoring the activity below were about fifteen feet above the heads of the men visiting the urinal. As one garda said after a stakeout on the railway bridge, "I could see the penis of anyone in the lavatory quite plainly."[63]

The testimonies of the 1950 vice squad reflected the purpose and intent of the stakeout. The gardaí often indicated that watching the public lavatory was their primary objective. As Cullen noted, "I took up position immediately over the gents public urinal in Beresford Place."[64] Their intent to arrest same-sex-desiring men was clear. Almost all of the testimonies describe observing men masturbate in urinal stalls for upwards of fifteen minutes. Under the laws governing public conveniences, such behavior was itself criminal. But the gardaí waited for autostimulation to develop into fondling.

Gardaí, either in answering questions from the prosecution or in anticipating this possible defense, almost always included in their testimony whether the accused urinated. This established for the listening jury whether the visit to the lav was a "legitimate" one. As Garda Cullen testified, one man "entered the lavatory and. . . . took out his penis, did not urinate, but began rubbing it up and down, until it was in a state of erection and he kept looking at other people who were using the urinals while he was doing this."[65] When accused of visiting too many lavatories—and revisiting too many lavatories—in the course of an evening, another man was arrested but denied "the charges on the grounds that" he was "suffering from kidney and bladder

62. NAI, Dublin Circuit Court, State Files, V14-30-27, docket 4, 18-Jun-1951, the State v. Henry Percival Pollard and Thomas Hughes, Deposition of Garda Frederick Ryan.

63. NAI, Dublin Circuit Court, State Files, 1D-28-124, docket 18, 10-Oct-1950, the State v. Robert Brennan, Deposition of Garda Michael Byrne.

64. NAI, Dublin Circuit Court, State Files, 1D-28-123, docket 38, 10-Oct-1950, the State v. Samuel Jones and Christopher O'Connor, Deposition of Gd. James Cullen.

65. NAI, Dublin Circuit Court, State Files, 1D-28-123, docket 40, 10-Oct-1950, the State v. Richard Kelly and Michael O'Connor, Deposition of D./O James Cullen.

trouble."[66] The jury dismissed his claim of an overactive bladder. They saw his frequent lav visits as a penchant for the casual sex available in the public conveniences and found him guilty just for spending too much time in and around toilets.

The frank and descriptive testimonies given by the gardaí laid bare the erotic element of their police work. There was danger in haunting lavatories to catch men in the act. Detective Brendan Maher took the stand in the courtroom of the circuit court judge McCarthy on August 3, 1954. He was asked by the prosecution to recall the events of the previous evening, which resulted in the arrest of John Poynts and Joseph Gilligan. Maher obliged. In their patrol car, Maher and two other officers pulled up to the lavatory at Eden Quay. The lav at Eden Quay was a small, one-stall conical structure on the sidewalk overlooking the River Liffey. Maher and his colleagues were likely searching for gross indecency offenders leaving the pubs and haunting the lavs of the quays in the wee hours of the night. On the evening of August 2, 1953, Maher thought they were in luck.

> I opened the . . . door of the car and I looked in through the . . . bottom of the urinal. I saw a mans foot moving. I then got out of the car and . . . saw a man, whom I now know to be the deft. Joseph Gilligan, with his penis out. A gentleman in front of him and in the far cubicle, whom I now know to be the def John Poynts, and his right hand back handling Gilligan's penis. I watched them for about 2 minutes, I was . . . lying flat on the ground. I then got up and Gda. Halloran and myself lay on the ground watching them for about another minute.[67]

This testimony seems, in retrospect, much like that given in any of the gross indecency cases of the 1940s or 1950s. Two reputable gardaí gave testimony in court against two men seen fondling each other. There was even photographic evidence to set the scene for the jury. Yet Poynts and Gilligan were found not guilty. Maher was pushed in his testimony to explain his motivation, his procedure, where he lay on the ground, and why he stopped at the lavatory if he was in a patrol car. Unlike the task force of the summer of 1950, which established a procedure for observation and a formula for testimony, there were no clearly defined boundaries between the officers and the offenders in this case. Stopping at a random lavatory to lie on the ground and peer up at men engaged in sex acts was not readily accepted as reliable testimony.

---

66. NAI, Dublin Circuit Court, State Files, 1D-28-123, dockets 41 and 42, 10-Oct-1950, the State v. Patrick Seery and Phillip O'Connor, Statement of Patrick Seery.

67. NAI, Dublin Circuit Court, State Files, V15-14-20, docket 1, 1-Febr-1954, the State v. John Poynts.

After the high conviction rate of the arrests made over the summer of 1950, convictions became more difficult to obtain even as (or because) the number of men arrested declined. The ease with which juries seemed to be able to overlook the policeman-voyeur broke down. From 1924 to 1950, only 26 percent of the 296 men charged with gross indecency were able to evade conviction; from 1951 to 1972, 43 percent of 42 men were found not guilty or the case was thrown out. There was never a moment when a judge or jury questioned the veracity of a garda's testimony outright. Presiding over the case of Joseph Byrne in 1931, Judge Davitt stated that the evidence had only one possible outcome, a guilty verdict, because either the defendants were guilty or the court would have to charge the garda with perjury.[68] There are no records of cases being thrown out or overturned on the basis of a garda's perjury. Yet, cases where the gardaí provided testimony were not assured of a conviction. The success of the vice squad was in their systematic presentation of their evidence, as a clearly defined team of seven officers who worked formulaically together to identify and arrest gross indecency offenders. This was such a precipitous assignment that the gardaí in 1950 had a minimum of four but often six gardaí working on the stakeout of a single lavatory. Policing same-sex-desiring men left the gardaí vulnerable to association with such behavior. In 1950, the Garda seemed aware that extreme lengths were needed to create a starker division between the offender and the officer. Garda Maher failed to take extreme lengths to protect his testimony from scrutiny, and so his effort failed in 1954.

These peculiarly erotic courtroom testimonies reveal more than just the efforts to police same-sex-desiring men. The frank discussions of the mechanics, possibilities, and locations of same-sex sex from the gardaí quoted here, but also from defendants themselves when they took the stand, constructed knowledge and a discourse about same-sex desire. These testimonies also reveal that the gardaí were not infallible or fully removed from their involvement in the same-sex-desiring world, and great lengths were necessary to create an artificial boundary between offender and officer to lend greater credibility to a garda's testimony. In a state that created fear and ignorance of sex, even the police had to be wary of how they engaged in the queer world of Dublin.

There is no simple answer to explain the decline in both arrests and convictions for gross indecency or sodomy from 1952 to 1972. Perhaps policing shifted more permanently to less serious charges—loitering, disorderly conduct, and the like—because those lesser charges required less overall follow-through for the gardaí. Maybe state resources were redirected toward dealing with economic issues to stave off the waves of emigration, or emigration

---

68. "Grave Offences," *Irish Independent*, 25 April 1931, 6.

itself was a solution that same-sex-desiring men embraced in the 1950s. In the mid-1950s there was a massive shift in the Garda, with most of the men who were recruited directly after independence retiring and a new generation replacing them. For many young men in the 1950s, they felt that their only option in life was to either join the Garda, which would provide a steady (if menial) wage and pension, or emigrate.[69] Historians have called the 1950s the "lost generation" because four out of five people born in the 1930s emigrated in the 1950s. In 1958 alone, sixty thousand emigrated.[70] Particularly in the late 1950s, when the Wolfenden Commission Report was released and the British Parliament began the debates that would decriminalize homosexuality in 1967, men and women who sought to embrace sex, in general, and same-sex sex, specifically, would have found more welcoming social conditions beyond the Republic of Ireland.

Change abroad was not the only factor to chip away at social conditions in Ireland. The cracks in the dominance of the Catholic nationalist moral order appeared after the upset of the Mother and Child Scheme. In 1950, the minister for health Dr. Noel Browne led the introduction of a health care scheme to provide free health care to all mothers and their children. Resistance from private physicians and the Catholic hierarchy—which asserted that health care was the responsibility and right of the father according to Church doctrine—crushed the bill and resulted in Browne's resignation. The defeat of the Mother and Child Scheme was, at the time, both controversial and discussed as inappropriate interference of the Church in the affairs of government. Historian John Whyte, in particular, has identified this moment as the point in which state and church began to diverge, allowing for the "thaw" of the 1960s and major social change through the end of the twentieth century. Dissatisfaction with the rigid social and sexual regime of the church-state relationship may have trickled down to the Garda, with the impetus to uphold that Catholic nationalist ideal of sexual morality and masculinity disintegrating in the 1950s. Or it may reflect the disinterest of the new gardaí generation in policing sexual immorality, because the men recruited in that decade were not forged in the Catholic nationalist ideologies of the War of Independence and Civil War, nor were they signing up for the Garda to fulfill a sense of duty or honor. They were there to get a regular paycheck and a promise of retirement and pension.

Equally unclear from the existing records is what motivated the gardaí to embark on that campaign in 1950. In their courtroom testimonies the vice squad did not discuss why they were on the patrol that sought to identify and arrest "gross indecency" offenders. It is possible that they were hand-

---

69. Conway, *Policing Twentieth Century Ireland*, 78.
70. Ferriter, *Transformation of Ireland*, 463.

selected by their supervising officer, and the motivation was a simple matter of following orders, or that they believed they were upholding a sense of justice and righteousness, as dictated by the laws and ethos of the independent state for which they had fought in the War of Independence. In 1952, two-thirds of the force was made up of men who had joined before 1926 and were over forty-five years of age.[71] By the mid-1950s, over half of the force retired.[72] The men who replaced them had not taken part in the War of Independence or grown up in the tumultuous height of the nationalistic fervor that led to that conflict.

Conversely the vice squad were all pre-1950 enlistees, perhaps more committed to the original mission of the force, or at least the commissioners and taoiseachs they served. The sporadic but persistent policing of same-sex sex in the 1920s through the 1950s could be understood as a reflection of the Garda enforcing a Catholic nationalist conceptualization of appropriate masculinity. The decline over the course of the 1950s and 1960s in vice policing efforts makes sense with the loss of the Gardaí whose sense of duty and purpose was forged in the Republican struggle against British imperialism. That was particularly true of Byrne and Cusack, who joined under O'Duffy, but it was also true of the "newer" officers. All the vice squad members had been serving for at least a decade, and they were born and raised in the fiery postcolonial Republic.

Contextually, there are several plausible explanations for the 1950 vice squad's campaign. In 1950, the force was modernizing and experimenting with more efficient modes for policing sex.[73] The 1950 campaign may have been a demonstration of what concerted vice policing *could* look like with modern procedure and technology. In March of that year the Department of Justice also launched an inquiry to determine if the state could cut costs—and Garda positions—and continue to effectively police the country. The vice squad's work may have been their commanding officer's preemptive response to that threat: by demonstrating the resources needed to truly police vice in Dublin, the Garda actually needed *more* officers. Almost certainly the 1950 summer campaign was a strain on the resources of the DMD.

The policing campaigns in 1931 and 1950 may represent the efforts of the Garda leadership taking measures in both 1931 and 1950 to answer criticisms from Fianna Fáil, in 1931, and from the public, in 1950, about Garda efficiency, cost, and need.[74] If there was an ongoing ideological slant to the 1950 campaign, it was not preserved in the court records. The Garda commis-

71. McNiffe, *History of the Garda Síochána*, 159.

72. Conway, *Policing Twentieth Century Ireland*, 77.

73. "Dublin May Have Modern Police Contact Service," *Irish Independent*, 23 March 1948, 6.

74. See Chapter 1 for a discussion of 1931.

sioner from 1940 to 1953 was Michael Kinnane, a lifetime civil servant who took on the job in 1940 quite reluctantly.[75] But 1950 was a tense moment for the organization; recruitment had been suspended citing, again, economic concerns. After the gushing praise lauded on the gardaí during World War I, op-eds died down in the late 1940s, and there was talk in the Dáil of reducing the force.[76] In the mid-1950s, the Garda had to fight for an increase in pensions to meet living costs and for better working conditions, both causes which were supported—and largely resolved positively for the gardaí—by the Catholic hierarchy. Archbishop McQuaid's hand may have been in the brief but significant spike in policing same-sex sex in the summer of 1950. Though there are few records of McQuaid's thoughts or ideas about same-sex desire, there was a single missive in the 1950s that indicated he was, at the very least, concerned with the presence of sex between men in Ireland.[77]

The answer may also be in the unrecorded conversations between the Garda leadership, the discarded records of what "special duty" meant and how particular gardaí were selected for it. Some answers may never find their way out of the past. Similarly, the official or underlying causes of the decline in policing and convicting gross indecency over the course of the 1950s are not to be found in the records of the NAI. Yet the contextual conditions surrounding the Garda institution and Irish society after the 1950s are indicative of reluctance by both gardaí and juries to employ or accept tactics so morally questionable. The potential and actual danger of policing same-sex desire was evidenced in the rejection and refinement of tactics for surveillance from independence until the peak of policing in the summer of 1950. Even the distanced participation of watching sex between men was just a bit too erotic. Like any witness in a gross indecency case, they had to present themselves carefully in the court lest they be implicated by their role in these cases.

75. Allen, *Garda Síochána*, 134.
76. "Gardai Force May Be Reduced," *Leinster Express*, 12 February 1949, 4; "Sharp Cut in Garda Strength Is Expected," *Irish Press*, 5 February 1949, 11.
77. Ferriter, *Occasions of Sin*, 223–224.

7

The Lovers

In 1928, two English men cofounded the Gate Theatre Company in Dublin.[1] According to Éibhear Walshe, Alfred Willmore made his way to Ireland because he was fleeing either military conscription or a wealthy older lover, or both.[2] Whatever his motivations, when he returned, Willmore adopted an Irish identity and accent, started telling people he was born in Cork, and Gaelicized his name. "Alfred Lee Willmore" became Micheál Mac Liammóir. Mac Liammóir met Hilton Robert Hugh Edwards when the two were in the same traveling theater company, and their connection must have been instantaneous. When Edwards fell ill, Mac Liammóir elected to stay behind with him when the rest of the company moved on to the next city.[3] Edwards didn't change his name, but he also became, in a way, Irish. Certainly, by the end of their lives and successful careers, Ireland had adopted both as its own. Together Mac Liammóir and Edwards elevated Irish-language theater, often with Mac Liammóir writing and starring in productions, and Edwards directing. A former Irish president, the taoiseach, and several members of parliament attended Mac Liammóir's funeral in 1978.[4] They were Irish celebrities in their time: Mac Liammóir handsome and campy, and Edwards a

---

1. With two colleagues: Daisy Bannard Cogley, an Irish-French actress, and Gearóid Ó Lochlainn, an Irish actor.
2. Walshe, "Importance of Staging Oscar Wilde," 217–230.
3. Fitz-Simon, *The Boys*, 49, 266.
4. Fitz-Simon, 301.

bit dourer in comparison but just as charismatic. They lived, as Walshe put it, as "Ireland's only openly gay couple" before 1973.[5] They fell in love in their twenties and spent the rest of their lives together. Their biographers have chronicled their impressive careers as leaders in the Irish theater, acknowledged their partnership as more than business, and even noted the rumors and affairs with other men in their time together; despite having access to their full correspondences and estates, however, none have focused on the intimate, beautiful, and moving love the two shared.[6]

For fifty years Mac Liammóir and Edwards were leaders in Irish theater, and more importantly, they were partners. Publicly and without reservation, they were business partners. For his seventieth birthday in October 1969, Mac Liammóir joined Gay Byrne on the popular Raidió Teilifís Éireann (RTÉ) program *The Late Late Show*. When Byrne asked Mac Liammóir for his reaction to the recorded well-wishes and exaltations of his career that *The Late Late Show* prepared for the occasion, Mac Liammóir gave a mock look of primness. "Exquisitely embarrassed," Mac Liammóir quipped, "And I think it had all the charm of a great work of fiction. I only wished my partner had heard it. Oh, I'm delighted he didn't, because life at home would have been unbearable, 'oh, that Late Late Show has made you even more impossible!'"[7] What did the Irish viewers that night think about Mac Liammóir's reference to life at home with his partner? When Mac Liammóir spoke of Edwards, he offered up a glimpse into their domesticity. By 1969, the two had, indeed, been joined in both love and creative partnership for over four decades. They lived together, with two Siamese cats completing their little family, on Harcourt Terrace in a posh Georgian area of south Dublin. Mac Liammóir spoke of Edwards as one would of a spouse.

When Judge Cahir Davitt commented that "vice" seemed to be spreading in the city in 1931, he echoed the broader state concerns about the visibility of sex in Ireland and how that undermined the postcolonial moral project.[8] Eradicating the visibility of sex, generally, and queerness, specifically, guided the efforts of the Garda in dealing with sex workers and cruising men. The culture of containment encouraged families to send their daughters to

5. Walshe, "Importance of Staging Oscar Wilde," 218.

6. Fitz-Simon, in *The Boys*, is open about their relationship (and their affairs with various other men), but he almost always quoted from the least interesting parts of their letters, leaving out the parts that evidenced their love and affection; even Éibhear Walshe's brief piece on them takes their relationship as a given without exploring the sweet and enduring love of Mac Liammóir and Edwards, parallel though it ran to their theater careers. For two men who defied the publicly acceptable in their self-representations to the world, exploring the evidence of their love both in public and private is essential.

7. RTE Archives, Micheál Mac Liammóir on *The Late Late Show* (1969), available at https://www.rte.ie/archives/2013/0306/374380-michael-mac-liammoire-an-irishman-from-london/.

8. "Vice Prevalent in Dublin," *Irish Times*, 13 February 1931, 13.

Mother and Baby Homes and Magdalene laundries, and to ignore or discipline children who tried to speak up about priest sexual abuse.[9] The state and church did not take any actions or encourage the kind of social change that would address teen pregnancy, unsafe public sex practices, or sexual abuse; the modus operandi was instead hide, suppress, and silence. The collective memory in the first four decades of Irish independence, explored in the work of the sociologists Tom Inglis and Paul Ryan as well as historians like Roy Foster, Diarmaid Ferriter, and Mary Daly, was of sexual repression, violent homophobia, and crushing misogyny.[10]

How, then, to account for the likes of Mac Liammóir and Edwards' ability to live openly in a long-term same-sex relationship? Some might argue that their profession was a safe space for visible queerness. Inglis suggests, "They were part of an esoteric, artistic, and urban literary élite, they did not pose a threat to the Catholic Church's monopoly over morality."[11] But as Walshe has argued, Mac Liammóir and Edwards actually grew quite careful with their mobilization of queerness on stage. Though they launched the Gate Theatre with productions of Oscar Wilde plays, fully aware of what association with Wilde would mean in 1930s Ireland, by the 1960s, they'd gone to great lengths to dehomosexualize Wilde's name and legacy.[12] Though the theater was a significant space for queer community building prior to 1973, it was the socioeconomic class they constructed around themselves, as bourgeoisie bachelors, that protected Edwards and Mac Liammóir from censure and state violence.

When they arrived in Ireland, both Mac Liammóir and Edwards came from modest means. Mac Liammóir was middle class, though, as their biographer Christopher Fitz-Simon notes, perhaps on the lower end of the middle class.[13] He was the son of a forage-buyer and lived in a decent neighborhood in Kensal Green, London. He didn't bother with college, as he and his sister started acting young and he never stopped. Hilton Edwards's journey was a bit more complicated. His father worked for the government in India, he had an ayah as a boy and lived with his nurse on an estate called Nether-

9. For a discussion of the cultural "architecture of containment," see Smith, *Ireland's Magdalen Laundries*; for a brief history of priest sexual abuse in Ireland, see Averill Earls, "The Catholic Church and Child Sexual Abuse in Twentieth-Century Ireland," *Notches Blog*, 14 July 2016, available at https://notchesblog.com/2016/07/14/who-knew-catholic-institutional-power-and-child-sexual-abuse-in-twentieth-century-ireland/; and the recent oral history project at Queen's University Belfast investigating the Mother and Baby Homes and Magdalene laundries, available at https://quote.qub.ac.uk/mother-and-baby-homes-and-magdalene-laundries-oral-history-project/.

10. Ryan, *Asking Angela MacNamara*; Inglis, *Moral Monopoly*; R. Foster, *Modern Ireland*; Ferriter, *Occasions of Sin*; Daly, *Battle to Control Female Fertility*.

11. Inglis, "Origins and Legacies of Irish Prudery," 21–22.

12. Walshe, "Importance of Staging Oscar Wilde," 223–227.

13. Fitz-Simon, *The Boys*, 22.

woods until he was seven. That was when his father died suddenly while in Agra, India; his mother returned to England, moved them to a smaller home, and enrolled her son in what Fitz-Simon calls the "poor man's Ampleforth" of the public school system.[14] Edwards's mother had been his father's second wife, and seems most likely to have been from a lower class than his father. It seems too that she was left with little after her husband's death, because she pulled Hilton out of school after only a few months, probably because she couldn't afford the fees. Years later Edwards would claim that he went to Cambridge, found it not to his liking, and then returned home to get a job so he could help out his mother.[15] Despite these humble or humbling beginnings, the two men were able to reinvent themselves in Ireland. They were, in some ways, wild and unconcerned with "respectability" in their twenties and thirties. They took risks with the Gate Theatre program that could very well have put them in danger of censorship or worse, particularly in foregrounding Oscar Wilde as a voice of their theater group. But, as they aged, even as they settled into a kind of queer domesticity, they wrapped themselves in gossamer bourgeois respectability. The theater, then, was a tool for constructing and interpreting their public personas but not necessarily the institution that protected them from the moral project of the Free State.

At some point in the shared language of queer Irish men, the association between the theater or "arts and culture scene" and safety became part of the community lexicon. An older couple I had the privilege of speaking to—Jim Harkin and Ian Fox—echoed similar ideas when discussing their own experiences in Dublin's 1960s queer pubs.[16] They'd been together fifty-eight years when I met them in January 2024. Though they were very active in Dublin's queer social scene, hitting bars like Davy Byrne's, Bartley Dunne's, and Rice's regularly, they don't remember being worried about the police or that people might turn them in for "gross indecency." In their estimation, that was because they were also connected to the "arts," and so the crowds they socialized with were accepting of men like them. Jim worked as a commercial artist, doing ads and marketing campaigns, and Ian worked for RTÉ. When I was listening to them, I was struck by the way the umbrella of the "arts" could stretch and bend to encompass an awful lot of professions— and that those occupations were decidedly, in Dublin socioeconomic terms, middle class. Their community may have been built on the arts and culture scene and its peripheral expressions, but it's just as important to acknowl-

---

14. Fitz-Simon, 34–35.

15. Fitz-Simon, 35–36.

16. Unrecorded conversation with Dr. Averill Earls's Love and Sex in Modern Irish History Class and Sam McGrath (*Come Here to Me*, available at https://comeheretome.com/), Jim Harkin, and Ian Fox, 28 January 2024, at Davy Byrne's Pub; discussed here with permission of Jim Harkin and Ian Fox.

edge the class boundaries associated with those professions. It was their class status that actually protected them, even if it were through the "theatre people" and "bohemian types" that spaces were made queer in the 1950s and 1960s. When he spoke to my students in January 2024, Kieran Rose echoed these ideas: he, as an urban planner and middle-class man, didn't hide who he was or worry about being arrested in the 1970s and 1980s, and he acknowledged his class status as the root of his sense of invulnerability.[17]

Class was both nebulous and deeply entrenched in Ireland in the twentieth century. According to Ferriter, socioeconomic class distinction was central to Irish life before the 1960s.[18] According to Marilyn Silverman, who conducted a microhistory and ethnography of Thomastown, Ireland, Irish class was organized around occupational categories like landlords, farmers, shopkeepers, tradesmen, and laborers.[19] Though occupational in nature—and thus potentially transgressible—the class system was fixed, with little social mobility. Sons tended to follow in their father's footsteps—as did both James Hand the cabbie and Ronald Brown the solicitor—and marriage tended to be endogamous, in terms of both class and religion.[20] According to both Silverman and Maura Cronin, socioeconomic class was also strictly hierarchical, and enforced by the expansion of Catholic influence throughout the island.[21] Sodalities, weekly pastoral letters read aloud at Mass, and secret organizations like the Knights of St. Columbanus served to police and reinforce social class divisions.[22] Of course, though exogamous marriage and social climbing were rare, urban and rural Irish people did both. Men like Hand and North socialized across class boundaries.[23] Occasionally, too, depending on larger political and economic trends, an occupation might itself cross class boundaries. For example, farmers in the nineteenth century were landless tenants with little political or social collateral; with the Land Acts of the 1880s and Irish independence, farmers became one of the most powerful social and political classes in Ireland.[24] But, for the most part, the gendered and class-based expectations that governed daily life enforced those clear divisions.

---

17. Interview with Kieran Rose, 26 January 2024, YWCA, Baggot Street Dublin, with Dr. Averill Earls's students for Love and Sex in Modern Irish History. Paraphrased here with permission from Rose.

18. Ferriter, *Transformation of Ireland*, 505.

19. Silverman, *Irish Working Class*, 7.

20. Silverman, 70–76; though Ruth Coon and Alison Garden are investigating the underreported and oft ignored commonality of exogamous marriage, or "intermarriage," in Northern Ireland and Ireland. Garden and Coon, *Mixed Marriages and Mixed Relationships*.

21. Silverman, *Irish Working Class*, 7; Cronin, "Class and Status," 33–43.

22. Silverman, 365.

23. See Chapter 3, "The Cabbie."

24. Silverman, *Irish Working Class*, 10–27.

Because class in Ireland was largely occupation based, and it was possible that an occupation might shift in its positionality on the hierarchy, it's harder to speak broadly about occupations that are "working class" or "middle class." According to Joseph Ruane and Jennifer Todd, the Irish "middle" class, in all of its fuzziness, referred to a largely urban-based "commercial, white-collar and professional stratum with a relatively high educational level and distinctive lifestyle and values."[25] The persistence of a small landed gentry, and the blurred boundary between middle class and gentry, added additional complications to class and status in Ireland. Most of the "Big House" families left Ireland after independence, and their homes were sold off or stripped for parts by foreigners and locals alike.[26] The Irish upper middle class moved into some of those houses. Someone like the author John Broderick, whose family owned a commercial bakery, might be considered "middle class," but his family bought homes like "The Moors" and spent lengthy time abroad in a facsimile to traditional gentry behavior. We might call these people "bourgeois," people like Mac Liammóir, Edwards, and Broderick, who projected gentility and respectability either through actual economic capital or cultural capital. The working class could range from the day laborers who were under or unemployed for part of the year to those skilled laborers who had permanent and nearly year-round employment, like shop assistants, barrel makers, brewers, longshoremen, and the like. Despite these murky and sometimes mutable boundaries, class was a defining feature of Irish life in the twentieth century. What separated the middle class/bourgeoisie/gentry from the working class/working poor was a sense of deference dividing the strata. The majority of men who joined the Garda were from the working classes, and many were from rural communities where these social divisions reigned supreme. Further, the judges and solicitors who oversaw the courtrooms treated men of their same social class differently than those they considered socially inferior. While some may have been empowered by their law enforcement positionality to overcome those social norms, the court records reveal a clear division in how and who were most likely to be arrested, and how they were likely to be treated in the courtroom.

The vast majority of those arrested for whom there is evidence of their occupation/class would have fallen under the category of either poor or working class. Of the 291 records I have from 1922 to 1972, I have been able to determine the class status of 239. Some of their occupations were listed in the

25. Joseph Ruane and Jennifer Todd, "The Changing Role of the Middle Classes in Twentieth-Century Ireland," in *The Cambridge Social History of Modern Ireland*, eds. Eugenio Biagini and Mary E. Daly (Cambridge: Cambridge University Press, 2017), 177.

26. Terrence Dooley, "The Big House," in *The Cambridge Social History of Modern Ireland*, eds. Eugenio Biagini and Mary E. Daly (Cambridge: Cambridge University Press, 2017), 170.

arrest forms or announced in the newspaper summaries of cases. Others I've traced to their working-class neighborhoods throughout Dublin. It's not particularly surprising that the majority were working class or poor. Many of the men seeking sex in Dublin's public spaces did so because they didn't have access to private spaces. The unemployed and underemployed were more likely to live in the crowded tenement houses of the Liberties or North Dock, renting a room from a family or, worse, sharing a room with one or more other lodgers or family members.[27] Conversely, Dublin's solicitors, bank managers, and celebrated actors occupied the finer neighborhoods and posh houses south of the River Liffey, like Rathmines and Ranelagh. But that's not to say that bourgeois bachelors didn't cruise, as there is evidence of all kinds of men—from the poor and indigent to the middle class to the landed gentry—who were arrested in lavatories and parks in this period. But the public cruising culture was most dangerous for working-class men, as they were most likely to get caught, most likely to be convicted, and most likely to get the harsher sentences compared to their bourgeois counterparts.

Of the 239, just over 20 percent were "middle" class, living in the affluent neighborhoods like St. Peters Terrace in Howth or Ranelagh Road, or employed as solicitors, bakery owners, publicans, medical students or doctors, Anglican priests, bank officers, dentist assistants, or land stewards. Of those, 42 percent were found guilty. For those found guilty, 28 percent were given the option to pay a fine and avoid prison, and 50 percent were given sentences under nine months. Thirty of these middle-class men were exonerated, or the prosecution threw out their case. One man, Caleb Wallace, was sent to the Bloomfield Private Lunatic Asylum for "treatment."[28] Psychiatric institutionalization wasn't common for men associated with gross indecency crimes prior to 1960 in Ireland, in part because Irish psychiatry did not follow the same timeline in developments as the United Kingdom or the United States, where commitment for homosexuality was quite common. But it is significant that this middle-class man was given over to the private asylum in Bloomfield, which didn't accept many patients and typically only those who could pay; the two working-class men who were sent to institutions were committed to the state-run Grangegorman Mental Hospital in Dublin.[29] Similarly, Victor Walter Sinton, a doctor, was found guilty, in 1945, and sentenced

27. Brady, *Dublin, 1930–1950*, 54–56.

28. NAI, Dublin Circuit Court, State Files, 1C-95-126, 20-Jan-32, the State v. Caleb Wallace.

29. Maunger, *The Cost of Insanity*, chap. 1. NAI, Dublin Circuit Court, State Files, 1D-24-136, 11-May-39, the State v. Harry Noel; and NAI, Dublin Circuit Court, State Files, #27, 10-Oct-49, the state v. John Grennan, 1D-28-115.

to ten months imprisonment, but, after four months, he was sent to a clinic in London for "treatment."[30]

Significantly, at least 62 percent of those charged with gross indecency were working-class men, and almost all were caught in those public spaces best known as cruising sites.[31] The Garda caught men in lavatories, parks, and alleyways all over the city. Of the 147 working-class men arrested, 94 were found guilty (63 percent), and only 18 percent were given the option to pay fines. With higher rates of arrest, higher rates of conviction, and lower likelihood of the judge offering a working-class man the opportunity to avoid prison, the contrast could not be more revealing. Though the law specified sex between men in both public and private, the gardaí concentrated almost all of their efforts on public spaces. That already set working-class men, who often had no option but to pursue sexual relationships in public spaces, at a disadvantage. Middle-class men shared public spaces with working-class men, from the pubs to the parks to the highly trafficked cruising spots like Beresford Place or the Quays, but they didn't share equally in the consequences for being caught out in those places.

The unequal dynamic of policed sex between men has been evident throughout this book. In 1931, Frank North, an insurance man—middle class—was charged alongside James Hand. Hand was accused of procuring rent boys for North, for "conducting a male brothel."[32] But, by all accounts, it was North who had sex with those young men. And yet, the judge, Cahir Davitt, gave North a lesser sentence than Hand. As reported in the *Irish Times*:

> Mr. Wood, in an appeal for leniency, stated that North had occupied a responsible position with an insurance company in the city for the past sixteen years. Inspector Beggs, of the Civic Gardaí, said that North had been engaged in practices such as that of which he had been

---

30. NAI, Dublin Circuit Court, State Files, 1D-27-8, 11-Jan-1945, the State v. Victor Walter Sinton.

31. Men who were poor or indigent were often caught having sex inside Dublin's institutions for the poor, like the Dublin Union Workhouse. Significantly, rather than gardaí lying in wait in cruising grounds, men arrested for having sex in the former workhouses were turned in by supervisors of the institutions. But not all poor men were granted shelter in the city's welfare homes. In total, forty men listed as having "no address" or "no business" were charged, and 63 percent of them were found guilty. Four (10 percent) were given the option to pay fines—which, presumably, they were unable to do—and the rest all got sentences of six months or more.

32. NAI, Dublin Circuit Court, State Files, 1C-94-89, dockets 63, 64, 20-Jan-1931, the State v. Frank North. There was another insurance agent arrested, charged, tried, and found guilty of gross indecency, for which he received a fifteen-month sentence, but his victim was a ten-year-old, and, per the parameters of this project, I haven't included the data of men who had sex with children under fifteen. See NAI, Dublin Circuit Court, State Files, 1D-33-112, docket 23, 4-Jul-1933, the State v. Alphonsus Keaney.

found guilty for some time past. Judge Davitt, in passing sentence, said that the maximum sentence for the offence was two years with hard labour. "The offence," proceeded his lordship, "is filthy, unnatural and detestable. To any man who still conceals about his mentality any shred of self-respect the conviction should be sufficient, but I must have regard to the community. The offence must be stamped out, and so far as I can contribute to stamping it out I will endeavour to do so. The only circumstance I can discover for not imposing the maximum sentence on you, North, is the restrained way in which your counsel conducted the defence. I impose a sentence of twenty-one calendar months, with hard labour, and you can thank your counsel that you have escaped the other three months."[33]

North, with the means to hire counsel, and with the backing of his sixteen years working in a respectable job, was granted a leniency unimaginable for a working-class man in his position. Indeed, Hand, who was a working-class man, didn't have the socioeconomic capital to pay for his own release on bail, to hire an effective counselor to plead his case, or to earn a modicum of grace from a "disgusted" judge.

There's no denying that men who were charged with gross indecency faced dire consequences, whether or not they were given lesser sentences or even acquitted in these cases. Association with a gross indecency offense could be life ruining. As any genealogist of Ireland knows, many people shared the same name, and that could lead to some sticky situations. When the *Evening Herald* published an announcement in 1931 of Patrick Byrne's "serious charge," the editors included Byrne's age (twenty-nine) and address (North Richmond St.) with a disclaimer that he was not in any way connected with "Mr. P. Byrne, the well-known coach upholsterer, of 17 North Richmond St."[34] Exoneration might be enough to ameliorate a situation, and middle-class men were more likely to be exonerated than working-class or poor men, even when they were cruising the same public spaces. Ultimately, though, having control of the more semipublic spaces, like the "artsy" pubs Harkin and Fox recall from the 1960s, was better. Ideally, though, it was the private bourgeois flat or house, in a firmly middle-class or gentrified neighborhood, unlikely to be disturbed by the gardaí, that protected Dublin's "bachelor" and "spinster" couples.

Respectability, tied intimately to class, allowed men, like Mac Liammóir and Edwards or Patrick Hennessy and Henry Robertson Craig, and women, like Kathleen Lynn and Madeleine ffrench-Mullen or Margaret Skinnider and

33. "Vice Prevalent in Dublin," 13.
34. "Serious Offence," *Evening Herald*, June 30, 1931, 8.

Nora O'Keeffe, to maintain comfortable domestic same-sex partnerships, and not because they were so secretive that they avoided detection by *anyone*.[35] Perhaps for some of their neighbors and colleagues, the idea that two people of the same gender would be in a loving and sexual relationship was inconceivable and so they didn't see what was right before their eyes. But it is clear that many people were aware of the nature of Mac Liammóir and Edwards' relationship—not least of all *The Late Late Show* viewership in 1969. Similarly, Hennessy (an Irishman) and Craig (a Scot) were artists and lived together in Dublin from 1947 until their deaths. Today, they are known popularly (and acknowledged) as life partners and lovers, though little has been written on them academically.[36] Though, as Sean Kissane suggests, they lived a "quiet life" in Ireland together, it seems likely that they ran in the same circles as Mac Liammóir and Edwards, and their connection to the "arts" strengthened their immunity to Irish moral policing.[37]

The association of theater and art serving as insulation for gay men is a kind of popular mythology in Ireland. When I talk with Irish people about Ireland's famous queer men, they tend to repeat the idea that it was their association with the arts that protected men like Mac Liammóir, Edwards, Hennessy, and Craig. And it is true that artistic cultural institutions like the theater have long served as sanctuaries for those unable or unwilling to conform to the gender and sexual expectations of the era, in Ireland and around the world.[38] Ireland had a vibrant theater scene throughout the nineteenth and twentieth centuries.[39] Men who desired men found community and a tacit acceptance in Irish theater, in sharp contrast to the political rhetoric and "habitus and ethos" that coalesced in Ireland through cultural nationalism and state building. And for Mac Liammóir and Edwards, being sensations in theater brought them in contact with the affluent and respectable. As Fitz-Simon recounts, before they bought their home at Four Harcourt Terrace, they lived in "bachelor disarray in an upstairs flat at 60 Harcourt Street."[40] In the 1930s, they

---

35. For information about the open secrets of Lynn/ffrench-Mullen and Skinnider/O'Keefe, see McAuliffe and Wheelock, *Diaries of Kathleen Lynn*; and McAuliffe, *Margaret Skinnider*.

36. Sean Kissane, "Unearthing the Gems That History Has Mistakenly Written Out," *Curtain: The Artpool Magazine*, 3 March 2021, available at https://curtain.artcuratorgrid.com/sean-kissane/.

37. Kissane, "Unearthing the Gems."

38. See, e.g., Woods, *Homintern*; Dirk Gindt, "Sky Gilbert, Daniel MacIvor, and the Man in the Vancouver Hotel Room: Queer Gossip, Community Narrative, and Theatre History," *Theatre Research in Canada* 34, no. 2 (2013): 1; Farfan, *Performing Queer Modernism*.

39. And still today! See, e.g., Christopher Fitz-Simon, *The Irish Theatre* (London: Thames & Hudson, 1983); Barry Houlihan, *Theatre and Archival Memory: Irish Drama and Marginalised Histories, 1951–1977* (New York: Springer International, 2021); and Christopher Morash, *A History of Irish Theatre, 1601–2000* (Cambridge: Cambridge University Press, 2002).

40. Fitz-Simon, *The Boys*, 69.

were fast friends with Edward and Christine Longford. Edward, Earl of Longford, bought the majority of shares in the Gate Theatre in 1930 and was quickly elected the chairman of the board and remained an invested partner for decades, even when the company was in dire financial straits.[41] He and Christine would take Mac Liammóir and Edwards out to fine restaurants in the 1930s. Though Fitz-Simon suggests that the two wouldn't have found their acquired respectability necessary, it may have protected them from overt criticisms from Catholic Ireland's domineering institutions.[42]

In theory, the theater should have been a space and place where Mac Liammóir and Edwards could pull off more public transgressions that would align with their sexuality. But, it seems, particularly in their creation and production of *The Importance of Being Oscar*, that they attempted to unqueer one of Ireland's queerest legends. Edwards and Mac Liammóir wrote *The Importance of Being Oscar* based on Oscar Wilde's writings and excerpts from his plays, and, as one reviewer noted, the playwrights "painted Wilde's life with a gentle brush . . . [though] all of Wilde was not shown to us, that his sins were smoothed over by his regret."[43] A caricature of a talented and repentant man that leaves the audience feeling sorry for all Wilde had been through in the years after his imprisonment, *The Importance of Being Oscar* was a hit in Ireland and England. Edwards directed its debut in 1960, starring Mac Liammóir, and, ultimately, took the play on the road and to television between 1960 and 1970. As Walshe points out, Mac Liammóir's representation of Wilde in the play was intentionally dehomosexualized, emphasizing instead his love for his wife, and presented a heterosexually palatable version of Oscar Wilde to audiences.[44] The play was broken into two halves, with his "tiger life"—a phrase meant to signal his affair with Lord Alfred "Bosie" Douglas and the London rent boys—left out completely. Mac Liammóir skipped over the already well-known story of Wilde's gross indecency trial. Instead, the second half of the play invited the audience to sympathize with the fallen hero, picking up with the broken Wilde after his imprisonment. It's a notable and telling feature of Mac Liammóir and Edwards' negotiation of Irish society. The public reception of *The Importance of Being Oscar* during the show's run was approving. The reminiscences on the play after his death, in a period of more open discussions of same-sex desire and gay rights organization-led activism to transition Ireland to the acceptance of gay men and women, echoed Walshe's critiques. After Mac Liammóir's death, one journalist noted:

41. Fitz-Simon, 66, 206–208.
42. Fitz-Simon, 69.
43. "Three Hours of Triumph for Mac Liammóir," *Irish Press*, 20 September 1960, quoted in Walshe, "Importance of Staging Oscar Wilde," 224.
44. Walshe, 225.

His final masterpiece, the one-man show on Wilde, was by any standard a great tour de force, and from 1960, when it was first presented,
to his death brought him international acclaim. The great success of
Oscar was probably due, in some measure at least, to his own identifi-
cation with Wilde, and this lent to his portrayal a force and poignancy
it otherwise could scarcely have had. . . . He shared the loneliness of
being forever different from the mass of his fellows; the ultimate sadness of being forever apart from those he loved, whose entertainment
and joy was his life's work, in whose plaudits he lived and had his being.[45]

While Mac Liammóir and Edwards attempted to "dehomosexualize" Wilde,
the author of this obituary made an overt queer connection between Wilde
and Mac Liammóir. In the end, they succeeded only in relegating Wilde's
queerness to the same liminal space of their own queerness: into the realm
of open secret. But, in reviving Wildean respectability, Mac Liammóir and
Edwards (perhaps unwittingly) constructed the same kind of armor around
Wilde that they had for themselves. The theater itself may have normalized
Mac Liammóir's camp command of Irish parties and stages, but the acceptance of his domestic life with Edwards, discussed nonchalantly on live television a decade before his death, was the armor of respectability that class
and social capital afforded Ireland's cultural icons and elite.

Granted, neither the arts scene nor class status was a complete shield from
the moral policing project. George Thompson, a singer with an address of
Twelve Eaton Square, was arrested in 1950, found guilty, and sentenced to
three months imprisonment with hard labor.[46] He pursued sex with another
man in the lavatory at St. Stephen's Green, Gordon McWilliams, who was—
of all things—a Church of England priest.[47] McWilliams was also found guilty
and sentenced to four months with hard labor. Though caught, tried, and
found guilty, the judge's caveated sentencing was in deference to their class and
occupational statuses. Each was permitted to pay a fine and keep the peace
instead of serving the prison sentence. Thompson was given the option to

---

45. "Micheál Mac Liammóir," *Strabane Chronicle*, 18 March 1978, 5.

46. Twelve Eaton Square in Monkstown is valued today at over 1.4 million euros, and, in
1950, the commuter suburbs of Salthill and Monkstown, connected to the city by railroad from
the 1830s, were predominantly middle class and wealthy, see Property Price Registry Ireland,
available at https://propertypriceregisterireland.com/details/12_eaton_square_monkstown
_co_dublin_ireland-218840/; Twelve Eaton Square in Terenure was a southern middle-class sub-
urb of Dublin that was developed in the late nineteenth century. I'm not sure which Twelve Eaton
Square Thompson belonged to, but either option would have cast him as a middle-class man.

47. NAI, Dublin Circuit Court, State Files, 1D-28-125, 10-Oct-1950, the State v. Gordon
McWilliams.

pay £25 and keep peace for two years. McWilliams was permitted to pay £100 and keep peace for three years.[48] I can't measure their suffering, because I don't know what happened to them in the years after their conviction. Still, they were fortunate in comparison with other men who got longer prison sentences they had to serve.

The significance of class seems even more poignant among middle class and elite Irish women who loved women. The historian and gender studies scholar Mary McAuliffe has written about a number of revolutionary Irish women who loved women, whose partnerships were both certainly known to their family members and friends and observed and impressed upon even the most willfully ignorant colleagues and acquaintances.[49] In January 2024, I brought a group of students to University College Dublin to hear McAuliffe speak about Ireland's revolutionary lesbians. McAuliffe discussed Kathleen Lynn, and how one of the most beautiful aspects of Lynn's diaries (held at the Royal College of Irish Physicians) is the way Madeleine ffrench-Mullen is present every day in Lynn's otherwise brief diary entries, even after ffrench-Mullen died. One of Lynn's hospital employees recalled how you never saw the doctor without ffrench-Mullen.[50] Though Lynn's family didn't have much to do with her partner, ffrench-Mullen seems to have welcomed the two for holidays and visits as a couple. In the case of Margaret Skinnider, McAuliffe discovered her personal diaries—which were undoubtedly open and effusive about her love for Nora O'Keefe—were destroyed by her nephew in his capacity as the executor of her estate.[51] The nature of their relationship was quite obviously known by friends and family, but they were not subjected to the barbaric Irish culture of containment. In a country where women were committed to institutions and Magdalen laundries by family members, priests, and gardaí for far lesser sins than taking another woman as a lover, it's clear that the boundaries of class and respectability were particularly powerful in independent Ireland.

It bears repeating here, as I have said elsewhere, that the love and sexual dimension of these couples' relationships was not and still is not taken for granted.[52] Journalists and historians have been trying (purposefully or sim-

---

48. NAI, Dublin Circuit Court, State Files, 1D-28-127, docket 64, 10-Oct-1950, the State v. George Thompson.

49. McAuliffe, *Margaret Skinnider*; and McAuliffe, *Diaries of Kathleen Lynn*.

50. Lecture from Mary McAuliffe to St. Olaf College Love and Sex in Modern Irish History, 29 January 2024, at University College Dublin.

51. Lecture from Mary McAuliffe to St. Olaf College Love and Sex in Modern Irish History, 29 January 2024, at UCD.

52. Averill Earls, "Irish Hero, Queer Traitor, Gay Icon: Roger Casement over Time," *Dig: A History Podcast*, 2 July 2023, available at https://digpodcast.org/2023/07/02/roger-casement-over-time/.

ply out of ignorance) to erase the queerness of Ireland's national heroes—men like Padraic Pearse and Roger Casement, women like Skinnider and Lynn—for decades.[53] As recently as 2000, the *Irish Times* referred to Patrick Hennessy and Henry Robertson Craig as just "life-long friends."[54] There are several biographies of Roger Casement written explicitly to refute the idea that his diaries are "authentic."[55] And, in 1988, Gifford Lewis wrote a biography of Eva Gore-Booth and Esther Roper just to "prove" that the two were not "deviant."[56] These (often ridiculous) attempts at erasure are rooted in the lingering belief that queerness and Irishness are incompatible, no matter the evidence to the contrary.[57] But the efforts backfire. What they protest too much against is the overwhelming evidence of queer love and sex. When scholars or people with opinions try to "rescue" these nationalists and cultural icons from the "taint" of association with same-sex desire, all they really do is highlight the obviousness of those relationships and sexualities.

None of these people—Casement, Mac Liammóir, Hennessy, Skinnider, or anyone else—were giving public interviews about the people with whom they had sex. Mac Liammóir's 1969 interview aside, these men and women lived in a time when no one really talked openly about their sex lives, unless they were writing and promoting guides to family planning and married love.[58] Mac Liammóir and Edwards may have been discreet about the full dimension of their partnership between 1928 and 1968, but their relation-

---

53. Scholars who deny the legitimacy of the diaries, and thus Casement's same-sex desire, include Angus Mitchell, E. Ó Máille, M. Payne, and R. McHugh. In *Kathleen Lynn: Irishwoman, Patriot, Doctor* (Irish Academic Press, 2006) Margaret Ó hÓgartaigh refutes the idea that Lynn and her partner were anything more than friends.

54. Robert O'Byrne, "Idyllic Warmth in Work by Landscape Artist Craig," *Irish Times*, 10 June 2000. For another example of fame and class status exempting queer people from legal or social ostracization, see Tom Hulme and Maurice Casey, "Queer Men and Networks of Communication in Northern Ireland before the 1970s," *Journal of the History of Sexuality* 34, no. 3 (2025), which includes a section on Peter Stephen Montgomery, one of the most well-known confirmed queer Northern Irish men of the twentieth century.

55. See, e.g., William Maloney, *The Forged Casement Diaries* (Dublin: The Talbot Press, 1936); Alfred Noyes, *The Accusing Ghost or Justice for Casement* (London: Victor Gollancz Ltd, 1957); Roger McHugh, "Casement: The Public Record Office Manuscripts," Threshold, 4, no. 1 (Spring–Summer 1960): 28–57; Herbert Mackey, *Roger Casement: The Truth about the Forged Diaries* (Dublin: C.J. Fallon Ltd, 1966); Angus Mitchell, *Casement*, (London: Haus Publishing, 2003); E. Ó Máille and M. Payne, *The Vindication of Roger Casement: Computer Analysis and Comparisons* (Dublin: privately printed, 1994); and Michael O'Sullivan, "Lies, Damn Lies and Forensics: The Ghost of Roger Casement," *History Ireland* 10, no. 2 (Summer 2002): 5–6.

56. Gifford Lewis, *Eva Gore-Booth and Esther Roper: A Biography* (London: Pandora, 1988).

57. Earls, "Unnatural Offenses of English Import."

58. For example, Margaret Sanger, *Happiness in Marriage* (New York: Brentano's, 1926) and Marie Stopes, *Married Love* (New York: The Critic & Guide Company, 1918), both of which were banned by the Irish Board of Censors.

ship was not a secret. Mac Liammóir was a prolific writer, both of published works and in his correspondence with friends, family, and, of course, Edwards. The intimacy of their partnership was communicated both in the ways they talked about each other with friends and in the ways they presented as a family unit in their correspondences and—at least in 1969, if not earlier—in public.

Most of the surviving letters preserved at the NLI are from Mac Liammóir either to Edwards or to one of a handful of friends, especially Molly Mac Ewen, a talented set designer. Writing to her in 1967, Mac Liammóir described the activities of their recently adopted Siamese cats, saying that "the cats have gone raving mad & fly in & out of the room when they are not gorging themselves, making messes on the stairs (a new & deeply unattractive activity) or mercifully lying in slumber wrapped in each others paws & looking like something by Marie Mawrencin."[59] The couple doted on their cats, talking about them with equal parts exasperation and love. When the cats passed away, by June 1977, both felt the loss. In a letter to Mac Ewen, Mac Liammóir, feeling his age and the loss of their furry family members, lamented, "We haven't even our Siamese cats now so I have no news for you even of them so I'll shut up."[60] In a few lines, Mac Liammóir could paint a picture of their domesticity and draw friends into their circle. They conducted their correspondence with friends as any couple might.[61] They signed off with "love from us both" or "love from Hilton and Micheál." They sent Christmas cards, postcards, and regular correspondence to friends they made over the years. I've no doubt that dozens, if not hundreds, of their friends and colleagues were firmly aware of the full nature of their "partnership."

Certainly, too, their neighbors on Harcourt Terrace knew that the two men lived together. Harcourt Terrace is a beautiful street lined with grand homes, some Regency-era Greek revival, some brick Victorians, with direct access to the pedestrian path along the Grand Canal and just a stone's throw from the National Concert Hall. Their home at Four Harcourt Terrace was semidetached, a large Georgian-era house with small wrought-iron terraces for the second-floor rooms and a grand foyer. They purchased it together in 1945 from Donald Whiteside, and both of their names were recorded in the Valuation and Rate Books.[62] Co-ownership is significant; a more cautious couple might have one owner, with the other occupant listed as a tenant. But Mac Liammóir and Edwards did not hide. They owned it together from 1945

59. NLI, MS 36,071/2, Undated, Micheál Mac Liammóir/Molly MacEwen papers, Dublin, Ireland.

60. NLI, MS 36,071/3, 1 June 1977, Micheál Mac Liammóir/Molly MacEwen papers. Dublin, Ireland.

61. For a deeper, more nuanced exploration of queer domesticities, see Cook, *Queer Domesticities*; and Upchurch, *"Beyond the Law."*

62. Tailte Eireann, Dublin, Property Details for 4 Harcourt Terrace, Fitzwilliams 1939–1947.

until 1978 when Mac Liammóir died; it is unclear who lived there between Edwards's death in 1982 and its purchase in 1988 by Timothy Riordan.[63] The other half of the building, number Five, was owned by George Coffey when they first moved in, but, for the next twenty years, it was vacant. Harcourt Terrace, in the years they lived there, was a mix of owner-occupied rentals and single-owner homes. At one point, investors tried to move in and demolish homes to put up new construction, but Mac Liammóir and Edwards, along with their neighbors, resisted. Lilian Stephens, who lived at number Two nearly as long as Mac Liammóir and Edwards lived at number Four and regularly had tea with them, recalled that Mac Liammóir "was the best kind of neighbour one could wish for. He helped us save the Terrace from the builders."[64] Another neighbor, perhaps Louisa Daly or Christina Cahill, spoke fondly of Mac Liammóir and Edwards, whom she'd run into when she was walking her dog. The garda from across the road sent a Mass card upon Mac Liammóir's death. Though they were stars in some ways, they were very much at home on Harcourt Terrace and had nothing to fear from their neighbors, new and old.[65] (See Figure 7.1.)

One might allow for friends, family, and neighbors to be aware of the enduring love of two men living together in Dublin. But, as Fitz-Simon notes, there were ample rumors about both Mac Liammóir and Edwards from very early on in their Dublin era. Fitz-Simon suggests that Mac Liammóir was "more friendly than was seemly" with the army chief of staff.[66] Mary Kenny, referring to oral histories collected from Mac Liammóir's friends Patrick Bedford and Mary Manford, suggests that it was O'Duffy, the commissioner of the Garda, who waited for Mac Liammóir outside the theater in an armored car, "its engines throbbing expectantly."[67] Since O'Duffy was the army chief of staff in 1922, it's likely that the two authors refer to the same man, though Fitz-Simon offered no citation. Whether O'Duffy or Maurice Twomey, one might imagine such enforcers of Irish nationalist ideals would've made an example of these two young queer Englishmen. But, like most middle-class and "respectable" Irish men, the gardaí conveniently overlooked the illegal activities of these men. To that end, Ireland's queer men and women among the theatrical, the musical, the RTÉ hosts, the marketing professionals, the architects, the doctors, the painters, the city planners, and all manner of middle-class or bourgeois professions—whether "arts and culture" or not—were the Free State and Republic's "open secrets."

---

63. Tailte Eireann, Dublin, Property Details for 4 Harcourt Terrace, St. Kevin's 1970–present.

64. Jim Farrelly, "Mac Liammóir, the Kindliest Neighbour on the Terrace," *Irish Independent*, March 8, 1978, 12.

65. Farrelly, "Mac Liammóir, the Kindliest Neighbour," 12.

66. Fitz-Simon, *The Boys*, 70.

67. Kenny, *The Way We Were*, 76–77; Fitz-Simon, 70.

Figure 7.1 House on Harcourt Terrace. Note the Greek mythological reliefs carved under the eaves; two male figures (one a centaur and one a man) grapple, as if the man plans to ride the centaur. *(The Wiltshire Photographic Collection. Reproduced courtesy of the National Library of Ireland.)*

In some ways the justice system, which was designed to harshly punish working-class men, worked to protect the middle-class men. For example, based on the lengths the gardaí went to collect evidence that he *wasn't* a gross indecency offender, it seems likely that State Solicitor Ronald Brown's love affair with Leslie Price would have gone unremarked if not for Price's association with the less savory type from Dublin's slums.[68] I've already discussed in this book the human resource limitations to the postcolonial state's moral project. The Garda simply didn't have the men needed to effect a true elimination of public sex between men. But the nonmolestation of couples like Mac Liammóir and Edwards reveals the class-based limitations of the postcolonial moral project. The target of policing tended to be visible sex, which meant that those most likely to be caught in the crosshairs were working-class and poor men. Class could and did exempt hundreds, maybe thousands, of queer Irish men and women from legal and social consequences. Finding evidence of that exemption, and of the lived experiences of those who were exempted, has been the greatest challenge in my research.

---

68. NAI, AGO, 2002-16-466, the State v. Ronald H. Brown.

Sporadic policing and class-based discrimination means that when it comes to archival material, it is really challenging to find evidence of same-sex love in the NAI. And, of course, we have to acknowledge the inherent problems of state archives to begin with. State bodies, including government-funded archives, are reflective of the policies and norms of the state, the archivists, and the cultural moment of preservation. The court records for gross indecency cases may not be filed with the general criminal court files because archivists or court officials found the content too shocking or disturbing to keep. Undoubtedly, there are case files that have been lost or even destroyed. Further, the things cataloged there are records of state activity; in the case of same-sex-desiring people, trans people, women, people of color, and people with disabilities, the materials collected in state archives tend to be records of state surveillance, control, and restriction of bodies. Silence and silencing is built into the physical body that is the archive.[69] The voices of the surveilled, controlled, and restricted are often unrecorded or unrepresented in the archival records.

If they were significant figures in Ireland's arts and culture scene, like Mac Liammóir and Edwards, some of their papers may be preserved at a place like the NLI. If they were significant leaders in medicine, like Dr. Kathleen Lynn, their papers might be preserved at the Royal College of Physicians in Ireland. But, for the average Irish person, it's unlikely that their life and love have been preserved for future generations.[70] The diffuse nature of the Republic of Ireland's private collections, deposited with either local historical societies or libraries or not at all, makes the quest to fill in Ireland's queer history all the more challenging.

Finding Mac Liammóir and Edwards' personal correspondence at the NLI was, perhaps, the most rewarding moment of my decade of research in Ireland. Before we used email or gave in to the convenience of texting, my partner and I exchanged dozens of handwritten letters over the first few years of our relationship. From a quick update on the mundanity of the day to penning the wrenching pain of being apart for long stretches when he was in the Navy, those letters—which we both kept and still have stashed away at home—are evidence of a youthfully passionate, and sometimes ridiculous, love. Though I can't be sure when Mac Liammóir and Edwards started,

---

69. See, e.g., Trouillot, *Silencing the Past*; and editors Michael S. Moss and David Thomas, *Archival Silences: Missing, Lost, and Uncreated Archives* (Abingdon, UK: Routledge, 2021).

70. It seems that the Public Records Office of Northern Ireland accepts more private collections than the NAI and NLI, which means that there's an almost untapped treasure trove held there. Tom Hulme, Leanne McCormick, Charlie Lynch, and Maurice Casey are taking great strides in making use of those materials with their Queer Northern Ireland: Sexuality before Liberation Research Council project, with several books, articles, and public-facing products already out or in the works.

as the letters at the NLI only go back to the late 1950s, in their fifty years together, it seems they never stopped writing to one another.

When Mac Liammóir wrote to Hilton, he always opened his letters with either "my darling Hilton" or, more frequently, "my own darling Hilton."[71] In the course of their long careers in theater and, for Mac Liammóir, even film, the two traveled the world extensively, bringing their little theater company to London, South Africa, and Egypt, but always returned, in the end, to their adopted home in Ireland.[72] Some projects required that they be separated. Mac Liammóir traveled most of the two. He used hotel stationery for his letters to his partner. Once, when he had only the lined pages that he clearly ripped out of a notebook, he joked that he knew Edwards would be laughing at him for the ridiculousness of the tiny paper, but he just had to write, and anything would do to send off the written declaration of his care and thought for Edwards.[73] Mac Liammóir was a prolific writer. Just based on the snippet of his life and scrawl captured in the NLI, he wrote daily, in his diary, letters to friends, scripts for plays, or one his memoirs.[74]

The letters Mac Liammóir sent to Edwards were ordinary, often recounting the odd or funny encounters he had while traveling for movie filming or with a stage production. On October 2, 1962, writing on a Geneva hotel's stationery, Mac Liammóir opened a letter as usual with "My darling Hilton." He described the fiasco that was their journey from France to Geneva, in which the people who were supposed to be taking him to and from hired a guide who didn't speak English, and no one thought to bring any francs with them. Mac Liammóir had to pay for their transport to the hotel, and, by the time they arrived, some of their companions had departed without them.[75] They managed to make their train to Geneva, temporarily mislaid their tickets until "*some* (only some)" of the tickets were "discovered in Humptey's [his nickname for the manager traveling with them] shoes or somewhere." Short the appropriate tickets, which were supposed to be single sleeper cars, one of their companions "wedged some strange woman in with him & Brendan Matthews ended up in the top bunk as there was nowhere else for him & heard

71. Examples in the NLI, MS 45,866/5— Micheál Mac Liammóir papers, Dublin, Ireland.

72. Fitz-Simon's *The Boys* is a comprehensive history of Mac Liammóir and Edwards illustrious theater and film careers.

73. NLI, MS 45,866/5, letters from Micheál Mac Liammóir to Hilton Edwards, letter dated Monday 14 October 1963.

74. Memoirs included *All for Hecuba* (Boston: Branden Press, 1967), *An Oscar of No Importance* (London: Heinemann, 1968), *Put Money in Thy Purse* (Malton, UK: Methuen Publishing Ltd, 1976), and *Enter a Goldfish* (London: Thames and Hudson, 1977). He wrote thirteen plays, including *Diarmuid agus Gráinne* (1928), *The Ford of the Hurdles* (1929), *Easter 1916* (1930), *Where Stars Walk* (1940), *Dancing Shadows* (1941), *Ill Met by Moonlight* (1946), *Home for Christmas* (1950), and *The Importance of Being Oscar* (1963).

75. NLI, MS 45,866/5-Micheál Mac Liammóir Papers, 2 October 1962, Dublin, Ireland.

Marshall & strange woman making love all night which he said had a fright-ful effect of nausea on him." Sometime the next morning they discovered that Humptey was missing—"no sign of him." For five pages, Mac Liammóir detailed his adventures for Edwards—acknowledging that it was just the sort of chaos that Edwards would hate but Mac Liammóir loved. "I'm quite all right," he finished his letter, "on 75 a week & maybe will have enough to bring you home a Windmill from Holland, with some Edelweiss for Brian & a—small—bottle of Schnapps for PB [Paddy Bedford]. God bless you darling, I'll write again soon . . . all my love to you, Micheál."[76] Mac Liammóir often included the most ridiculous things he did and saw in his letters, not just to Edwards but also to his friends. But with Edwards it wasn't just about relay-ing the ridiculous. Sometimes Mac Liammóir would sit down and write out a note just to let his lover know that he was thinking of him. "My own dar-ling Hilton—I came home specially early tonight in order to telephone you: did so, no answer. So I am writing this to send you my love."[77] Through their many dalliances and affairs, Mac Liammóir's love for Edwards was deep, demonstrative, and enduring.

As Fitz-Simon notes, in their last decade or so, Mac Liammóir and Ed-wards argued more frequently—perhaps over Paddy Bedford, perhaps over their goals for the Gate Theatre. But an argument was not enough to dimin-ish one's love for the other. After one fight, Mac Liammóir left on a business trip but then wrote a note to send to Edwards, opening with "I am, my dear-est & only love, worried about you. . . . That reminds me: I bought for you an Avocado Pear for a present but when you were so cross it fled from my mind—Do get it from basket in kitchen larder. Scoop out: dice: ordinary salad dress—eat it for me!!! . . . Try to keep calm, my dearest, my only, true love. Don't let the tiny flies & fleas of life obscure the sum for you. I love you so much, I can't express it. For ever devoted, . . . PS, Love to Panjas & Ban [cats]."[78]

After thirty years together, Mac Liammóir still expressed a deep and earnest passion for his partner. With the exception of some undated letters, there aren't any letters between the two in the NLI that predate 1945. I won-der what happened to their older letters. What did they write to each other in the earliest years of their love story? What parts of their sometimes tur-bulent but, ultimately, enduring relationship are missing, destroyed, or inac-cessibly tucked away somewhere? In the 1960s, their letters allude to an ongoing tension over Edwards's infatuation with Patrick Bedford, a hand-some young actor who lived with the couple for a time at Harcourt Terrace. Did they fight about Mac Liammóir's alleged lovers from the 1930s and 1940s?

---

76. Micheál Mac Liammóir Papers.
77. Letter undated, NLI, MS 45,866/6.
78. Letter undated, NLI, MS 45,866/6.

Or Edwards's fling with a young man that their friends all referred to as "Miss S"?[79] Or were those brief interlopers part of their romance? Though Fitz-Simon spends a lot of time on those years in tracing their mutual and individual careers, and even mentions the rift Bedford caused in their household, he doesn't spend much time on their love and lovers; they're brief mentions in what is mostly a history of their theater careers.

Mac Liammóir's glib reference to his relationship with Edwards in 1969 on *The Late Late Show* was an interesting moment in what the sociologist Paul Ryan identifies as a longer shift in Irish public discussions around sexuality. Throughout the 1960s, people challenged the restrictive environment around talking about sex, sexuality, and women's role in society. For example, Angela McNamara offered teens advice about sex and sexuality, within the parameters of Catholic education.[80] In 1971, Nell McCafferty and Máirín Johnston, members of the Irish women's liberation movement (IWLM), appeared on *The Late Late Show* to talk about contraception.[81] That same year the IWLM made a highly publicized run for contraceptives across the border in Northern Ireland, bringing back the illegal condoms and diaphragms that Irish women desperately needed to control their own reproduction. On *The Late Late Show*, the IWLM spoke more openly about sex, reproduction, and birth control than any public broadcast in Ireland had before.

As noted, in his 1969 *The Late Late Show* interview, Mac Liammóir didn't talk about same-sex desire explicitly. Mac Liammóir and Edwards would never speak openly about the full complexity of their relationship, which included other lovers at times, and, from the content of their letters, their passionate and abiding love for one another. Instead, these benign public-facing declarations fit into a kind of queer respectability that had served the Mattachine Society in the United States decades earlier and would serve the Irish marriage equality movement decades later.[82] The way that Mac Liammóir spoke about his domestic partnership with Edwards was almost shocking in its ordinariness. If he implied love, desire, or sexuality, it was not in the explicit manner of that the IWLM did two years later on *The Late Late Show*. He talked about Edwards the way any man on the show might speak about his spouse.

When Mac Liammóir died in 1978, Edwards was devastated. In a shaky hand that revealed his own age and arthritis, Hilton Edwards inscribed the funerary registry of Micheál Mac Liammóir.

---

79. Fitz-Simon, *The Boys*, 139.
80. Ryan, *Asking Angela MacNamara*.
81. Ryan, "Asking Angela," 334.
82. Martin Meeker, "Behind the Mask of Respectability: Reconsidering the Mattachine Society and Male Homophile Practice, 1950s and 1960s," *Journal of the History of Sexuality* 10, no. 1 (2001): 78–116; and Sonja Tiernan, *Marriage Equality in Ireland: A Social Revolution Begins*, (Oxford: Oxford University Press, 2020).

Born, Cork October 25th, 1899
Died, Dublin March 6th 1978: at seven P.M.
Rest in Peace.
To the beloved memory
Of a great actor
Artist, Irishman
+
the best friend, partner
and companion
that a man could
wish for for 51 years.
Micheál MacLiammóir
from his devoted
Hilton Edwards
+
Micheál's friends
+
admirers
Gate Theatre,
Dublin, 11th March, 1978[83]

With perhaps a touch of humor—preserving the mythology of "Mac Liammóir" Cork origins—Edwards inscribed a tribute to his love for all to see. Best friend, partner, and companion for fifty-one years. Hilton Edwards, devoted to Micheál Mac Liammóir.

Hundreds signed the book of condolences, and hundreds more sent Hilton Edwards notes and cards expressing their sympathy for his loss.[84] At the funeral, attendees deferred to Hilton Edwards as the chief mourner, a courtesy normally granted to a spouse.[85] According to the *Irish Independent*, "Hilton Edwards, clad in black, was embraced and consoled as he tried to discipline tears threatening to make their way down his cheeks."[86] Though same-sex sex was still illegal, the newspapers reporting on the funeral wrote around and implicitly about Mac Liammóir's sexuality. "A working man named John who had known Mac Liammóir 20 years ago in what circumstances he would not disclose shook the hand of a distraught Hilton Edwards. He had traveled a long distance to be there for the final goodbye to a man who had been a friend."[87]

83. NLI, MS 45,872/2, Micheál Mac Liammóir / Hilton Edwards Papers, Dublin, Ireland.
84. Micheál Mac Liammóir / Hilton Edwards Papers; also Farrelly, "Mac Liammóir, the Kindliest Neighbour," 12.
85. Walshe, "Importance of Staging Oscar Wilde," 219.
86. Farrelly, "Mac Liammóir, the Kindliest Neighbour," 12.
87. Farrelly, 12.

Their complicated home life and relationships were briefly put on public display when the papers reported on Patrick Bedford. "Many of the embraces were reserved for Paddy Bedford, the Edwards-Mac Liammóir protege and star of the box office Hollywood success 'Up the Down Staircase.' He was visibly upset at the parting of the master."[88] Fitz-Simon couldn't say for sure just how close Edwards and Bedford got; he insinuates that it was a one-sided admiration on Edwards's part. Whatever Bedford once was to Edwards, though, he wasn't enough to stem the tide of consuming grief that swept the older man away in the wake of Mac Liammóir's passing.

Politicians, journalists, artists, actors, and all of his many friends around the world expressed what a great loss Mac Liammóir's death posed to Ireland. The Fine Gael leader Garret FitzGerald (who served as taoiseach from 1982 to 1986) said that for over half a century Mac Liammóir "enriched in a unique way Ireland's cultural life and its world reputation. . . . Both at a personal and national level, he is irreplaceable."[89] But no one felt his loss as acutely, as heartrendingly, as his life partner and true love, Hilton Edwards.[90] Just a month after he lost Mac Liammóir, Edwards responded to a note from their friend Molly Mac Ewen. "Yes, I have lost poor Micheál. I need hardly say that I am desolate and my only consolation is that—after all our frequent clashes, which were after all the sparks which lit a conflagration which burned up into the Gate—we were nearer together at the end than ever before. I will not now tell you the details of his passing which was, I think and pray, peaceful enough. . . . For the moment—and for once!—Hilton is speechless and very lonely."[91] Characteristically, Edwards spent most of his letter discussing business, for Molly Mac Ewen was a set designer as well as a longtime friend. On the third page of his typed letter, Edwards turned at last away from peppering her with ideas for paint colors and props. He invited Mac Ewen to Dublin for the duration of the production. "Not to work: I would like your work to be strictly of the supervisory nature—but to stay as my guest. I dread doing the play, but I must do it in Micheál's honour. . . . All my affection, dear Molly, and my respectful greetings to your sister. I am too desolate to write more." He signed the letter "Your old and battered friend, Hilton Edwards."[92]

To cope with—or put off the pain of—the loss of his love, Edwards threw himself back into work until he could no more. But, for three years, the toil was empty. He wrote to Mac Ewen in October 1981 that "the real fact of the matter is that since Micheál's going I have, let me whisper it to you, lost heart

88. Farrelly, 12.

89. Farrelly, 12.

90. Farrelly, 12; "The Stage in Mourning at the Master's Funeral," *Irish Independent*, 8 March 1978, 12.

91. NLI, MS 36,017/4, Hilton Edwards Papers, Dublin, Ireland.

92. Hilton Edwards Papers.

in the Gate. I am just pushed along by an impetus which is the alternative to falling down."[93] He wasn't alone at the home he'd previously shared with Mac Liammóir, as Patrick Bedford was staying with him, but he let the emptiness of Mac Liammóir's absence seep into his bones. "I have not been out of Ireland for well over a year and do not expect I ever will again. Things are a bit lonely and never having had a hobby other than my work I am not very good at handling life at the moment." Though, he said he wasn't "ill" but only "uncomfortable," as one might be at nearly seventy-nine, Edwards's prolonged mourning period clearly took a toll on his health. He finished his letter to Mac Ewen, "I will end now before I burst into tears. . . . I am grateful for your letter, it served as a kind of life-line and I am, always, yours affectionately and gratefully, Hilton."[94] These are the words of a man who has lost the love of his life.[95] When Edwards died in 1982, he was buried at St. Fintant's graveyard, next to the love of his life.[96]

In many ways, Mac Liammóir and Edwards represent a sharp contrast to the other same-sex-desiring men featured in this book. Their lives were not disrupted by policing or the violence of arrest, trial, and imprisonment. The archival evidence of their love and sex lives are not in the court records but in the love letters their estate deposited at the NLI. Their fifty-one-year relationship seemed, for all intents and purposes, above the law and order in Ireland. And yet, they were men who loved, desired, and had sex with other men. While James Hand, Frank North, Leslie Price, John Bodkin, and the gardaí of the 1930s sting operations and the 1950s vice squad are revealing of the extent and damage of the postcolonial moral project, men like Ronald Brown, Micheál Mac Liammóir, and Hilton Edwards demonstrate its limitations.

The limitations of the postcolonial moral project weren't merely human resources and the will to police; there were quite clearly different rules for the privileged. As I've already demonstrated throughout this book, the overwhelming majority of policing focused on public sex, with only a few illustrative exemptions. If we compare the treatment of Hand and Brown, for example, it is clear that class and status were central factors in deciding how and when policing resources were used. The gardaí went to great lengths to exonerate Brown, a state employee from a respectable Irish family. When the opportunity arose to make an example of Hand, a working-class cabbie, the Garda dedicated an unusual amount of time and human resources to throw-

---

93. Hilton Edwards Papers.

94. Hilton Edwards Papers.

95. If you know someone who lost a spouse, you will recognize the shattered hollowness captured in these words. Despite, or maybe especially, if that love endured for over fifty years.

96. Fitz-Simon, *The Boys*, 309.

ing the book at the man. In the Brown case, it seems clear that if Brown's lover hadn't been associated with the seedy character Tom Levins, Brown might have avoided detection altogether. Hand's destruction was a warning to men like him: working-class, same-sex-desiring Dubliners who might be hiding their activities behind closed doors most of the time, but who participated in the visible sexual subculture of the city. Though both cases took place in particularly turbulent moments of postcolonial Irish state building, the results of their cases were dictated by power and privilege.[97]

Mac Liammóir and Edwards moved to Ireland early in the state's postcolonial history. Their ability to glide through the world together, to share a home, and to speak publicly about a quiet domesticity, while professing deep and abiding love in private letters, are evidence of the limitations of the postcolonial moral project. While there's no archival evidence that they flaunted their love with public displays of physical intimacy, Mac Liammóir nodded to their domestic partnership on television at a time when men were still being arrested and imprisoned for acts of gross indecency. They took up residence at their home on Harcourt Terrace in 1945; in all the time they lived there, they were never harassed by the Garda. It's clear that their positionality and privilege afforded them exemption from the law. Which, of course, is not the same thing as feeling free to love and be loved. Even for those with the privilege of socioeconomic capital to spend, there was a great deal of loneliness in Ireland's culture of silence and shame.

---

97. NAI, AGO, 2002-16-466, the State v. Ronald H. Brown.

Conclusion

The Writer

n the novel *The Trial of Father Dillingham*, John Broderick unfolds a story of
love, loss, and lust. Eddie Doyle veers off his normal path home to stop in the
obviously named Rainbow Inn for a drink.[1]

> Friday was Cole Porter night at the Rainbow Inn. Saturday evening was
> given over to the tunes associated with Judy Garland and Marlene Die-
> trich. But Eddie Doyle did not know this. He had never been to the
> place before—although he was well aware of the special reputation
> it enjoyed in the half-world of Dublin—and he passed it every after-
> noon on his way home from work.[2]

He takes a seat at the bar, orders a pint, and stares into its foamy depths. He's
heartsick and restless. His long-term partner, Maurice, is ill with leukemia.
They can't be physically intimate, and, for Eddie—who craves the touch of his
lover—it's become nearly unbearable. With the threat of losing Maurice hanging over him and his pent-up frenetic energy, he's spiraling. Though he won't
admit it to himself, he knows exactly why he's turned up at the Rainbow Inn,
where rough men are readily available for semianonymous sex. He doesn't
want to betray Maurice like that, but he almost can't help himself.

---

1. Broderick, *Trial of Father Dillingham*, 20–22.
2. Broderick, 22.

When Abraham Gillepsie, a six-foot-three longshoreman "built like a Cretan bull," approaches him at the bar, he's startled briefly from his brooding. "Does that tune get you below the belt?" Abraham asks, referring to "Everytime We Say Good-Bye" coming through the speakers. When Eddie doesn't quite get it, Abraham remarks, as insinuatingly as his sandpaper Dublin voice would allow, "Mild weather for this time of year," to which Eddie gave a "shy but friendly smile" and ordered the first of "a long row of pints to be set in front of the delighted connoisseur of the national beverage." They spend the evening together drinking, mostly Eddie talking and Abraham listening. It's hours before Eddie is shocked into the realization of what he is doing in engaging this sweet, slow Dubliner in the Rainbow Inn. With an apology and shame, he backs out of the pub and hurries home to Maurice.[3]

When Maurice dies, Eddie finds his way back to Abraham. He knows he shouldn't. He should control himself. He should walk away from the Rainbow Inn. But instead he takes the rough man back to his rooms, and every Saturday for two months after. For Abraham, his relationship with Eddie is so different from all the other one-night stands with fancy businessmen who frequent the Rainbow Inn. He opens up. He shows parts of himself that he hasn't ever before because the men who buy him drinks just want a big dumb man who can give them a good ride. Eddie seems different; but, in the end, he isn't.

After two months, Eddie knows he should call it off. But wanting to dull the pain of Maurice's loss, and the guilt of leading poor Abraham on, Eddie "reached forward suddenly, took the glass from Abraham's hand, drank half of it, stood up and held it to the other man's lips. He felt his hands covered as the glass was drained. It fell on the carpet between them as his wrists were grasped and he allowed himself to be mercifully drawn down and held with strangely gentle fingers." The two are entwined in an embrace in a desperate moment. "'That isn't enough,' whispered Abraham later, lifting the hot disheveled body by the armpits and stroking the naked chest with his palms. Eddie shivered and looked up with gratitude into eyes as glazed as his own. Slowly, like two people shocked by an accident, they made their way into the hall and through the kitchen into the bedroom."[4]

Class, Dublin's queer urbanscape, pain, and love between men are at the center of John Broderick's *The Trial of Father Dillingham*—much as they've been at the center of this book. Most of the men I've discussed had their lives disrupted by the Irish policing of same-sex sex. Over 350 men were arrested in Dublin between 1922 and 1972 for crimes of "gross indecency."[5] Perhaps hun-

---

3. Broderick, 23–25.

4. Broderick, 184.

5. This number is estimated from the Dublin Circuit Court State Books and State Files for 1922–1965, newspaper reports from 1922 to 1972, and the Garda commissioner reports from

dreds more were subjected to extrajudicial harassment and violence without documentation. In addition to the formal policing of same-sex desire, the Catholic habitus and ethos of postcolonial Ireland created informal systems of self-policing and social pressure to reject one's "unnatural" sexual desires.[6] Though Dubliners like Edward Payton and Matthew Nyhan's father might have been willing to overlook or ignore the queerness of friends, neighbors, and family members, the messaging from the Catholic hierarchy and Irish state was clear in its opposition to sex, generally, and same-sex sex, especially.[7] Undoubtedly, the informal self-policing and community pressure was, at times, more suffocating than the actual threat of legal sanctions. Those stories are harder to uncover in state archives.

There were hundreds, perhaps even thousands, of same-sex-desiring men and women who were never arrested or harassed by the gardaí. There were husbands who took secret lovers and were never caught, and bachelors who roomed together to make ends meet—for their entire lives. There were most certainly unrelated "spinster" aunties who built lives together in quiet domesticity, and women like Rosemary Curb and Nancy Manahan, former religious sisters who took vows and then found each other.[8] While many found happiness and pleasure within Ireland, *despite* the Catholic nationalist postcolonial project, there were still others who suffered under the regime without ever coming into contact with the laws: same-sex-desiring women who resigned themselves to unhappy, perhaps abusive, marriages; and same-sex-desiring men who denied themselves the love of another man because they feared for their livelihood, reputation, or souls. The formal and informal systems of repression took their toll. An undetected queer life, like that of John Broderick, was not necessarily a happy one.

John Broderick Jr., author of *The Trial of Father Dillingham*, was born in 1924, not long after the Irish Free State was founded. He would be his parent's only child. John Sr. and Mary Katherine Broderick ran a bakery in Athlone, Broderick's Sunshine Bakery. After John Sr.'s death in 1927, his mother astutely turned the family business into the biggest bakery in the midlands. Nine years later, she married the bakery manager, a "handsome rogue" named

---

1965 to 1972. The Garda commissioner reports don't isolate Dublin data, but, based on previous years/decades, I estimate that at least 25 percent of the country's total was in Dublin.

6. Inglis, "Catholic Identity in Contemporary Ireland," 205–220.

7. Ferriter, *Occasions of Sin*, 338.

8. Manahan and Curb were American but appeared on RTÉ, in 1985, to promote a book they wrote that included interviews with forty-five religious sisters and nuns about their sexuality. The book—and the women's feature on RTÉ—caused an immense stir in Ireland. They had to change their hotel reservation when the hotel proprietor refused to house them on the grounds of their "immorality." Available at https://www.upi.com/Archives/1985/09/14/Lesbian-ex-nuns-cause-furor-in-Ireland/1194495518400/.

Paddy Flynn, known as much for his womanizing as for his management skills. John did not get along with his stepfather, though he lived with his mother and her husband until her death in 1974. After his mother's remarriage, John was sent away to boarding school, first to Summerhill College in Sligo, and when he was expelled from there for "raiding the kitchen," to St. Joseph's College just outside Ballinasloe, where he remained until leaving with his Intermediate Certification.[9]

John was close with his mother, even after she remarried.[10] After he finished school, without taking the Leaving Certificate, he and his mother traveled together and attended parties, the theater, and society events, from Athlone to Dublin to Paris. Their thriving bakery allowed the otherwise middle-class Brodericks to play at midland aristocracy. They bought and lived in properties with grand names like The Willows and The Moorings.[11] A talented actor, John joined the Athlone Musical Society and Athlone Little Theater, appearing in dramatic productions in 1949 and 1950.[12]

Though he was involved in the family business, writing was John's true passion. In 1951, he spent a year or two in Paris, where he met and became close friends with Julien Greene, and rubbed elbows with a number of the twentieth century's great—and mostly gay—writers who found community in Paris, including Gore Vidal, Truman Capote, James Baldwin, and Ernest Hemingway.[13] By 1956, John's first piece of writing was published in the *Irish Times*.[14] He wrote travel pieces and book reviews for twenty-five years.[15] He lived briefly in Dublin, Paris, Rome, and London, and for much longer stretches in Athlone and, at the end of his life, Bath, England.[16] At one point, John probably considered staying in France with Julien Green permanently, and Julien may have invited him to do so, but John always returned to his mother, until he couldn't anymore.[17]

John Broderick's lifework rejected Ireland's denial of homegrown same-sex desire through the characters in his novels. His controversial discussions of homosexuality did not fare well in Ireland. "Only three favorable reviews in Ireland in 20 years!" he told the *Westmeath Independence* in 1981. "But it is fatal to be praised in this country in your lifetime; it means that you are

---

9. Kingston, *Something in the Head*, 24–26.

10. Kingston, 32.

11. Gray, "If One Is Lonely One Prefers Discomfort," 251–262.

12. Kingston, *Something in the Head*, 35.

13. Kingston, 38.

14. "Oedipus at Epidaurus," *Irish Times*, 14 August 1956, 5.

15. *Irish Times*, 1956–1981.

16. "A Profile of John Broderick," *Westmeath Independent*, March 16, 1973, 9.

17. "Broderick Revisited," Athlone Community Radio, available at https://athlonecommunityradio.ie/tag/john-broderick/.

considered 'harmless.'"[18] He described the negative receipt of his books as a sort of badge of honor in his later years. When his novel was banned by the Board of Censors for "immoral themes," Broderick didn't appeal or challenge the decision. He disapproved of the censors but decided that trying to reason with people "as stupid and narrow-minded" as the Board of Censors was fruitless and so did not bother.[19]

The United States, United Kingdom, and most European states in the 1930s, 1940s, and 1950s were grappling with the idea that same-sex desire was more than just a behavior and act, that it was a defining characteristic of a kind of person—a sexuality. In some ways, the Irish state was (distantly) involved in that conversation too. Judges commented on the problem of "men like you" with a kind of casual acknowledgment that the men having sex with other men were not quite "normal."[20] But sexology, psychology, and sexuality studies were explicitly targeted and hindered by the activities of the Board of Censors. Librarians and doctors had to write requests to be able to import books like Havelock Ellis's *Studies in the Psychology of Sex* or Richard von Krafft-Ebing's *Psychopathia Sexualis*.[21] Ordinary people were flat-out denied personal access to those kinds of texts as well as novels like Radclyffe Hall's *Well of Loneliness*, queer pulp, and the novels with "homosexual" protagonists of Irish authors like John Broderick.[22] Libraries that did have copies were instructed to keep them in a restricted section.[23]

It was just as likely, more so in most cases, for an Irish person, judge or otherwise, to frame same-sex desire not as identity but as sin or vice until well

---

18. Margaret Grennan, "John Broderick Says Farewell to Athlone," *Westmeath Independent*, 28 August 1981, 16.

19. Quoted in Kingston, *Something in the Head*, 46.

20. E.g., "Vice Prevalent in Dublin," *Irish Times*, 13 February 1931, 13; "Sentence of Seven Years Penal Servitude," *Irish Times*, 14 February 1931, 15; "Strong Comment by Dublin Judge," *Irish Times*, 1 August 1931, 9; and "Not Uncommon in This City," *Irish Times*, 7 February 1931, 6.

21. Averill Earls, "Explicit: Censorship, Sexology, and Sexuality in Independent Ireland," *Nursing Clio*, 13 February 2018, available at https://nursingclio.org/2018/02/13/explicit-censorship-sexology-and-sexuality-in-independent-ireland/.

22. Havelock Ellis, *Studies in the Psychology of Sex*. Volumes 1–6 were originally published between 1896 and 1910. Volumes 1 and 2 were reprinted in 1942 (New York: Random House, 1942). Richard von Krafft-Ebing, *Psychopathia Sexualis*, was originally published in 1886 in German, and then translated into English by Charles Gilbert Chaddock in 1892, with multiple editions being released throughout the twentieth century (Philadelphia: The F.A. Davis Company, 1894; New York: Arcade Publishing, 1998); Radclyffe Hall, *Well of Loneliness* (London, Jonathan Cape Publishing, 1928).

23. NAI, Department of Justice, Committee on Evil Literature, Report, JUS/3/2/1. For a discussion of the queer public fiction that proliferated in the 1940s, 1950s, and 1960s, see Susan Stryker, *Queer Pulp: Perverted Passions from the Golden Age of the Paperback* (San Francisco: Chronicle Books, 2001).

into the 1960s. Keeping the public discourse mired in the weeds of sin allowed the state to ignore the shifts in other countries where same-sex-desiring people were advocating for rights and recognition: for instance, the German rights movement of the 1920s, led by figures like Magnus Hirschfeld, or later, the homophile movements in the United States and the United Kingdom. The Mattachine Society used a combination of radical politics and conformity/respectability politics to advance the ideas both that same-sex-desiring people couldn't change who they were and that they deserved the freedom to marry, have families, and be in love like any opposite-sex attracted person. Those conversations were aided and sometimes initiated by the sexological studies published in the 1890s through the 1960s. By outlawing public access to those materials, the Free State stagnated productive and iterative conversations about things like sexuality and sexual identity.

Though Irish people did not with any frequency bring same-sex-desiring men to the attention of the Garda, they did bring "offensive" publications to the attention of the Board of Censors.[24] There are hundreds of letters in the NAI from grannies, housewives, and self-congratulatory businessmen who either sought out or stumbled upon material in bookshops and newsstands that they felt contravened the censorship laws. Pretty frequently the board agreed and issued the required paperwork to ban those publications. Broderick knew, of course, that having "homosexual" characters in *The Pilgrimage* would result in its banning. The same had happened to Kate O'Brien's *Land of Spices* two decades earlier, and that for just a single sentence in the entire book.[25] The *Pilgrimage* has a main character who was a bourgeoisie gay man, seemingly on his deathbed; on top of that, there are bizarre vignettes about Tommy Baggot, a young man who lives in Dublin in a flat he shares with another young man. The two are reportedly "known homosexuals" who run around town getting into trouble.[26] The possibility of banning didn't seem particularly troubling to Broderick. In 1961, he told an interviewer that "nobody now takes the Censorship Board seriously—at worst it is an irritating exhibition of public hypocrisy."[27] Knowing the likely consequences, he went ahead with his story and characters as written.

John Broderick was not publicly "out" about his sexuality for most of his life, and he didn't leave many records of his own feelings or self-perceptions of life as an Irish same-sex-desiring man. He wrote same-sex-desiring characters but did not (in a legal sense) fight for same-sex-desiring people to exist

---

24. I discuss the apparent blind eye that Dubliners turned to what was obviously a robust queer subculture in the city in Chapter 3.

25. Dalsimer, *Kate O'Brien*, 89.

26. Broderick, *The Pilgrimage*, 119–120.

27. John Broderick, "Under the Counter," *Irish Times*, 11 November 1961, 8.

in Ireland. He acknowledged that he wrote from a position of privilege; if his family bakery hadn't been one of the largest employers in Athlone, he might've faced more severe social consequences for publishing the books that he did.[28] And yet, though he didn't tussle with the law or advocate for his own books to be able to circulate in Ireland or serve as a sort of public figure for queer Irish youths, he persisted in publishing works that challenged the postcolonial moral regime. Even if he wouldn't have self-identified as an activist, his books did that work for him.

In interviews, Broderick claimed that he wrote homosexual characters to be purposely provocative. He told one interviewer, "I think the Irish are pathological about homosexuality. That was one of the reasons I chose it as a theme for my books, because it never had been done before."[29] Undoubtedly, he did strive to be provocative. He claimed to be the first Irish author to write about homosexuality.[30] Writing about same-sex-desiring men—always men, never women—set him apart from other Irish writers of his time. *The Land of Spices* has a single sentence that describes two men in an intimate sexual embrace. Brendan Behan discussed queer people nonchalantly that he encountered in juvenile prison in *Borstal Boy* (also banned).[31] And many writers—from Oscar Wilde to Elizabeth Bowen—hinted at or alluded to or could be read as homoerotic or queer. But Broderick wrote main characters, protagonists, and titular characters who were gay. And as evidenced by the landscapes, the personalities, and the themes of his novels, Broderick also wrote what he knew.

Broderick rarely talked about his own sexuality. In a 1979 interview with Campbell Spray, features editor of the *Irish Press*, Broderick said he'd lived an "active" life as a young man. He drank, he smoked, and he had sex. "I did everything I wanted to, in every conceivable way." After dire news from the doctors, warning that he'd die if he kept up with his drinking and smoking, he gave it all up. "I remember going to a Turkish bath in Rome and being surrounded by old men with fat bellies chasing young male prostitutes—[and thinking] that's not going to happen to me."[32] Broderick was good at deflecting and giving half answers. He never said what he actually *was* doing in that Turkish bath. Generally when asked about his own sexuality, he demurred. He told Spray that "as far as sexuality is concerned I think that most men are bisexual—as are most women." In June 1988, just a few months before Broderick had a stroke, and less than a year before he died, he sat down with David Hanly for RTÉ. Interviewers almost always asked Broderick about his sexu-

---

28. Campbell Spray, "I Did It All," *Irish Press*, 16 August 1979, 9.

29. Quoted in Kingston, *Something in the Head*, 48.

30. Spray, "I Did It All."

31. Donal Ó Disceoil, "Irish Books Banned under the Censorship of Publications Act, 1929–67," in *The Oxford History of the Irish Book* (New York: Oxford University Press, 2011), 645–649.

32. Spray, "I Did It All."

ality—how could they not, when he was the only Irish writer writing gay characters regularly?—and Broderick gave his usual answer. He told Hanly that he was not homosexual but bisexual, but that he had never been sexually promiscuous, and it had not made life more difficult because he "had not been ruled by sexual impulse."[33] He wrote frankly about his characters' sex lives but never ventured beyond dropping hints or deflecting from discussions about his own.

I have no concrete evidence that he took a lover or had any romantic entanglements. Unlike Mac Liammóir and Edwards, Broderick didn't leave personal diaries chronicling affairs or correspondences with lovers behind. The bits and pieces of himself that are preserved at the Westmeath Library in Athlone are ideas for stories, lists of names from obituaries for his characters, and occasional insights into his literary imagination. What Madeleine Kingston has managed to reconstruct in terms of biography and insights into Broderick's writing is remarkable. But there are other more intimate things that we will never know about John Broderick. We know that he desired men but have little evidence that he ever acted on his feelings. We know that he imagined a Dublin that gave men like him a place to build a life and a family, but we can't know if he wanted that for himself or knew others for whom that fantasy was a reality.

While he didn't keep a diary or leave documents that would help us better chronicle his life, we do know that he wrote what he knew. When he was living in Athlone, nearly every novel he wrote took place in some unnamed midlands Ireland town with all the obvious landmarks and physical features of Athlone. When he lived in Bath—but wished he lived in London—he wrote picturesquely of London and unflatteringly of Bath. As a teen, he lived in Dublin for a bakery apprenticeship and returned there many times as an adult. When he set his stories in Dublin, he captured the walkability of the city, the character of the subdivided but still grand Georgian homes, and the particular homosociality of the Dublin pub. His novels almost always have two older women who gossip shamelessly while trying to outdo each other in piousness or martyrdom. His lead women are flawed, beautiful, and strong willed. In half of his twelve published novels there are men who desire men, openly or obviously. As Broderick told Spray in 1979, "I have written about both sides of the coin, my attitudes [about sexuality] are known."[34] How many of the relationships and caricatures that he wrote about were similarly inspired by the world and people around him? How many of the female protagonists he wrote about were inspired by his mother? How much of the longing and loneliness felt by his characters was drawn from his own pain?

---

33. Kingston, *Something in the Head*, 155.
34. Spray, "I Did It All."

Most scholars agree that his best work was *The Waking of Willie Ryan*, published in 1965, a novel in which an elderly man escapes the asylum he's been held in for decades and returns to his hometown. As a young man, he had an affair with another man, and his sister-in-law, who learned of this embarrassment, accused him of sexually assaulting *her* so that he would be sent away. Most of Broderick's early novels are critiques of the things he hated about the Irish midlands: the insularity, the Catholic performativity rather than genuine personal faith, and the unending hypocrisy. *The Waking of Willie Ryan* is a poignant example of this. Despite his homosexuality, the titular character is the only person in his hometown who maintains real personal religion; everyone around him merely performs the rituals and public piety of Catholicism.

Arguably, Broderick's second best novel was his first, *The Pilgrimage*. The debut was published in 1961 and promptly banned in Ireland for its frank discussion of sex (without love and often without pleasure), depiction of gay characters, and, most damningly, the final chapter, a single sentence deemed blasphemous by the Board of Censors. The Board of Censors must've read *The Pilgrimage* in sanctimonious horror when the bedridden gay man, who continued to pursue sexual relationships with young men throughout the novel, returned from Lourdes completely healed.

Though he didn't write about love so much as sex, and few of his characters had healthy or fulfilling relationships, there are glimpses that Broderick was a bit of a romantic, or at least indulged in romantic fantasies. The Dublin he built in his novels, whether it was based in reality, purely fiction, or somewhere in the middle, was practically a haven for same-sex-desiring men. After his mother passed, Broderick spent the rest of his life looking for his place in the world. In 1981, wanting to be closer to the intellectual hub of London, he moved to Bath, England. Though the setting inspired some of his later novels, he continued to feel restless and out of place. In the 1988 interview with David Hanly, Broderick discussed plans to return to Ireland. He wanted to go, not to Athlone, but to Dublin or Wicklow, "returning to live among the amusing, quick-witted, honest Irish people with their awareness of Christian values," which Kingston rightly points out was as "romantic" (and ridiculous) an idea as "moving to Jane Austen's Bath had been in 1981."[35] The romantic Dublin that he set his sights on in 1988 was probably the Dublin he'd imagined in his fiction.

Some of the characters in Broderick's novels enjoyed a far greater degree of joy and romantic companionship than the author. Between 1961 and 1965, Broderick published four novels. Though his novels are set in the 1950s and 1960s, which were periods of high unemployment and constant emigration,

---

35. Kingston, *Something in the Head*, 155–156.

his characters live comfortably in Dublin, either able to share a house of apartments with their loved ones or find rooms to share with a lover without the press of prying eyes in overcrowded slums. As the slums were cleared and new homes constructed between the 1930s and the 1960s, opportunities to rent or buy a flat or cottage increased, but the demand for housing still surpassed the supply for most of that period.[36] In reality, some men (like James Hand and Ronald Brown) were able to maintain private spaces that offered regular shelter from the dangers of pursuing sex in the streets, but certainly not all. All of Broderick's gay characters are that fortunate.[37] There was queer joy to be found in midcentury Dublin—both in the imagination of its writers, in the private nooks of the city's Georgian edifices, and in the alleys, pubs, and even the lavatories, where men could find a bit of love if they went looking.

There was also plenty of sorrow and fear in Dublin.[38] For some, like Ronald Brown in 1941, the allegations of intimacy with another man obliterated his career and drove him out of Ireland. Of the hundreds arrested and tried, Brown was among the fortunate; yes, he lost much, but he served no time and was ultimately exonerated. For men without means or connections, the consequences were far more dire. Men like James Hand spent months or even years in prison with hard labor. A few were made into examples to instill fear and loathing in the public. Newspapers published names, employers, and addresses of the accused, alongside veiled details of the crimes. Judges gave statements to journalists decrying the vice of the city and reminding readers that the gardaí were always watching. In the 1930s and 1940s, word likely spread of the undercover gardaí who would lure an unwary man into an arrest. In the summer of 1950, with nearly forty men hauled to the Garda station by the vice squad at Bottesford Place, the danger—and dangerous opportunity—of Dublin's public lavatories was hammered home at the October assizes and in the newspapers. Though the Garda may not have had the manpower necessary to truly eradicate same-sex sex from the streets, cinemas, cars, parks, or public urinals of Dublin, they certainly cultivated a legacy of fear and loneliness among the Irish men who hadn't the familial, financial, or spiritual freedom to live queer lives. For men who feared the rejection of family, for men who couldn't afford to live alone or beyond the family home, and for men who were unable to separate their private Christian identity from the official word of the Catholic Church, the weight of state homophobia was enormous. While the moral policing project was neither consistent nor successful in eradicating homosexuality in Ireland, it *was* successful in creating a hostile environment for Ireland's queer people.

---

36. See Brady, *Dublin, 1950–1970*, 62–300.
37. Broderick, *The Pilgrimage*, 119–120; Broderick, *Trial of Father Dillingham*, 22–25.
38. O'Carroll and Collins, *Lesbian and Gay Visions*, 18–21.

Beginning in the early 1960s, John Broderick struggled with alcohol abuse. His friends loathed when John was drinking, and, by his own admission, when he drank it was always to excess. He tried to dry out, several times, but always fell off the wagon, taking secret trips to local hotels just to drink. His mother's death in 1974 further unmoored John. He was very lonely after she died but seemed unable to forge a connection to replace her role in his life. He moved to Bath in 1981, where his loneliness was compounded; according to Kingston, he was trying to get back to Ireland for the rest of his life, but his liquid assets got tied up in real estate law. He died in Bath, perhaps never experiencing the joy and love he crafted for some of his characters. It seems likely that his experience was more like those characters who were lonely, cynical, and viewed sex as distasteful.

Broderick was forged by the Ireland that made examples of men who expressed their sexual desire for other men. He was seven years old when James Hand was arrested, when judge Cahir Davitt told journalists that the vice of homosexuality was prevalent in Dublin and needed to be eradicated, when judge George Shannon assured the reading public that the gardaí were always watching. He was seventeen when Leslie Price—also seventeen—was sent to prison and Ronald Brown's career was blown up because of their romance. His cousins, Patrick and Mary Hunt, noted a change in him starting in 1946–1947, which Kingston suggests would have been Broderick's era of realizing his desire for men. He was twenty-six and a regular visitor to Dublin with his mother when the gardaí staked out Beresford Place and sent forty men to prison in October 1950.

From 1951 to 1972, 43 percent of men charged with gross indecency in Dublin were exonerated in court, and most of those convicted were released with a fine and charge to keep the peace. As the conviction rate declined, so too did the overall arrests for gross indecency and sodomy in Dublin.[39] For example, Francis Dermody and Thomas O'Shea were charged with having sex with each other in 1962. Dermody was found guilty but allowed to pay a fine and "keep the peace" for two years. Bizarrely, O'Shea—Dermody's sexual partner—was found not guilty.[40] Their story is representative of the majority of cases in the 1960s, when juries were less likely to convict alleged gross indecency offenders unless children were involved, and judges commuted most sentences to fines. In the same period, sex was discussed for the first time on national television on *The Late Late Show*, and the "Asking Angela" column

---

39. I found twenty-three court files in the NAI, and, as far as I can tell, there were no cases that went to trial between 1968 and 1972. That doesn't mean men weren't still being harassed and arrested, but the Gardaí may have used the loitering charge more liberally in that period.

40. NAI, Dublin Circuit Court, State Files, V14-16-5, docket 4, 18-Jan-62, the State v. Francis Dermody and Thomas O'Shea.

in the *Sunday Press* was helping Irish couples, singles, and families navigate all kinds of challenging questions about love, marriage, and sexuality.[41] Historians earmark the 1960s as the start of a "thaw" in Irish culture, especially around issues of sex and sexuality. As Páraic Kerrigan has demonstrated, in the 1970s, activists seized on the thawing to open up conversations about same-sex love, domestic violence, sex education, and gay rights.[42] The visibility of the IGRM was a pivotal moment for young queer people in Ireland.

But the thawing of Irish society also created thin spots and cracks that could swallow some people whole into the nation's icy depths. As expressed by activists in the 1970s and 1980s and captured in the fever dream of Aodhán Madden's memoir, cruising same-sex-desiring men continued to be harassed extrajudicially.[43] The Catholic Church's moral monopoly persisted, led by Archbishop McQuaid. In 1965, John McGahern published his acclaimed novel *The Dark*, which lays bare the sexual impropriety of a Catholic priest. In response, the archbishop had McGahern sacked from his teaching position in Clontarf.[44] Certainly, like the 1982 example of Declan Flynn, queer men could even be murdered with no consequences for the murderers.[45] Being gay and Irish was dangerous and could be deeply lonely in the 1960s and early 1970s. Fewer men were arrested, and fewer still convicted, but the legacy of policing and the persistent religiocultural homophobia left many same-sex-desiring Irish men—and women—feeling like outsiders in their country.

It's true that the Garda didn't police Dublin with the kind of rigor they would have needed to eradicate the city's public queer life. But when gardaí did organize campaigns to target same-sex-desiring men, as in 1931, the 1940s, and 1950, they were exceedingly effective. The scattered but zealous efforts of 1931's gardaí resulted in the arrest of thirty-nine men and the conviction of nineteen over the course of a year. Wartime patrolling of the Dublin streets led the gardaí to arrest forty men in five years. And the targeted and detached efforts of the 1950 vice squad sent over forty-seven men to prison in just a few months. Those highly publicized efforts had an impact beyond the immediate prison rolls.

41. Ryan, "Asking Angela," 317–339.
42. Kerrigan, *LGBTQ Visibility, Media and Sexuality*.
43. NAI, Department of Justice, JUS/3/116, Norris v. Ireland. David Norris requested the arrest/conviction totals for 1973–1985 when he lodged his suit against the Irish government in the European Human Rights Court. For the 1980s and late 1970s, the report shows that 75 percent of men arrested for "homosexual offences" were dealt with "summarily."
44. Noel Ward, "When a Teacher Was Engulfed by 'The Dark,' and His Union Failed," *Irish Times*, 18 June 2002, available at https://www.irishtimes.com/news/education/when-a-teacher-was-engulfed-by-the-dark-and-his-union-failed-1.1061023.
45. See Kerrigan, *LGBTQ Visibility, Media and Sexuality*; and McDonagh, *Gay and Lesbian Activism*.

As Madden describes in his memoir, knowledge that the gardaí were watching, that the consequences would flay him before family, coworkers, and country was enough to induce fear and panic well into the 1970s. Madden describes most vividly a fear of the public lavatory in Phoenix Park, a known haunt of men seeking sex with other men. He stumbles there drunkenly one day, hypnotized by the grotesquely writhing bodies and his attraction to them. But he flees, chased by the fear of being caught, of his father finding out, of his employer finding out.[46] For those like Madden, the state-led violence and culture of Catholic nationalist morality instilled persistent self-loathing. For those like Broderick, even as he wrote about men like him in an explicit challenge to the nation's antigay agenda, he seemed to friends to be an exceptionally lonely man. Loneliness, fear, and self-loathing in a homophobic country could lead to self-destruction, alcoholism, and early deaths. John Broderick died at sixty-five in 1989; Aodhán Madden died at 68 in 2015.

Though Michael Mac Liammóir and Hilton Edwards represent a different potential outcome, one rippling with love and joy and the beautiful chaos of a life shared, it's hard to say which was the norm for same-sex-desiring Irish men. In the collective memory of Ireland's LGBTQ community in the 1970s and 1980s, the norm was pain, shame, and suffering. Certainly, that was an experience that Broderick shared with men like James Hand, Ronald Brown, John Bodkin, Frank North, Michael Corr, and the hundreds of others arrested for crimes of gross indecency. Even if Broderick never faced a trial in court himself, the laws and cultural prejudices did their damage.

The gay rights movement took shape in Dublin, Cork, and rural Ireland in the early 1970s.[47] Broderick was known for his pointed critique of Ireland's hypocrisies and sexual backwardness—but only in his writing. He did not participate in the queer social opportunities of institutions like Flikkers at the Hirschfeld Center in Dublin.[48] There is no evidence that he was a member of any of the gay rights organizations that formed across the country. But he wrote queer characters who were whole people, main characters, even protagonists, which was not something any other Irish writer was doing openly or quite so boldly at the time, and even for decades on.

Maybe he felt too old or too aristocratic or too buttoned-up or simply too uninterested to participate in the movement for gay rights. Instead, he left the country entirely in 1981, hoping to find a more "cosmopolitan" and worldly community in England. He didn't find what he was looking for, and seemed

---

46. A. Madden, *Fear and Loathing in Dublin*, 92–93.
47. McDonagh, *Gay and Lesbian Activism*.
48. McDonagh, 44; Páraic Kerrigan, "Waking the Hirschfeld: An Oral History and Archival Study of Dublin's Hirschfeld Centre," available at https://wakingthehirschfeld.com/the-project/.

to regret his departure almost immediately.[49] He died in Bath, though, a year after David Norris won the European Human Rights court case against Ireland's anti-homosexuality laws, and four years before the Irish Dáil would finally decriminalize same-sex sex. When asked whether he was happy, more tellingly, Broderick told Hanly that no life was entirely happy or unhappy and that it was misguided to search for happiness.[50] The words, I think, of a lonely man.

There is no narrative of progress here. Things got bad, then a little better, then worse still. The public persecution of men who had sex with men would have been imprinted on Broderick and the other men of his generation. When he took up drinking in the 1960s, he asserted it was to overcome a terrible shyness, a bit of "Dutch courage."[51] His fear and discomfort with his sexuality were, undoubtedly, only part of the challenges that shaped Broderick's life. Alcohol abuse, his educational limitations, social anxiety, and his personal religious belief were equally influential. But the conditions in Ireland that made it a hostile place for the same-sex-desiring were developed as policies, procedures, and an ethos during his formative years; those realities cannot be ignored.

Those born twenty or thirty years after Broderick benefited from his persistent, sometimes sloppy, but always important work. He gave the world queer *Irish* characters and their struggles. In the twentieth-century, discourse was important in the process of forging sexual identities. In *The Well of Loneliness*, Hall's semi-autobiographical Stephen Douglas is relieved and empowered when they find the works of Richard von Krafft-Ebing in their father's study, knowing then that their father saw them and gaining a language for their own desire and identity.[52] Media scholars Alexander Dhoest, Lukasz Szulc, Bart Eckhout, and Páraic Kerrigan have all demonstrated the importance of media representations of queer people to LGBTQ identity formation and civil rights in late twentieth century. Kerrigan in particular argues that without television, the IGRM would not have been successful.[53] Like Broderick, the young gay Irish men born in the 1950s and 1960s suffered the indignities of Ireland's Catholic nationalist moral regime, but they came of age at a time when the consequences of same-sex sex were less publicized in splashy

---

49. Kingston, *Something in the Head*, Part III.

50. Kingston, 156.

51. Kingston, 79.

52. Radclyffe Hall, *The Well of Loneliness*, chap. 27, Australian Project Gutenberg, available at https://gutenberg.net.au/ebooks06/0609021h.html.

53. Alexander Dhoest, Lukasz Szulc, and Bart Eckhout, *LGBTQs, Media, and Culture in Europe* (Abingdon: Routledge, 2016); and Kerrigan, *LGBTQ Visibility, Media, and Sexuality*.

court cases and news reports.[54] There were fewer actual cases, and none nearly as publicized as Hand's, high profile as Brown's, or as concentrated as the 1950s cases of Beresford Place. They grew up in a world with Broderick's *The Pilgrimage* and the *Waking of Willie Ryan*, the former made all the more exciting to read for its banned status. Perhaps the next generation was able to do more than just imagine a better world: they were empowered to fight for one.

---

54. NAI, Department of Justice, JUS/3/116, Norris v. Ireland.

Epilogue

After two decades of organizing, building community, claiming public space and airwaves, marching, and fighting the legal battles to decriminalize sex between men, the IGRM won a major victory in 1993. A decision passed down from the European Court of Human Rights in 1988 validated queer Irish people's human rights. The legislation to decriminalize five years later was an important milestone. But the ethos of the Catholic nationalist state was not erased with the legislative decision. It took decades more to change hearts and minds. Tourism books continued to warn queer travelers about PDA into the 2010s. When I was doing research in 2013, I was told by some archivists that there wasn't anything about *that* in their collections. I had to be evasive, in some cases, when asked about my research goals.

But hearts and minds are changing. By 2023, my email inquiries have been answered with friendly helpfulness. The Irish Queer Archive, curated by Tonie Walsh and held at the NLI, has been active and growing since 2008. There are dissertations, books, and major research council-funded projects in Ireland *and* Northern Ireland. There are enough academics working on these topics now both to form entire (small) panels at conferences and to give government-sponsored public talks. And over the past year or so, I've even had the opportunity to serve on the advisory committee for the Irish government's initiative to disregard past convictions. The men whose stories I've attempted to reconstruct here can now have their records cleared, and hopefully there will be reparations projects in the coming years.

I've been working on this research for a decade. When I started, I got funny looks from the people helping me pull records in the archives. Now it seems like there would be state-level support for a major project to catalog and collect queer archival material dating before the IGRM. I hope that the next book published about same-sex desire in Ireland will be built on oral histories, personal letters, and diaries instead of the cold and heartbreaking records of crime and punishment. The limitations of this book don't mean the records of queer joy, love, and pleasure in Ireland's preliberation period don't exist, just that we haven't found them yet. But we will.

Bibliography

ARCHIVES

Houses of the Oireachtas, Dublin
    Parliamentary Debates. Accessed 7 February 2024. Available at http://debates.oireach
        tas.ie/.
Irish Newspaper Archive, online
    Anglo-Celt
    Connaught Telegraph
    Donegal News
    Drogheda Independent
    Dublin Evening Mail
    Evening Echo
    Evening Herald
    Irish Examiner
    Irish Independent
    Irish Press
    Leinster Express
    Leinster Observer
    Longford Leader
    Meath Chronicle
    Post
    Strabane Chronicle
    Sunday Independent
    Ulster Herald
    Westmeath Independent
Irish Times Archive, online

National Archives of Ireland, Dublin (NAI)
    Census of Ireland, 1901/1911. Available at http://www.census.nationalarchives.ie/.
    Department of Foreign Affairs
    Department of Justice (JUS)
        Carrigan Report, JUS/2004/32/105
        Censorship materials, including 2019/144/3, 2005/25/10, 2006/148, 90/102/12
        Report on juvenile and sexual offenses, JUS/8/451
        State Books, City and County of Dublin, 1922–1972
        State Books, County Galway, 1922–1972
        State Files, City and County of Dublin, 1922–1965
    Irish Genealogy, Civil and Church Records. Accessed 6 February 2024. Available at
        irishgenealogy.ie.
    Office of Attorney General (AGO)
        David Norris v. Ireland, 116/1305/2 or 2023/16/1
        Indecent Assault Case File, 5-2002-16-466
    Wills and Probate Office
National Library of Ireland, Dublin (NLI)
    Hilton Edwards Papers
    Micheál Mac Liammóir Papers
Raidió Teilifís Éireann (RTÉ) Archives
Tailte Eireann, Rate and Valuation Office, Dublin
University College Dublin (UCD)
    Dublin Metropolitan Police and Temporary Garda Registries

FICTION, MEMOIR, AND PUBLISHED PAPERS

Behan, Brendan. *Borstal Boy*. London: Gorgi Books, 1961.
Broderick, John. *The Pilgrimage*. Dublin: Lilliput, 2006. Originally published in London:
    Weidenfeld and Nicolson, 1961.
———. *The Trial of Father Dillingham*. London: Sphere Books, 1982.
———. *The Waking of Willie Ryan*. Dublin: Lilliput, 2004. Originally published in Lon-
    don: Weidenfeld and Nicolson, 1965
Clarke, Austin. *Twice Round the Black Church*. London: Routledge, 1962.
De Valera, Éamon. "The Ireland That We Dreamed Of." In *Speeches and Statements by
    Eamon de Valera 1917–1973*, edited by Maurice Moynihan. New York: St. Martin's Press,
    1980.
Madden, Aodhan. *Fear and Loathing in Dublin*. Dublin: Liberties, 2009.
McCourt, Frank. *Angela's Ashes*. New York: Scribner, 1996.
McGahern, John. *All Will Be Well: A Memoir*. New York: Alfred A. Knopf, 2006.
———. *The Barracks*. London: Faber and Faber, 1963.
———. *The Dark*. London: Faber, 1965.
O'Brien, Kate. *The Land of Spices*. New York: Doubleday, Doran & Company, Inc., 1941.
O'Callaghan, Sean. *Down by the Glenside*. Dublin: Mercer, 1992.
O'Connor, Frank. *An Only Child*. New York: Alfred A. Knopf, 1961.

SECONDARY LITERATURE

Allen, Gregory. *The Garda Síochána: Policing Independent Ireland 1922–1982*. Dublin: Gill
    and Macmillan, 1999.

Angelides, Steven. *The Fear of Child Sexuality: Young People, Sex, and Agency*. Chicago: University of Chicago Press, 2019.

Bakshi, Sandeep. "Fractured Resistance: Queer Negotiations of the Postcolonial in R. Raj Rao's The Boyfriend." *South Asian Review* 33, no. 2 (2012).

Barry, Aoife. "Hidden Dublin: Supplying a 'Long Felt Want'—Dublin's Public Toilets." *The Journal*, 20 Jan 2013. Accessed on 6 June 2015. Available at http://www.thejournal .ie/public-toilets-dublin-755462-Jan2013/.

Beatty, Aidan. "From Gay Power to Gay Rights." *Jacobin Magazine*, 29 May 2015. Accessed on 20 November 2015. Available at https://www.jacobinmag.com/2015/05/ireland-gay -marriage-referendum-rights-movement.

———. "'The Life That God Desires': Masculinity and Power in Irish Nationalism, 1884– 1938." Unpublished manuscript, Ph.D. diss., University of Chicago, June 2015.

Beaumont, Caitriona. "Women, Citizenship and Catholicism in the Irish Free State, 1922– 1948." *Women's History Review* 6, no. 4 (1997): 563–585.

Beriss, David. "Introduction: 'If You're Gay and Irish, Your Parents Must Be English.'" *Identities: Global Studies in Culture and Power* 2, no. 3 (1996): 189–196.

Biagini, Eugenio, and Mary E. Daly, eds. *The Cambridge Social History of Modern Ireland*. Cambridge: Cambridge University Press, 2017.

Boag, Peter. *Same-Sex Affairs: Constructing and Controlling Homosexuality in the Pacific Northwest*. Berkeley: University of California Press, 2003.

Bourke, Joanna. "The Ideal Man: Irish Masculinity and the Home, 1880–1914." In *Reclaiming Gender: Transgressive Identities in Modern Ireland*. New York: St. Martin's Press, 1999.

Boyce, David George. *Nineteenth-Century Ireland: The Search for Stability*. Dublin: Gill and Macmillan, 1990.

Boyd, Clodagh, Declan Doyle, Bill Foley, Brenda Harvey, Annette Hoctor, Maura Molloy, and Mich Quinlan. *Out for Ourselves*. Dublin: Women's Community Press, 1986.

Boyd, Nan Alamilla. *Wide-Open Town: A History of Queer San Francisco to 1965*. Berkeley: University of California Press, 2003.

Brady, Joseph. *Dublin, 1930–1950: The Emergence of the Modern City*. Dublin: Four Courts Press, 2014.

———. *Dublin, 1950–1970: Houses, Flats and High-Rise*. Dublin: Four Courts Press, 2016.

Breathnach, Ciara. "Handy Women and Birthing in Rural Ireland, 1851–1955." *Gender and History* 28, no. 1 (April 2016): 34–56.

Brickell, Chris. "Court Records and the History of Male Homosexuality." *Archifacts* (2008): 25–44.

Buckley, Sarah Anne. *The Cruelty Man*. Manchester: Manchester University Press, 2013.

Campbell, Fergus. *Land and Revolution: Nationalist Politics in the West of Ireland, 1891– 1921*. Oxford: Oxford University Press, 2005.

Campbell, Hugh. *Interpreting the City: An Urban Geography*. Dublin: Trinity College Dublin, 1994.

Canaday, Margot. "'Who Is a Homosexual?' The Consolidation of Sexual Identities in Mid-Twentieth-Century American Immigration Law." *Law and Social Inquiry* 28, no. 2 (2003): 351–386.

Carrington, Tyler. *Love at Last Sight: Dating, Intimacy, and Risk in Turn-of-the-Century Berlin*. Oxford University Press, 2019.

Chauncey, George. *Gay New York: Gender, Urban Culture, and the Making of the Gay Male World, 1890–1940*. New York: Basic Books, 1994.

Cleary, Joe. "Postcolonial Ireland." In *Ireland and the British Empire*. Edited by Kevin Kenny. Oxford: Oxford University Press, 2004.

Cleves, Rachel Hope. *Unspeakable: A Life beyond Sexual Morality*. Chicago: University of Chicago Press, 2020.

Cocks, H. G. *Classified: The Secret History of the Personal Column*. Random House, 2009.

———. *Nameless Offences: Homosexual Desire in the 19th Century*. London: I. B. Tauris, 2010.

Coleman, Jonathan. "Rent: Same-Sex Prostitution in Modern Britain, 1885–1957." PhD diss., University of Kentucky, 2014.

Connell, R. W. *Masculinities*. Cambridge: Polity, 1995.

Connell, R. W., and James W. Messerschmidt. "Hegemonic Masculinity: Rethinking the Concept." *Gender and Society* 19, no. 6 (December 2005): 829–859.

Connolly, Claire. "Postcolonial Ireland: Posing the Question." *European Journal of English Studies* 3, no. 3 (1999): 255–261.

Conrad, Kathryn. *Locked in the Family Cell: Gender, Sexuality and Political Agency in Irish National Discourse*. Madison: University of Wisconsin Press, 2004.

———. "Queer Treasons: Homosexuality and Irish National Identity." *Cultural Studies* 15, no. 1 (2001): 124–137.

Conway, Vicky. *Policing Twentieth Century Ireland: A History of An Garda Síochána*. Abingdon: Routledge, 2014.

Cook, Matt. *London and the Culture of Homosexuality, 1885–1914*. New York: Cambridge University Press, 2003.

———. *Queer Domesticities: Homosexuality and Home Life in Twentieth-Century London*. New York: Palgrave Macmillan, 2014.

Cooney, John. *John Charles McQuaid: Ruler of Catholic Ireland*. Dublin: O'Brien, 2009.

Cronin, Maura. "Class and Status in Twentieth-Century Ireland: The Evidence of Oral History." *Saothar* 32 (2007): 33–43.

Curtin, Nancy J. *The United Irishmen: Popular Politics in Ulster and Dublin, 1791–1798*. New York: Clarendon, 1994.

Dalsimer, Adele M. *Kate O'Brien: A Critical Study*. Dublin: Gill and Macmillan, 1990.

Daly, Mary. *The Battle to Control Female Fertility in Modern Ireland*. Cambridge: Cambridge University Press, 2023.

———. *Slow Failure: Population Decline and Independent Ireland, 1920–1973*. Madison: University of Wisconsin Press, 2006.

———. "Women in the Irish Free State, 1922–39: The Interaction between Economics and Ideology." *Journal of Women's History* 7, no. 1 (1995): 99–116.

Davidson, Roger. "Psychiatry and Homosexuality in Mid-Twentieth-Century Edinburgh: The View from Jordanburn Nerve Hospital." *History of Psychiatry* 20, no. 4 (2009): 403–424.

De Nie, Michael. *The Eternal Paddy: Irish Identity and the British Press, 1798–1882*. Madison: University of Wisconsin Press, 2004.

Denton, Morgan. "Open Secrets: Prostitution and National Identity in Twentieth-Century Irish Society." PhD diss, State University of New York at Buffalo, 2012.

Dickson, David. *Dublin: The Making of a Capital City*. Boston: Belknap Press, 2014.

Duberman, Martin. *Luminous Traitor: The Just and Daring Life of Roger Casement, a Biographical Novel*. Oakland: University of California Press, 2019.

Dukova, Anastasia. *A History of the Dublin Metropolitan Police and Its Colonial Legacy*. London: Palgrave Macmillan, 2016.

Earls, Averill. "Profiling the Pedophile Priest: A Study of Sexological Classification and Declining Catholic Power." Master's thesis, University of Vermont, 2010.

———. "Solicitor Brown and His Boy: Love, Sex, and Scandal in Twentieth-Century Ireland." *Historical Reflections/Réflexions Historiques* 46, no. 1 (2020): 79–94.

———. "Unnatural Offenses of English Import: The Political Association of Englishness and Same-Sex Desire in Nineteenth-Century Irish Nationalist Media." *Journal of the History of Sexuality* 28, no. 3 (September 2019): 396–424.

Evans, Jennifer. "Bahnhof Boys: Policing Male Prostitution in Post-Nazi Berlin." *Journal of the History of Sexuality* 12, no. 4 (October 2003): 605–636.

Farfan, Penny. *Performing Queer Modernism.* Oxford University Press, 2017.

Ferriter, Diarmaid. *Occasions of Sin: Sex and Society in Modern Ireland.* London: Profile Books, 2009.

———. *The Transformation of Ireland, 1900–2000.* London: Profile Books, 2004.

Finnane, Mark. "The Carrigan Committee of 1930–31 and the 'Moral Condition of the Saorstát.'" *Irish Historical Studies* 32, no. 128 (November 2001): 519–536.

Fitzpatrick, David. *The Americanisation of Ireland: Migration and Settlement, 1841–1925.* Cambridge: Cambridge University Press, 2020.

Fitz-Simon, Christopher. *The Boys: A Biography of Michael Mac Liammóir and Hilton Edwards.* London: Nick Hern Books, 1994.

Foster, John Wilson. "Masculinities in Life and Literature." In *Irish Masculinities: Reflections of Literature and Culture*, edited by Caroline Macgennis and Raymond Mullen. Dublin: Irish Academic Press, 2011.

Foster, Roy. *Modern Ireland, 1600–1972.* New York: Penguin, 1990.

Garden, Alison, and Ruth Coon, "Mixed Marriages." *The Honest Ulsterman* (September 2024). Available at https://www.humag.co/features/mixed-marriages.

Garvin, Tom. *Preventing the Future: Why Was Ireland so Poor for so Long?* Dublin: Gill Books, 2005.

Gray, Peter. "'If One Is Lonely One Prefers Discomfort': The Lives of John Broderick." *Studies: An Irish Quarterly Review* 97, no. 387, (Autumn 2008): 251–262.

Gustav-Wrathall, John Donald. *Take the Young Stranger by the Hand: Same-Sex Relations and the YMCA.* Chicago: University of Chicago Press, 1998.

Hanna, Erika. *Modern Dublin: Urban Change and the Irish Past, 1957–1973.* Oxford: Oxford University Press, 2013.

Hartman, Saidaya. *Wayward Lives, Beautiful Experiments: Intimate Histories of Riotous Black Girls, Troublesome Women, and Queer Radicals.* New York: W. W. Norton & Company, 2019.

Healy, Dan. *Homosexual Desire in Revolutionary Russia.* Chicago: University of Chicago Press, 2001.

Helleiner, Jane. "'For the Protection of the Children': The Politics of Minority Childhood in Ireland." *Anthropological Quarterly* 71, no. 2 (April 1998): 51–62.

Hindmarch-Watson, Katie. "Male Prostitution and the London GPO: Telegraph Boys' 'Immorality' from Nationalization to the Cleveland Street Scandal." *Journal of British Studies* 51, no. 3 (July 2012): 594–617.

Hoad, Neville Wallace. *African Intimacies: Race, Homosexuality, and Globalization.* Minneapolis: University of Minnesota Press, 2006.

Hopkinson, Michael. *Green against Green: The Irish Civil War.* Dublin: Gill and Macmillan, 1988.

Horgan, John. *Irish Media: A Critical History since 1922.* Abingdon: Routledge, 2001.

————. "Saving Us from Ourselves: Contraception, Censorship, and the 'Evil Literature' Controversy of 1926." *Irish Communications Review* 5 (1995): 61.

Houlbrook, Matt. *Queer London: Perils and Pleasures in the Sexual Metropolis, 1918–1957.* Chicago: University of Chicago Press, 2005.

Hug, Chrystel. "Moral Order and the Liberal Agenda in the Republic of Ireland." *New Hibernia Review* 5, no. 4 (Winter 2001).

————. *The Politics of Sexual Morality in Ireland.* London: Palgrave Macmillan, 1998.

Hulme, Tom. *Belfastmen: An Intimate History of Life Before Gay Liberation.* Ithaca: Cornell University Press, forthcoming.

————. "Queer Belfast during the First World War: Masculinity and Same-Sex Desire in The Irish City." *Irish Historical Studies* 45, no. 168 (2021): 239–261.

————. "Queering Family History and the Lives of Irish Men before Gay Liberation," *History of the Family* 29, no. 1 (January 2024): 62–83.

Humphreys, A. J. "Migration to Dublin: Its Social Effects." *Christus Rex* 4, no. 2 (1955).

Humphreys, Laud. *Tearoom Trade: Impersonal Sex in Public Places.* Chicago: Aldine, 1970.

Hutton, Clare, and Patrick Walsh. *The Oxford History of the Irish Book, Vol. V: The Irish Book in English, 1891–2000.* New York: Oxford University Press, 2011.

Inglis, Tom. "Catholic Identity in Contemporary Ireland: Belief and Belonging to Tradition." *Journal of Contemporary Religion* 22, no. 2 (2007): 205–220.

————. *Lessons in Irish Sexuality.* Dublin: University College Dublin Press, 1998.

————. *Moral Monopoly: The Rise and Fall of the Catholic Church in Modern Ireland.* Dublin: University College Dublin Press, 1998.

————. "Origins and Legacies of Irish Prudery: Sexuality and Social Control in Modern Ireland." *Eire-Ireland* 40, nos. 3–4 (May 2005): 9–37.

Jackson, Alvin. *Ireland, 1798–1998: Politics and War.* Oxford: Blackwell, 1999.

————. "Ireland, the Union, and the Empire, 1800–1960." In *Ireland and the British Empire.* Edited by Kevin Kenny. New York: Oxford University Press, 2004.

Jenkins, Philip. *Moral Panic: Changing Concepts of the Child Molester in Modern America.* New Haven, CT: Yale University Books, 2004.

Johnson, David K. *The Lavender Scare: The Cold War Persecution of Gays and Lesbians in the Federal Government.* Chicago: University of Chicago Press, 2009.

Kaplan, Morris B. *Sodom on the Thames: Sex, Love, and Scandal in Wilde Times.* Ithaca, NY: Cornell University Press, 2005.

Katz, Jonathan Ned. *Love Stories: Sex between Men before Homosexuality.* Chicago: University of Chicago Press, 2003.

Kayaal, Tuğçe. "'Twisted Desires,' Boy-Lovers, and Male-Male Cross-Generational Sex in the Late Ottoman Empire (1912–1918)." *Historical Reflections/ Réflexions Historiques* 46, no. 1 (March 2020): 31–46.

Keane, Elizabeth. *An Irish Statesman and Revolutionary: The Nationalist and Internationalist Politics of Sean MacBride.* London: I. B. Tauris, 2006.

Kearins, Evanna. *Rent: The Untold Story of Male Prostitution in Dublin* (Dublin: Marino Books, 2000).

Keating, Anthony. "Policing Culture, Gender, and Crime in the Irish Free State." In *Environmental Criminology,* edited by Liam Leonard. Leeds: Emerald, 2017.

————. "Sexual Crime in the Irish Free State 1922–33: Its Nature, Extent, and Reporting." *Irish Studies Review* 20, no. 2 (May 2012): 135–155.

Kennedy, Finola. "The Suppression of the Carrigan Report: A Historical Perspective on Child Abuse." *Studies: An Irish Quarterly Review* 89, no. 356 (2000): 354–363.

Kenny, Mary. *The Way We Were*. Dublin: Columba Books, 2022.

Kerrigan, Páraic. *LGBTQ Visibility, Media and Sexuality in Ireland*. Abingdon: Routledge, 2021.

Kiberd, Declan. *Inventing Ireland: The Literature of a Modern Nation*. New York: Random House, 2009.

Kincaid, Andrew. *Postcolonial Dublin: Imperial Legacies and the Built Environment*. Minneapolis: University of Minnesota Press, 2006.

Kinealy, Christine. *This Great Calamity: The Irish Famine, 1845–52*. Dublin: Gill and Macmillan, 1994.

Kingston, Madeleine. *Something in the Head: The Life and Works of John Broderick*. Lilliput, 2004.

Kissane, Bill. *The Politics of the Irish Civil War*. New York: Oxford University Press, 2005.

Lacey, Brian. *Terrible Queer Creatures: Homosexuality in Irish History*. Dublin: Wordwell Group, 2008.

LaPointe, Michael Patrick. "Between Irishmen: Queering Irish Literary and Cultural Nationalisms." PhD diss., University of British Columbia, 2007.

Larkin, Emmet. "The Devotional Revolution in Ireland, 1850–75." *American Historical Review* 77, no. 3 (June 1972).

Lee, Joseph. *Ireland, 1912–1985: Politics and Society*. Cambridge: Cambridge University Press, 1990.

Legg, Marie-Louise. *Newspapers and Nationalism: The Irish Provincial Press, 1850–1892*. Dublin: Four Courts, 1999.

Luddy, Maria. *Prostitution and Irish Society, 1800–1940*. Cambridge: Cambridge University Press, 2007.

Luddy, Maria, and James M. Smith. *Children, Childhood and Irish Society, 1500 to the Present*. Dublin: Four Courts, 2014.

Lumsden, Ian. *Machos, Maricones, and Gays: Cuba and Homosexuality*. Philadelphia: Temple University Press, 1996.

Madden, Ed. "Queering Ireland, in the Archives." *Irish University Review* 43, no. 1 (2013): 184–221.

Maguire, Moira J. *Precarious Childhood in Post-independence Ireland*. Manchester: Manchester University Press, 2009.

Marhoefer, Laurie. *Sex and the Weimar Republic: German Homosexual Emancipation and the Rise of the Nazis*. Toronto: University of Toronto Press, 2015.

———. "Untitled Job Talk." Research Presentation, State University of New York at Buffalo, March 2015.

Maunger, Alice. *The Cost of Insanity in Nineteenth-Century Ireland: Public, Voluntary and Private Asylum Care*. Basingstoke: Palgrave Macmillan, 2017.

Maynard, Steven. "'Horrible Temptations': Sex, Men, and Working-Class Male Youth in Urban Ontario, 1890–1935." *Canadian Historical Review* 78, no. 2 (June 1997): 191.

———. "Through a Hole in the Lavatory Wall: Homosexual Subcultures, Police Surveillance, and the Dialectics of Discovery, Toronto, 1890–1930." *Journal of the History of Sexuality* 5, no. 2 (1994): 207–242.

———. "'Without Working?' Capitalism, Urban Culture, and Gay History." *Journal of Urban History* 30, no. 3 (2004): 378–398.

McAuliffe, Mary. *Margaret Skinnider*. Dublin: University College Dublin Press, 2023.

McAuliffe, Mary, and Harriett Wheelock. *The Diaries of Kathleen Lynn: A Life Revealed through Personal Writing*. Dublin: University College Dublin Press, 2020.

McAvoy, Sandra. "Sexual Crime and Irish Women's Campaigns for a Criminal Law Amendment Act, 1912–1935." In *Gender and Power in Irish History*, edited by Maryann Gialanella Valiulis. Dublin: Irish Academic Press, 2009.

McDevitt, Patrick F. "'Muscular Catholicism': Nationalism, Masculinity and Irish Team Sports, 1884–1916." *Gender and History* 9, no. 2 (August 1997): 262–284.

McDonagh, Patrick. *Gay and Lesbian Activism in the Republic of Ireland, 1973–93*. Dublin: Bloomsbury, 2021.

McGarry, Fearghal. *Eoin O'Duffy: A Self-Made Hero*. Oxford University Press, 2005.

McGrath, Sam. "Bartley Dunnes." *Come Here to Me* (6 October 2013). Available at https://comeheretome.com/2013/10/06/rices-bartley-dunnes-dublins-first-gay-friendly-bars.

———. "Hotel Beresford and the Seafarer's Club." *Come Here to Me* (20 February 2014). Available at https://web.archive.org/web/20200718180055/http://comeheretome.com/2014/02/20/hotel-bereford-and-the-seamens-club/.

McLaren, Angus. *The Trials of Masculinity: Policing Sexual Boundaries, 1870–1930*. Chicago: University of Chicago Press, 1997.

McMahon, Timothy. *Grand Opportunity: The Gaelic Revival and Irish Society, 1893–1910*. Syracuse: Syracuse University Press, 2008.

McManus, Ruth. *Dublin, 1910–1940: Shaping the City and Suburbs*. Dublin: Four Courts, 2002.

McNiffe, Liam. *A History of the Garda Síochána: A Social History of the Force, 1922–52, with an Overview of the Years, 1952–97*. Dublin: Wolfhound, 1997.

Montgomery, Dale. "'They Were the Men Who Licked the IRA until They Squealed': Blueshirt Masculine Identity, 1932–36." In *Irish Masculinities: Reflections on Literature and Culture*, edited by Caroline Magennis and Raymond Mullen. Dublin: Irish Academic Press, 2011.

Mosse, George L. *Nationalism and Sexuality: Respectability and Abnormal Sexuality in Modern Europe*. New York: H. Fertig, 1985.

Moynihan, Sinéad. *Ireland, Migration and Return Migration: The "Returned Yank" in the Cultural Imagination, 1952 to Present*. Liverpool: Liverpool University Press, 2019.

Murphy, Brendon. "Deceptive Apparatus: Foucauldian Perspectives on Law, Authorised Crime and the Rationalities of Undercover Investigation." *Griffith Law Review* 25, no. 2 (2016): 223–244.

Murphy, James H. *Ireland: A Social, Cultural and Literary History, 1791–1891*. Dublin: Four Courts Press, 2003.

Ndjio, Basile. "Post-colonial Histories of Sexuality: The Political Invention of a Libidinal African Straight." *Africa: The Journal of the International African Institute* 82, no. 4 (2012): 609–631.

Nugent, Joseph. "The Sword and the Prayerbook: Ideals of Authentic Irish Manliness." *Victorian Studies* 50, no. 4 (2008): 587–613.

Ó Buachalla, S. *Education Policy in Twentieth Century Ireland*. Dublin: Wolfhound, 1988.

O'Carroll, Ide, and Eoin Collins, eds. *Lesbian and Gay Visions of Ireland: Towards the 21st Century*. London, 1995.

O'Donnell, Katherine. "St. Patrick's Day Expulsions: Race and Homophobia in New York's Parade." In *Irish Postmodernisms and Popular Culture*, edited by Wanda Balzano, Anne Mulhall, and Moynagh Sullivan. Basingstoke: Palgrave Macmillan, 2007.

O'Dwyer, Conor. *Coming Out of Communism: The Emergence of LGBT Activism in Eastern Europe*. New York: New York University Press, 2018.

O'Farrell, Fergus. *Catholic Emancipation: Daniel O'Connell and the Birth of Irish Democracy, 1820–30.* Dublin: Gill and Macmillan, 1985.

O'Malley, Thomas. *Sexual Offences: Law, Policy, and Punishment.* Dublin: Round Hall Sweet & Maxwell, 1996.

O'Sullivan, Michael. *Brendan Behan: A Life.* Dublin: Rinehart, Roberts Publishers, Inc., 1997.

Peniston, William A. *Pederasts and Others: Urban Culture and Sexual Identity in Nineteenth-Century Paris.* Abingdon, Routledge, 2004.

Petri, Olga. *Places of Tenderness and Heat: The Queer Milieu of Fin-de-Siècle St. Petersburg.* Ithaca, NY: Cornell University Press, 2022.

Ponzio, Alessio. "'What They Had between Their Legs Was a Form of Cash': Homosexuality, Male Prostitution, and Intergenerational Sex in 1950s Italy." *Historical Reflections/Réflexions Historiques* 46, no. 1 (March 2020): 62–78.

Punch, Aidan, and Catherine Finneran. "Changing Population Structure." *That Was Then, This Is Now: Change in Ireland, 1949–1999.* Central Statistics Office: Dublin, 2000.

Raferty, Mary. *Suffer the Little Children: The Inside Story of Ireland's Industrial Schools.* London: Continuum International Publishing Group, 2002.

Reidy, Conor. *Ireland's 'Moral Hospital': The Irish Borstal System, 1906–1956.* Newbridge, Ireland: Irish Academic Press, 2009.

Rey, Michel. "Parisian Homosexuals Create a Lifestyle, 1700–1750: The Police Archives." In *Tis Nature's Fault: Unauthorized Sexuality during the Enlightenment.* Edited by Robert Purks MacCubbin. Cambridge: Cambridge University Press, 1987.

Robertson, Stephen. "What's Law Got to Do with It? Legal Records and Sexual Histories." *Journal of the History of Sexuality* 14, nos. 1–2 (2005): esp. 161–169.

Robinson, Stephen. "Bringing It All Back Home." *Gay Community News,* March 1998, 18.

Rose, Kieran. *Diverse Communities: The Evolution of Lesbian and Gay Politics in Ireland.* Cork: Cork University Press, 1994.

Ross, Andrew. *Public City/Public Sex: Homosexuality, Prostitution, and Urban Culture in Nineteenth-Century Paris.* Philadelphia: Temple University Press, 2019.

Ryan, Paul. "Asking Angela: Discourses about Sexuality on an Irish Problem Page, 1963–1980." *Journal of the History of Sexuality* 19, no. 2 (2010): 317–339.

———. *Asking Angela MacNamara: An Intimate History of Irish Lives.* Dublin: Irish Academic Press, 2011.

———. "Coming Out of the Dark: A Decade of Gay Mobilisation in Ireland, 1970–80." In *Social Movements and Ireland,* edited by Linda Connolly and Niamh Hourigan. Manchester: Manchester University Press, 2007.

Ryle, Martin. "John McGahern: Memory, Autobiography, Fiction, History." *New Formations* 67 (Summer 2009): 35–45.

Said, Edward W. "Afterword: Reflections on Ireland and Postcolonialism." In *Ireland and Postcolonial Theory.* Notre Dame, IN: University of Notre Dame Press, 2003.

Sheppard, Barry. "'As a Gael Should Meet Gaels,' The Gaelic Athletic Association and the Irish Free State." *Irish Story,* 21 Aug 2012. Accessed 20 November 2015. Available at http://www.theirishstory.com/2012/08/21/as-a-gael-should-meet-gaels-the-gaelic-athletic-association-in-the-irish-free-state/#.Vk-Kzt-rQb0.

Silverman, Marilyn. *An Irish Working Class.* Toronto: University of Toronto Press, 2001.

Sinfield, Alan. *The Wilde Century: Effeminacy, Oscar Wilde, and the Queer Moment.* New York: Columbia University Press, 1994.

Smith, Helen. *Masculinity, Class and Same-Sex Desire in Industrial England, 1895–1957.* London: Springer, 2015.

Smith, James. *Ireland's Magdalen Laundries and the Nation's Architecture of Containment.* Notre Dame, IN: University of Notre Dame Press, 2007.

Stoler, Ann. *Carnal Knowledge and Imperial Power.* Berkeley: University of California Press, 2002.

Strauss, Erich. *Irish Nationalism and British Democracy.* London: Methuen, 1951.

Syrett, Nicholas L. *An Open Secret: The Family Story of Robert and John Gregg Allerton.* Chicago: University of Chicago Press, 2021.

Tewksbury, Richard. "Finding Erotic Oases: Locating the Sites of Men's Same-Sex Anonymous Sexual Encounters." *Journal of Homosexuality* 50, no. 1 (2008).

Thane, Pat. *Unequal Britain: Equalities in Britain since 1945.* London: Continuum Press, 2010.

Townsend, Camilla. *Malintzin's Choices: An Indian Woman in the Conquest of Mexico.* Albuquerque: University of New Mexico Press, 2006.

Trouillot, Michel-Rolph. *Silencing the Past: Power and the Production of History.* Boston: Beacon Press, 1995.

Upchurch, Charles. *"Beyond the Law": The Politics Ending the Death Penalty for Sodomy in Britain.* Philadelphia: Temple University Press, 2021.

———. "Full-Test Databases and Historical Research: Cautionary Results from a Ten-Year Study." *Journal of Social History* 46, no. 1 (Fall 2012): 89–105.

Valente, Joseph. *The Myth of Manliness in Irish National Culture, 1880–1922.* Urbana: University of Illinois Press, 2011.

Valiulis, Maryann Gialanella, editor. *Gender and Power in Irish History.* Dublin: Irish Academic Press, 2009.

Wahab, Amar. "Homophobia as the State of Reason: The Case of Postcolonial Trinidad and Tobago." *GLQ: A Journal of Lesbian and Gay Studies* 18, no. 4 (2012): 481–505.

Walkowitz, Judith. *Prostitution in Victorian Society: Women, Class, and the State.* Cambridge: Cambridge University Press, 1982.

Walshe, Éibhear. "The First Gay Irishman? Ireland and the Wilde Trials." *Éire-Ireland* 40, nos. 3–4 (Fall–Winter 2005): 38–57.

———. "The Importance of Staging Oscar Wilde: Wilde at the Gate." In *The Oxford Handbook of Modern Irish Theater.* Edited by Nicholas Grene and Chris Morash (Oxford: Oxford University Press, 2016): 217–230.

———. *Kate O'Brien: A Writing Life.* Dublin: Irish Academic Press, 2006.

———. *Oscar's Shadow: Wilde, Homosexuality and Modern Ireland.* Cork: Cork University Press, 2011.

———. "Sexing the Shamrock." *Anglo-Irish Studies: New Developments* 8, no. 2 (1996): 159–167.

Weeks, Jeffrey. "Inverts, Perverts and Mary-Annes: Male Prostitution and the Regulation of Homosexuality in England in the Nineteenth and Early Twentieth Centuries." In *Hidden from History: Reclaiming the Gay and Lesbian Past,* edited by Martin Duberman, Martha Vicinus, and George Chauncey. New York: New American Library, 1989.

Weigle, D. C. "Psychology and Homosexuality: The British Sexological Society." *Journal of the History of the Behavioral Sciences* 31, no. 2 (1995): 137–148.

West, Donald, and Richard Green. *Sociolegal Control of Homosexuality: A Multi-nation Comparison.* New York: Plenum, 1997.

Woods, Gregory. *Homintern: How Gay Culture Liberated the Modern World*. New Haven, CT: Yale University Press, 2017.

Worboys, Michael, Julie-Marie Strange, and Neil Pemberton. *The Invention of the Modern Dog: Breed and Blood in Victorian Britain*. Baltimore: John Hopkins University Press, 2018.

Index

Families: as endangered by vice, 29–31, 61, 130; estrangement due to homophobia, 1, 8–9, 15, 95, 110–111; as self-policing units, 79, 86, 121, 136, 165–166, 198; as supportive of same-sex-desiring men, 87, 120, 176, 191
Fascism, 62–64, 74
Fellatio, 133–134, 143–144
Ferriter, Diarmaid, 16, 18, 53, 64, 168
ffrench-Mullen, Madeleine, 91, 172–173, 176
Fianna Fáil, 19, 106; impact on the Garda, 62, 65, 68, 148, 162; Irish nationalist policies of, 27–29, 142
Fitz-Simon, Christopher, 166, 167, 173–174, 179, 183–184, 186
Flanagan, E. J., 124–125
Forde, Patrick, 132–136

Gaelic League, 121
Gannon, P. J., 45, 101
Garda Síochána, An: campaigns against same-sex sex, 31, 46–47, 58, 65, 89, 163, 171; Dublin Metropolitan Division (DMD) of, 25, 50; as enforcers of Catholic nationalism, 4, 24, 42, 141–142, 150, 162; generational divides within, 161–162; inequitable treatment of sex crimes, 33, 80–81, 90, 100–101, 110; modernization of, 145, 155–156; policing tactics of, 10, 46, 56–57, 66, 68, 156–157, 160; public's positive views of, 149–150; recruitment, 51–52, 59–60, 64–65, 146–148, 161; resource constraints of, 78–79, 98, 103, 139, 180, 198; vice squad of, 139–142, 157–158, 160–162, 187, 200
Gate Theatre Company, 164, 174; and Dublin gay subculture, 32, 62, 166, 167; and Mac Liammóir and Edwards' relationship, 91, 183, 186–187
Gaw, George, 133–136
Gender, 8, 19, 88, 168; as factor in sex crime arrests, 172–173, 176–177
Great Famine, 40n62, 52, 92
Grief, 84–85, 185–186, 199. *See also* loneliness
Gross indecency, 138; arrest statistics, 14, 26–27, 32–35, 43, 67, 77, 97, 145, 156–157; committed by gardaí undercover, 55, 66, 68; consequences of arrest for, 86, 98–99, 172; laws, 5, 19–20, 56, 98, 130; in the press, 61–62, 75–76, 89, 106–107; as undifferentiated from rape, 9–14, 135–136

Hackett, Michael: biography of, 83–85, 116n15; intergenerational relationships of, 127–129; leniency extended to, 115–120; testimony of, 85–86, 131, 135–136
Hand, James, 7; arrest and trial, 73–76, 86–87; as a facilitator of same-sex sex, 85–86, 127, 171; queer social life, 72, 77, 81–82, 88–89; socioeconomic status, 69–71; struggles with sexuality, 78–79
Hanna, Erika, 29, 31
Hennessy, Patrick, 172–173, 177
Heteronormativity, 39, 43–44, 55, 136, 174
Homophobia, 126, 166, 200–201; of authorities prosecuting sex crimes, 26–27, 103; state-sanctioned, 5–6, 15n40, 17, 68, 107, 198
Homosexuality, 4, 55; association with pederasty, 12–14, 126; endurance of, 15n40, 18, 89, 180; as English, 15, 17, 44, 45, 92; erasure of, 166, 174–175, 176–177, 198; decriminalization of, 9, 16, 19, 80, 81, 128, 202; as an identity, 4n9, 193–194; as illegal, 2–3, 10, 11–12, 44, 136, 193–194, 199; in literature, 194–195, 197; obscuring visibility of, 26, 57–58, 91, 138, 171; and oppression, 2, 8, 17–18, 43–44; as resistance to the state, 8, 73–75, 80, 178–179; self-repression of, 43–44, 62, 166, 190–191, 201; as sin, 1, 53, 80, 155, 163, 193–194, 199
Homosocial spaces, 74, 89, 96–97, 115–116, 196
Houlbrook, Matt, 26, 39, 125, 146
Hulme, Tom, 8
Humphreys, A. J., 29–30

Importance of Being Oscar, The (Micheál Mac Liammóir) 174–175
Institutionalization, 1, 79, 170, 197
Intercrural sex, 118
Intergenerational relationships, 12, 95–96, 108–109, 115–118, 126–127, 129
Intoxication, 23, 99, 109, 129, 201
Irish Civil War, 4, 50n35; and evolution of the Garda, 50, 52, 161; and high crime rates, 23; and nationalist vision, 27

Averill Earls is Associate Professor of History at St. Olaf College and Executive Producer of *Dig: A History Podcast.*

www.ingramcontent.com/pod-product-compliance
Lightning Source LLC
Chambersburg PA
CBHW020348270326
41926CB00007B/347